The Japanese Employee

ROBERT J. BALLON, EDITOR

CONTRIBUTORS

JAMES C. ABEGGLEN
Vice President, BOSTON CONSULTING GROUP

MAURICE BAIRY
Professor of Psychology, SOPHIA UNIVERSITY

PAUL TIMOTHY CHANG
Professor of Political Science, SOPHIA UNIVERSITY

HERBERT GLAZER
Professor of International Business
THE AMERICAN UNIVERSITY, WASHINGTON, D. C.

TADASHI HANAMI
Professor of Law, SOPHIA UNIVERSITY

RYOKICHI HIRONO
Assistant Professor of Labor Economics & Industrial Relations
SEIKEI UNIVERSITY

MOTOSHI ISOMURA
Chief Officer of the General Planning Dept.
THE TOYO TRUST & BANKING CO.

MAKOTO SAKURABAYASHI
Professor of Labor Economics, SOPHIA UNIVERSITY

IWAO TOMITA
TOHMATSU AWOKI & CO.

The Japanese Employee

ROBERT J. BALLON, *Editor*

PUBLISHED BY

SOPHIA UNIVERSITY · TOKYO

IN COOPERATION WITH

THE CHARLES E. TUTTLE COMPANY

RUTLAND · VERMONT & TOKYO · JAPAN

REPRESENTATIVES

Continental Europe: BOXERBOOKS, INC., *Zurich*
British Isles: PRENTICE-HALL INTERNATIONAL, INC., *London*
Australasia: PAUL FLESCH & Co., PTY. LTD., *Melbourne*
Canada: M. G. HURTIG, LTD., *Edmonton*

Published by Sophia University
7, Kioi-chō, Chiyoda-ku, Tokyo, 102
in cooperation with
the Charles E. Tuttle Company, Inc.
of Rutland, Vermont & Tokyo, Japan
with editorial offices
at Suidō 1-chōme, 2-6, Bunkyō-ku, Tokyo, 112

Library of Congress Catalog Card No. 75-99980
Order No. 8048-0871-6

PRINTED IN JAPAN

PETER BROGREN, THE VOYAGERS' PRESS, TOKYO

THIS BOOK IS

RESPECTFULLY DEDICATED TO

A MAN *who has given himself mind and body*
to the postwar economic reconstruction of Japan's economy

An INDUSTRIALIST *who has contributed immeasurably*
to the dynamic image
of Japan's private business enterprises

An INTERNATIONALLY-MINDED JAPANESE
who has represented his country superbly
in international meetings

MR. TAIZŌ ISHIZAKA
FORMER CHAIRMAN OF *Keidanren*
(JAPANESE FEDERATION OF ECONOMIC ORGANIZATIONS)

Preface

JAPAN's economic development 'is not so much a success story as a suspense story. Japan may be skating fastest where the ice is thinnest.' Thus wrote Max Ways in 'Why Japan's Growth Is Different' in the November 1967 issue of *Fortune*.

To build a 300,000 ton tanker in one year, to travel by train at 250 kilometers an hour, and, more fundamentally, to rank third in the world listing of GNP's within one decade—all this is indeed top speed. Often called 'Westernization', the Japanese phenomenon evokes the somewhat spectacular prodigy of a pupil surpassing his teacher. But is Westernization merely emulation of technological and material advances? If so, Japan is not different from many other countries in this respect. Nonetheless, the Japanese insist that she *is* different. If so, the difference is not to be sought only in her cultural past, nor in her technological present, for that matter. The difference is in the Japanese themselves.

In any industrial society, the key human relationship is the one determined by employment. Japan's industrial society is characterized by a view of the relationships of employment that is very different from the view that prevails in Western industrial societies. Generally speaking, as time passes and the benefits of industrial growth permeate a society more and more deeply, the more apparent become the sinews of its economic development. Nor are those sinews merely age-old customs and values transposed into an unfamiliar, new setting, preserved like amulets, or the age-old traditions of an agricultural economy surviving in an industrial environment. Certainly, in the case of Japan, while ancient values have been retained, they have been substantially assimilated in the new society by the institutions they are proper to, and they largely determine the basic dynamics of the national economy.

The Japanese Employee

Some ancient Japanese values, like employment security, exist also in the West. The difference is, however, that in the West they have not—or have not yet—acquired 'institutional' status; they remain pretty much just what they are: values of the past. But in Japan such values, although undeniably rooted in the past, nevertheless find revitalized strength in the present, in the dynamic present of an economic growth that has averaged 10% for over a decade and is not about to subside. A difference from the West is also revealed in this rate of growth, but the primary difference is revealed in the social and human aspects of the growth.

The one really caught up in the quandary of this phenomenon is not so much the Japanologist or the student of Asian affairs as it is the foreign businessman resident in Japan. Although, in the first place, it was the attraction of Japan's 'success story' that brought him to her shores, he soon found himself enmeshed in the drama of a 'suspense story', as Max Ways puts it. In this drama, as in all thrillers, the performances of the characters determine the conflict and excitement. And here the Japanese employees are central characters: all of them, from manual workers to managerial executives perform brilliantly—judged by the suspense they create. Resident foreign businessmen may wish they were in the front row enjoying the show, but instead they often find themselves in the center of the stage while the performance is going on. Some of them speak lines which, if heard at all, somehow sound out of tune. Understandably vexed, they stamp off the stage, predicting disaster. This type of businessman must soon be called home. Others, hardier souls, may not always like the drama, but they enjoy participating in it as though it were the challenge of their lives.

This volume is dedicated to these hardier souls. Large credit for it should go to a group of people, both foreign and Japanese, who believe that international business, for foreigners in Japan as well as for Japanese abroad, is a demanding test of open-mindedness and mutual consideration. Their contributions, herein printed, were originally prepared for the International Management Deve-

Preface

lopment Seminars sponsored by the Sophia University Socio-Economic Institute (Tokyo) and have been repeatedly submitted to the criticisms of their Japanese and foreign business partners or rivals. To these critics of our comments and interpretations go our sincerest thanks. Our prose, too, needed checking; it was the much appreciated task of Dr. Kenneth Scholes to smooth it out.

As Japan moves ever deeper into the arenas of business all over the world, her distinctive characteristics, whether strong or weak, must come increasingly under the scrutiny of potential foreign partners and actual competitors. At the level of her 'human know-how' as well as at the level of her technological know-how, it thus behooves her not only to draw upon but also to contribute to the international exchange of all relevant experience and achievement. In any case, in the arenas of world-wide industrialization, where human beings are hopefully advancing some of the greater values of contemporary life, an important actor is THE JAPANESE EMPLOYEE.

THE EDITOR
TOKYO, JULY 1969

CONTENTS

Part III

REMUNERATION OF THE JAPANESE EMPLOYEE

Part IV

JAPANESE INDUSTRIAL RELATIONS

Contents

Part V
FOREIGN MANAGEMENT AND JAPANESE EMPLOYMENT

LIST OF FIGURES

List of Figures

List of Figures

List of Figures

Part I

INTRODUCING THE JAPANESE EMPLOYEE

A

CHAPTER ONE

The Japanese dimensions of industrial enterprises

BY ROBERT J. BALLON

Industrialization and industrial enterprises—identity of the enterprise—organization of the enterprise—competition—the new forces

NOT so long ago—in fact, less than forty years ago—the West to its great surprise discovered that there was more to an industrial enterprise than had so far met the eye. As one of the 'discoverers' stated pungently:

'These examples show that industry has a social organization which cannot be treated independently from the technical problems of economic organization. An industrial organization is more than a plurality of individuals acting only with regard to their own economic interests. The individuals also have feelings and sentiments toward one another, and in their daily associations together they tend to build up routine patterns of interaction. Most of the individuals who live among these patterns come to accept them as obvious and necessary truths and to react as they dictate.'[1]

[1] F. J. Roethlisberger, *Management and Morale,* Cambridge: Harvard University Press, 1941, p. 53.

At long last, as a result of lengthy experiments conducted at the Hawthorne Chicago Works of the Western Electric Company from 1927 to 1933,[2] 'human relations in industry' became a new and vital dimension of enterprise—not that they had not been there all along, but now somehow Western scholars and managers started to give them explicit attention. Why did it take the West so long to make such a rather obvious discovery? Two main reasons come to mind. One is rather philosophical: the Western concept of the human person makes it primarily an individual entity only secondarily related to other similarly individual entities. This individualism assumes easily that the environment, whether industrial or other, has little impact on the 'individual'. The other reason has to do with the historical process of Western industrialization. By and large, it was started and developed by some especially clever individuals—'capitalists', or Marx's 'exploiters'—who, in order to satisfy their own personal ambitions, created agencies called enterprises. Enterprise was, in fact, the brain-child of entrepreneurs, and for a century or more employees were merely 'factors' like capital and raw materials, as indispensable as, but often much less tractable than other factors.

Even today, most Western thought concerning industrial enterprise starts from so-called 'formal organization,' which is actually a sort of mental blueprint in the mind of a manager. Stoutly clinging to his blueprint like Ariadne's thread, the manager then ventures to wade through the labyrinth of 'informal groups', 'grapevines', 'motivations', and so on.

In Japan, however, the same kind of economic institution, an industrial enterprise, moves in a different context. The philosophical postulates of individualism have, at best, flimsy roots in Japanese culture. Accordingly, industrialization has followed a rather dif-

---

[2] A fascinating description of these experiments is given by George C. Homans in *Fatigue and Workers, Its Relation to Industrial Production,* New York: Reinhold, 1941, as reprinted in H. R. Knudson (ed.), *Management and Human Resources, Concepts for Developing Nations,* Reading: Addison-Wesley, 1967, pp.355–376.

ferent path here. Succinctly stated, Japanese enterprise has been much less the brain-child of entrepreneurs than it has been a new social institution demanded by an entire nation whose survival was dependent upon its adoption.

Industrialization and industrial enterprises

DURING the Tokugawa Period (1603–1868), Japan knew a great number of commercial undertakings, some so prosperous that they even caused feudal lords, faced with staggering debts, to yield up their holdings to confiscation without hesitating. Many of these undertakings catered to more than the local market and covered most of the breadth of then contemporary economic activities; none, however, due to the seclusion policy, had any overseas connection or activity. At the local level, numerous private establishments, crafts and trade, bore witness to widespread market-oriented activities. Public undertakings were few, except for here and there the enlightenment of a feudal lord who timidly tried his wits on some industrial process. All craft and commercial ventures were family-owned, and by and large were able, together with the agricultural sector, to satisfy the daily needs of the population.

But to the leaders of the Meiji Restoration (1868), it was urgently clear that secluded Japan would not long survive unless something new was *added* to the existing economic life: namely, industry. Although initially industry was not felt as a need by the people, since traditional crafts and commercial activities had always taken adequate care of their necessities, it was plainly a need for the country. Open Japan required a new economic structure; industrialization was accordingly entered into not as an end in itself, but as an essential means towards Japan's survival, the truly necessary end. The same urgency still prevails one hundred years later. Today, the introduction of new technology is mostly justified in terms of catching up with other advanced nations (national policy) rather than in terms of comparative advantage (an economic law of enterprise).

Far from intending to disturb the economic order of Japan that existed at the daily level of economic needs, the Meiji leaders rather decided to add a new dimension, a superior level: industry. Thus it was that economic Japan laid the foundation of her coming dual structure. Industry would not be brought forth in some spontaneous generation, but by some deliberate import policy whereby industrial processes were to be acquired from the West. And for almost twenty years the government was left alone at this task; it went at it doggedly and clumsily, until the first stirrings of industrial entrepreneurship started to manifest themselves in the private sector. Notwithstanding later developments, Japanese industry would never repudiate its origins: it had been deliberately conceived by the government of the country and borne in great labor precisely in order that the continuity of the nation would be guaranteed. This newcomer in the international family of industrial states was thus not merely a stranger by virtue of its place of birth (the Orient, of all places!), but was also, contrary to the mores of the day, the offspring of an almost incestuous wedlock involving government!

Even at its own birthplace, the newborn was not readily accepted by everybody, nor, for that matter, successfully received by those courageous enough to adopt it: many industrial ventures turned out to be dismal failures. But in a few decades, a rapidly growing population turned to industrialization for employment; by World War I, Japanese industry was standing at the threshold of manhood. But industrial employment was again a new structure in a predominantly agricultural economy, a super-structure added to the existing order. Thus, for example, the majority of the Japanese industrial work force was female up until the 1920s. In fact, it was only in the inter-war period that industry and industrial employment started to sink roots into the infrastructure of the nation. Cottage industry mushroomed; subcontracting tapped the industriousness of the small producer; large industrial complexes monopolized the main sinews of economic activity, and... industrial strife fermented, until militarism galvanized the entire process by mobilizing all national energies for imperialistic conquest and the industry of war. Even then the pattern was not broken; the dual structure remained. At the upper level a relatively few 'modern' industries benefitted from the economies of large scale operations and catered primarily to the international (in the last instance, imperialistic) needs of the country; at the lower level myriads of small enterprises remained either expendable through dependence on the whims of subcontracting or somehow outside the industrialization process, absorbed in providing the populace with its daily necessities.

It was not until after World War II that a domestic market for industrially produced goods and services started to develop. Typically, some small firms, not very many, went 'modern' and emerged as large firms; the best known examples are Honda, Matsushita, and Sony. But it turned out that more than ever before the characteristic of a large firm was not just its size and the many advantages attached to size, economies of scale, easier financing, and the like. A large firm was also, as labor unions were discovering, the repository of security of employment! And thus duality of the economic structure came to be affirmed again. Modern technological innovation and stringency of the labor market, as well as capital liberalization, provided a new boost to industrial size.

When Japan opened her doors a hundred years ago, industrialization became by that very act a *sine qua non* of national policy if she wanted to survive. In other words, industrialization was and is a public policy not only required for domestic reasons like providing employment, but also absolutely required for reasons of international intercourse.[3] This view means that industrial enterprise— the working unit of industry, the actual manifestation of the policy of industrialization—fulfills a *public* function. Whether the result of government initiative or the fruit of private entrepreneurship,

---

3 From this point on, speaking of 'industrial enterprise', we refer to the enterprises that participated in the industrial policy often mentioned by Japanese scholars as the 'modern sector' of the economy. Unless otherwise indicated, the 'traditional sector' composed of small enterprises is excluded.

industrial enterprise is, more than by virtue of historical circumstances, constitutively in both inception and ulterior development an 'instrument' of public policy. Such a policy does not deny private initiative; on the contrary, great pains were taken by the government to generate entrepreneurship among former samurai. Government undertakings were eagerly yielded into private hands; tax and other incentives were generously bestowed, not to speak of what the Westerner considers an overprotective attitude of the government towards domestic industries. Even today this 'public' dimension of private enterprise is omnipresent, chiefly through the importance given to the balance of international payments. It is not that this 'international' problem is one whereby enterprise is expected to acquire an international dimension; it is solved by calling on enterprise's sense of 'public' responsibility to the Japanese community.

In the process of analyzing Japan's economic structure and trade today, Hollerman makes the following comment:

> '... Total trade has been unbalanced and Japan has been obliged to pay its debts by capital loans... Aside from the financial burden of the deficit, the nature of its structural repercussions on Japanese industry is of equal or even greater importance. These repercussions take effect through institutional action by which Japan's national need to export is transformed into actual exports by private firms. One of the principal ingredients of Japan's high growth rate in recent years is the relatively unnoticed and little known nature of this institutional action. Hitherto, the exchange control system has been one of its chief instruments. During brief periods, in order to obtain desirable import licenses, firms have been impelled to export almost without regard to profit or loss. The credit control system works in a similar manner. Because of the way in which domestic credit is restricted and channeled, firms are forced to obtain export contracts—accompanied by letter of credit—which they use either to finance production

[8]

or to finance short-term loans to others at high rates of interest.'[4]

Industrial enterprise has been the confluent of the expectations of the 'open' nation, as well as of its various components.

To the national economy, enterprise was expected to provide the goods and services that could be exported in order to acquire the foreign exchange essential for the import of much needed raw materials and technologies.

Except in armaments, the government soon learned that it was not qualified actually to manage industrial ventures. Private enterprise must do the trick, and government officials were and are eager to share with private entrepreneurs the burdens of industrialization.

The rural sector, in the initial stages of industrialization, contributed raw silk and tea that provided needed foreign exchange abroad, while in order to pay taxes now paid in cash, it grew deeply committed to the putting-out system. In return, farming families expected their second and third sons, as well as temporarily their daughters, to find industrial employment.[5]

Entrepreneurs were awakened less by some individual urge to start ventures along industrial lines than by the call of some national duty. They were expected to contribute to national survival by matching whatever wits they had with attempts at producing industrial goods and services. In return, they expected support and guidance from the national community at large: understanding officials, docile workers, cooperative financial institutions, and so on, knowing quite clearly that they could never succeed alone.

Employees, out from their rural origins and lost in the impersonal city, turned to industrial enterprise and their employers as to a new primary group where they would find the security of subsistence

---

[4] Leon Hollerman, *Japan's Dependence on the World Economy*, Princeton: Princeton University Press, 1967, p. 56.

[5] See Ezra F. Vogel, 'Kinship Structure, Migration of the City, and Modernization' in R.P. Dore (ed.), *Aspects of Social Change in Modern Japan*, Princeton: Princeton University Press, 1967, pp. 91–111.

that rural families could not provide any longer. What they expected was not so much gain as subsistence . . . It would take the recent 'consumer revolution' to change their outlook.

Even post-World War II labor unions turned to industrial enterprise for their *raison d'être,* their identification. Structurally they are enterprise-wide unions whose main object is to protect regular employees, i.e., those to whom the firm owes the security of lifelong employment. All other workers are left to themselves, or to other forms of labor organizations that cater to their needs for political or ideological reasons.

As the focus of so many expectations coming in from all sectors of the nation, industrial enterprise, even private, was spontaneously endowed with a high public responsibility. At a risk, however. The danger was, and is even today, that 'private' enterprise, or at least its entrepreneurs, considers itself a 'public' institution and arrogates to itself attitudes, actions, and even rights proper only to a genuine public institution. Being so much in public demand, industrial enterprise is tempted to consider its own 'private' pursuits 'public' interests. The temptation is formidable. Business accounting, by and large, still exists primarily for tax purposes, not for the information of investors. Business investment answers the call of expansion, but not the call of the market. Banks collect individual savings (but until very recently have completely overlooked individual credit) and extend loans to corporations, preferably large ones, and so on and on. The close relationship, one would almost say the partnership, between the government and enterprise in Japan is still another incentive to this sense of the 'public' responsibility of the private firm.[6] It has all been put into a *mot :* 'Whatever is good for Japan, Incorporated, is good; so whatever is good for, say, Mitsui, is good for Japan.'

---

[6] See the most enlightening study by James C. Abegglen, 'Japan Incorporated: Government and Business as Partners', Boston: Boston Consulting Group, Inc., 1967, 21 pages (mimeographed).

Chapter one: The Japanese dimensions of enterprises

Identity of the enterprise

IN the West, enterprises tend to be identified in themselves and in economic terms with only generic reference to their particular industrial line. It seems that recently rapid diversification of lines has weakened identification by industry and has marked a definite return to identification by innovator or by group of entrepreneurs boasting about their brain-child. In Japan, questioning a top executive about his firm rarely elicits talk about 'my' company; rather, it usually elicits talk about the state of affairs in the whole industry concerned and almost always culminates in references to the national economy, often in terms of balance of international payments. It is not that direct questions are dodged; the fact is that the identity of any enterprise is seldom, if ever, expressed in its own limited economic terms.

It would be wrong to imagine Japanese enterprise as some sort of entity existing in itself—say, a specific organization of people and their activities established for the production of goods and services. Of course, the identity of a firm is determined by its president,[7] its capital, its legal personality, and the like. But just as an individual shares with some others his family name, a Japanese enterprise is identified by its affiliation with a certain industrial grouping and the social position acquired thereby. Its identity is, therefore, expressed in a third dimension; its participation in an industrial grouping that itself contributes to the national economy.

The legal identification of a Japanese enterprise as stipulated in the Japanese Commercial Code, which has remained basically unaltered since its enactment in 1899, owes much to the French legislation from which it was derived. In view of the urgency of industrialization, and the lack of readily available capital, the Meiji government

[7] Today's advertisers are more concerned with having their names rather than their products kept in front of the customers. A few years back, even product advertising would inevitably mention the name of the company president concerned, if not also display his picture!

felt that incorporation had to be fostered by all means possible. It went through great lengths, for example, to encourage partnerships among former samurai, even to the extent of matching whatever amounts of capital had thus been marshalled.[8] The Commercial Code (Art. 17) determined three basic forms of incorporation: partnership *(gōmei kaisha),* association with limited responsibility *(yūgen kaisha),* and stock corporation *(kabushiki kaisha).* The first two forms being less popular, a company considered most respectable in Japan is a *kabushiki kaisha,* even to the extent that in the traditional sector a vast number of small family undertakings adopted this form of incorporation. Because, however, a 'company-in-the-form-of-stock,' as the four characters for *kabushiki kaisha* mean, is essentially legal terminology, what is actually involved is an altogether different matter.

For the common man, probably as much as for management and the work force, a firm is primarily known by its size. All entrants in the labor force have but one hope, to be hired by a 'big' firm; employees take an immense pride in the 'bigness' of the firm they work for, and managers compare the size of respective market shares. Historically, large size was always identified with belonging to the 'modern' sector of the economy, i.e., the upper level of the dual structure. The basic qualification for an undertaking's identification with the 'modern' sector was the use of modern technology, which remained for a long time something imported, even when it resulted from much original research. Even today, the first reaction of a Japanese industrialist faced with a new product or process may be to investigate whether he can acquire the pertinent license or patent and at what cost, and well before wondering whether he himself might not create a similar product. In the interwar period especially, this 'imported' aspect of modern technology often resulted in outright imitation. It was only after completion of this first step, whether

---

[8] See Johannes Hirschmeier, *The Origins of Entrepreneurship in Meiji Japan,* Cambridge: Harvard University Press, 1964, pp. 61–68.

taken by imitation or by license agreement, that a slow process of assimilation began: the foreign product was analyzed by a group of specialists who familiarized themselves with each and every component, in a way 'digested' each part. Japanese creativity thereby aimed, and still aims, not so much at a new product as at new uses of an already existing 'imported' product.[9] Modernity for a Japanese industrial enterprise had, then, from the very beginning, an almost exclusively technical meaning, and its most direct objective was to contribute to exports. This peculiarity of Japanese technology—to import from abroad in order to export abroad—has been changing rapidly from the early 1950s on. Japan's know-how is now at the threshold of maturity and, for a decade or so, has relied more and more explicitly on original research. Full confidence, however, has not yet been reached. On June 1 1968, the import of technology was 'freed', but seven fields remain still controlled: atomic energy, aircraft, space development, electronic computers, weapons, explosives, and petro-chemicals.[10]

Enterprises are identified by their capitalization, but the amount of capitalization is at best an elusive qualification. What is the true relevance of capital, when, as today, the average debt-equity ratio of private Japanese companies is 80:20 or worse? In the West, equity is a measure of a company's independence or, better, of its dependence on the brains of its entrepreneurs; such a concern has no place in Japan, where no company is the exclusive brain-child of an industrialist. Granted that the purpose of an enterprise is not capitalization but production, the fact remains that in Japan most of the requirements for such production—raw materials, technologies, and markets—have long been and have largely remained dependent on overseas contingencies and foreign exchange, over which an individual company has little control, if any. As a result, stockholding has in Japan dimensions different from those in the West, as is to be

9 See Hollerman, op. cit., p. 46 n.
10 *Nihon Keizai Shimbun,* Tokyo, May 14 1968, p. 1.

surmised from the presentation of financial statements.[11] It comes as a shock to the unprepared foreigner that Japanese profit-figures, and others, published in English for listings of American and European Depository Receipts (ADR and EDR) are different from the figures published in Japanese, or that the thirteen Japanese City Banks have all, for a decade, declared an annual dividend rate of 9%, the maximum permitted by the Ministry of Finance!

A Japanese enterprise is, therefore, not truly identified in absolute physical terms, like its equity capital. But a relative physical qualification looms large: its market share. In Japan, companies are ranked, especially the large ones, according to the share they command in their own product market. Each industry has its own 'Big Four' or 'Big Five', followed at a respectable distance by the spectrum of medium firms, where again ranking takes place, and these are followed by an undistinguished horde of small firms. This ranking, as will be shown later, is the yard-stick of competition. As a result, enterprises are predominantly production-oriented rather than consumption-oriented. The urge is not to win the market, but to conquer it, or at least to make sure that the 'growing pie', as long as the tempo of economic growth does not slacken, yields not only an absolutely but also a relatively larger portion.

It must also be understood that a Japanese industrial enterprise is identified by its relationship to some other enterprises or to an industrial grouping. The first relationship is of the *oyagaisha-kogaisha* type (parent firm-offspring firm). It takes many forms at all levels of the economic structure, from the *noren-wake* of the noodle peddler, whereby an employee is set up on his own and is allowed to advertise the patronage of his original employer, to full-fledged subsidiaries of large corporations. A cluster of firms may result from some vertical division of labor, as when manufacturers like Matsushita, Sony, Seiko run their own trading firms as *kogaisha*. Or it may

---

11 See T. W. M. Teraoka, 'Accounting Practices' in Robert J. Ballon (ed.), *Doing Business in Japan*, Revised Edition, Tokyo: Sophia-Tuttle, 1968, pp. 149–157.

result from mere diversification of operations, as when the Tokyo Electric Express Railway, Ltd., fathers Tokyu Construction Company, Tokyu Real Estate Company, Tokyu Department Stores, and so on. Such *kogaisha* are, as a rule, managed by retired executives of a parent firm and are used as training grounds for promising younger employees, often called *shukkō* (transferees). It is then fairly easy to shift from one offspring to another certain financial burdens which would otherwise be reflected in the balance sheets, although the recent decision of the Ministry of Finance progressively to enforce the consolidation of accounts may well deal a fatal blow to the practice.

Another type of group relationship was, in prewar years, the well known *zaibatsu*. Although the name is still used today, the institution, often carrying the same name as before—Mitsui, Mitsubishi, or the like—is fundamentally different. (Figure 1) Another term is often used, *keiretsu* (alignment). It consists in a controlling relationship among firms, either through stockholding, interlocking directorates, dispatch of directors, fund loaning, supply of raw materials, or supply of products; it may even cover subcontracting. (Figure 2) Some of the large commercial banks in Japan have attempted to 'align' a number of enterprises in various industries by calling on the prewar *zaibatsu* ties of solidarity backed by financial facilities. It is not that the bank 'runs the show'; postwar legislation has strictly limited a bank's shareholding in any given company, but much initiative has been taken by the banks in grouping around them firms hungry for capital to the extent that it has become current practice for commercial banks to lend working capital to their clients.

Such an industrial group is at best cemented by the following ties:
1 Preferential credit by the leading bank, but not entirely exclusive of competing banks. (Figure 3)
2 Interlocked directorates with representatives of the bank sitting on the board.

[15]

3 Overall coordinating committees.[12] (Figure 4)

It seems therefore that a Japanese industrial enterprise is much more easily identified by intangible qualifications than by 'tangible' equity. The hard facts of Western Economics are in Japan subsumed in environmental circumstances that 'give them a certain human warmth', the Japanese businessman would say, or 'water them down', the Western businessman would say. It may help the Westerner to remember the social custom that makes it difficult for Japanese to call one another by their first names; the family name followed by the honorific *san* should be used. The same could almost be said about enterprises; they should be called by their family names!

[12] See also Iwao Hoshii, *The Dynamics of Japan's Business Evolution*, Tokyo: Orient/ West, 1966, pp. 149–164, where a detailed composition of the major industrial groups is given.

Chapter one: The Japanese dimensions of enterprises

FIGURE I

BRIEF OUTLINE OF JAPAN'S INDUSTRIAL GROUPS (1967)

Names of groups	Central liaison organs	Number of member firms	Total paid-up capital[2]	Total sales[2]
Former *Zaibatsu groups*				
Mitsubishi	*Kinyōkai*	25	¥273,940	¥1,555,830
Mitsui	*Nimokukai*	17	113,000	583,590
Sumitomo	*Hakusuikai*	17[1]	158,690	736,930
Financial capital groups				
Dai-Ichi	Meeting of presidents *(Mutsumikai & Sansuikai)*	16	164,350	728,250
Fuji	*Fuyōkai*	25	309,840	1,684,710
Sanwa	*Sansuikai*	24	345,430	1,650,120
(Kōgin)	—	—	—	—
Industrial capital groups				
Nissan	*Shunkōkai*	14	187,040	1,167,210

Other groups: Matsushita, Toyota, Toshiba, Yawata, etc.

Source: *Nihon Keizai Shimbun,* Tokyo, April 25 1967, p. 10.

Notes: 1 Inclusive of Sumitomo Light Metal Co. which was due to join the group shortly.

2 In million yen: As of April 1, 1967 for paid-up capital and fiscal 1966 for sales, including some estimates; exclusive of member firms belonging to such industries as banking, insurance, real estate, trading, warehousing, etc.

FIGURE 2
"SCOPE" OF THE MITSUBISHI GROUP (1966)

1 Firms readily classifiable as those of the Mitsubishi Group because their activities strongly reflect their affiliation with the group:
 Member firms of *kinyōkai* gathering of presidents: Mitsubishi Bank, Mitsubishi Trust & Banking, Meiji Mutual Life Insurance, Tokio Marine & Fire Insurance, Mitsubishi Mining, Mitsubishi Cement, Mitsubishi Metal Mining, Mitsubishi Oil, Mitsubishi Heavy Industries, Mitsubishi Steel Mfg., Mitsubishi Electric, Mitsubishi Chemical Industries, Mitsubishi Monsanto Chemical, Mitsubishi Plastic Industries, Asahi Glass, Mitsubishi Rayon, Mitsubishi Petrochemical, Mitsubishi Chemical Machinery Mfg., Mitsubishi Paper Mills, Mitsubishi Edogawa Chemical, Kirin Brewery, Mitsubishi Shōji Kaisha, Mitsubishi Warehouse, Mitsubishi Estate, NYK Line, Chiyoda Chemical Engineering & Construction, Yūbetsu Coal Mining.
2 Firms whose conduct is akin to that of ex-*zaibatsu affiliates*: Nippon Kōgaku, Nichiro Fisheries, Lion Fat & Oil, Pacific Transportation, Yokkaichi Warehouse, Tōkai Gas Chemical, Tōkai Electrode Mfg., Nippon Carbide Industries.
3 Sub-groups:
 Shimadzu group: Shimadzu Seisakusho, Dai Nippon Toryo, Japan Storage Battery;
 Morimura group: Nippon Tōki Kaisha, Tōyō Tōki, Nippon Glass, Nippon Tokushu Tōgyo Kaisha;
 Tōkyū group: Tōkyō Electric Express Railway, Tōkyū Real Estate, Tōyoko, Tōei Motion Picture.
4 Firms simply related to the group on the basis of financing from Mitsubishi Bank: Ajinomoto, Fuji Spinning, Morinaga Confectionery, Honda Motor, Isetan, Dainichi-Nippon Cables, Kikkōman Shōyu, Ina Seito Kaisha, Shinetsu Chemical Industry.
5 Subsidiaries of Mitsubishi group firms other than Mitsubishi Bank:
 Subsidiary of Mitsubishi Chemical Industries: Nihon Suiso Kōgyō; Subsidiaries of Mitsubishi Shōji Kaisha: Kinsho-Mataichi, Meiji Sugar Mfg., Nippon Beet Sugar Mfg., Fuji Seitō.
6 Firms on the border line of the Mitsubishi group:
 Tōyōbō, Seibu Railway, Kinki Nippon Railway, Gunze Silk Mfg., Nippon Kayaku.

Note: Among the above groupings, only the following can be said to fall under the clear classification of the Mitsubishi group: 1,2, Shimadzu and Morimura groups of 3 and most of 5.
Source: *Nihon Keizai Shimbun,* Tokyo, January 31 1967, p. 10.

FIGURE 3

RATIO OF BORROWINGS BY FINANCING GROUP (1966)

Category	Mitsui Bank & Affiliates		Mitsubishi Bank & Affiliates		Sumitomo Bank & Affiliates	
Mining	Mitsui Mining	15.0	Mitsubishi Mining	18.6	Sumitomo Coal Mng.	39.2
Construction	Mitsui Construction	52.1	—		Kajima Construction	33.4
Foodstuffs	Taitō	44.5	Kirin Brewery	50.0	Asahi Breweries	13.4
Textiles	Kanegafuchi Spinning	17.2	Fuji Spinning	47.5	Kureha Spinning	27.9
	Tōyō Rayon	23.4	Mitsubishi Rayon	24.7	Asahi Chem. Ind.	28.0
Paper–Pulp	Ōji Paper	23.5	Mitsubishi Paper Mills	41.1	Daishōwa Paper	16.3
Chemicals	Tōyō Kōatsu Ind.	19.6	Mitsubishi Chemical	22.9	Sumitomo Chemical	39.0
	Mitsui Chemical Ind.	37.7	Shin-etsu Chemical Ind.	30.2	Sumitomo Bakelite	46.5
	Mitsui Petrochemical	32.8	Yoshitomi Pharmaceutical	46.5	Takeda Chem. Ind.	35.9
Ceramics	Onoda Cement	26.6	—		Sumitomo Cement	41.4
	Central Glass	31.5	Asahi Glass	29.8	Nippon Sheet Glass	60.1
Iron & Steel	Tōshiba Denkō	61.0	Mitsubishi Steel Mfg.	61.1	Sumitomo Metal Ind.	34.7
	Japan Steel Works	41.8	—		Kubota Iron & Mach.	29.3
Non-ferrous Metals	Mitsui Min. & Smelt.	27.1	Mitsubishi Metal Mining	41.3	Sumitomo Metal Mng.	60.4
	Fujikura Cable	50.1	Dainichi-Nippon Cables	45.5	Sumitomo Elec. Ind.	53.3
Machinery	Tsubakimoto Chain	34.7	Mitsubishi Chem. Mach.	72.2	Sumitomo Machinery	55.4
	Toyoda Machine Wks	22.8	Chiyoda Chem. Eng. & Const.	49.6	Komatsu Mfg.	20.1
Electric	Tōkyō Shibaura Elec.	21.8	Mitsubishi Electric	30.6	Matsushita Elec.	12.2
	Sony	44.9	Kyōsan Electric	34.4	Meidensha Elec. Mfg.	2.6
Transportation	Toyota Motor	9.3	Mitsubishi Heavy Ind.	24.2	Uraga Heavy Ind.	15.1
	Mitsui Shipbuilding	20.5	—		Tōyō Kōgyō	15.3
Prec. Mach.	—		Nippon Kōgaku	51.7	—	
Trading	Mitsui & Co.	24.7	Mitsubishi Shōji	36.4	Sumitomo Shōji	51.5
	General Bussan	34.2	—		C. Itoh & Co.	25.9
Real Estate	Mitsui Real Estate	43.6	Mitsubishi Estate	37.2	—	
Warehousing	Mitsui Warehouse	59.2	Mitsubishi Warehouse	74.3	Sumitomo Warehouse	63.0

	Fuji Bank & Affiliates		Sanwa Bank & Affiliates		Other Banks		
Mining	—		—		Furukawa Mining	Dai-Ichi Bank	28.9
Construction	Taisei Construction	40.8	Ohbayashi-Gumi	27.9	Shimizu Construction	"	33.5
Foodstuffs	Sapporo Breweries	6.0	Dai-Nippon Sugar	—	Dai-Nippon Sugar	"	17.3
Textiles	Japan Wool Textile	19.0	Nichibō	37.5	Tōyōbō	"	21.3
	Tōhō Rayon	30.3	Teijin	25.1	Kurashiki Rayon	Industrial Bk	23.2
Paper–Pulp	Kokusaku Pulp Ind.	21.3	—		—		—
Chemicals	Shōwa Denkō	21.9	Chisso	*19.8*	Nissan Chem. Ind.	Industrial Bk	31.8
	Kureha Chemical Ind.	21.1	Ube Industries	19.6	Denki Kagaku Kōgyō	Nippon Kangyō Bk	18.6
	Dai-Ichi Kōgyō Seiyaku	44.0	Tanabe Seiyaku	19.8	—		—
Ceramics	Nihon Cement	45.1	Osaka Cement	41.7	—		—
Iron & Steel	Nippon Kōkan	22.4	Nakayama Steel	51.7	Yawata Iron & Steel	Industrial Bk	14.5
	Yodogawa Steel Wks	47.9	Nisshin Steel Works	28.2	Fuji Iron & Steel	"	20.3
Non-ferrous Metals	Shōwa Aluminum	49.4	—		Nippon Mining	—	11.3
Machinery	Nippon Seiko	33.8	Hitachi Wire & Cable	36.0	Nippon Light Metal	Dai-Ichi, Ind.	15.0
	—		Tsukishima Kikai	52.3	Ebara Mfg.	Dai-Ichi Bk	29.9
	—		Tōyō Bearing	35.7	—		—
Electric	Oki Electric Ind.	41.7	Iwasaki Tsushinki	32.3	Hitachi	Industrial Bk	16.3
	Hayakawa Electric	46.8	Toyo Denki Seizo	44.1	Fuji Electric	Dai-Ichi Bk	10.4
Transportation	Hakodate Dock	15.7	Hitachi Shipbuilding	16.3	Nissan Motor	Industrial Bk	14.2
	Topy Industries	29.8	Daihatsu Kōgyō	33.0	Kawasaki Dockyard	Dai-Ichi Bk	19.6
Prec. Mach.	Canon Camera	32.4	—		Olympus Optical	Nippon Life Ins.	38.3
Trading	Marubeni-Iida	27.2	Nichimen	29.3	Nisshō	Sanwa Bk	26.5
	Okura Trading	53.8	Iwai & Co.	13.3	Gōshō	Bank of Tokyo	39.6
Real Estate	Tōkyō Tatemono	77.9	Heiwa Real Estate	—	Heiwa Real Estate	Long-Term Credit Bk	100.0
Warehousing	—		—		—		—

Note: (1) Large figures in italic show that the company's borrowings from the bank and affiliates rank second place or below in its total borrowings. Others first place.

(2) Surveyed at end of semi-annual settlement term which came during September, 1965-March, 1966. (April, 1965-March, 1966 for annual settlement term).

Source: "Tōkei Geppō (Statistics Monthly)", August 1966, Tōyō Keizai Shimpōsha (Oriental Economist)

FIGURE 4

MEMBER FIRMS OF PRESIDENTIAL MEETINGS OF THE 'BIG THREE' INDUSTRIAL GROUPS (1966)

Banking & Insurance	*Mining & Manufacturing*	*Trading & Others*
Mitsubishi Bank	Mitsubishi Mining	Mitsubishi Shoji Kaisha
	Mitsubishi Cement	Mitsubishi Warehouse
Mitsubishi Trust & Banking	Mitsubishi Metal Mining	Mitsubishi Estate
Meiji Mutual Life Insurance	Mitsubishi Oil	N.Y.K. Line
Tokio Marine & Fire Insurance	Mitsubishi Heavy Industries	
	Mitsubishi Steel Mfg.	
	Mitsubishi Electric	
	Mitsubishi Chemical Industries	
	Mitsubishi Monsanto Chemical	
	Mitsubishi Plastics Industries	
	Asahi Glass	
	Mitsubishi Rayon	
	Mitsubishi Petrochemical	
	Mitsubishi Chemical Machinery Mfg.	
	Mitsubishi Paper Mills	
	Mitsubishi Edogawa Chemical	
	Kirin Brewery	

"*Kinyō* (Friday) Club"
of Mitsubishi
Group

	Banking & Insurance	Mining & Manufacturing	Trading & Others
"*Hakusui Club*" of Sumitomo Group	Sumitomo Bank Sumitomo Trust & Banking Sumitomo Mutual Life Insurance Sumitomo Marine & Fire Insurance	Sumitomo Coal Mining Sumitomo Metal Mining Sumitomo Electric Industries Nippon Electric Sumitomo Metal Industries Sumitomo Machinery Sumitomo Chemical Nippon Sheet Glass Sumitomo Cement	Sumitomo Shoji Kaisha Sumitomo Real Estate Sumitomo Warehouse
"*Nimoku* (2nd Thursday) Club" of Mitsui Group	Mitsui Bank Mitsui Trust & Banking Mitsui Mutual Life Insurance Taishō Marine & Fire Insurance	Mitsui Mining Mitsui Mining & Smelting Mitsui Shipbuilding & Engineering Mitsui Chemical Industry Mitsui Petrochemical Industries Sanki Engineering Tōyō Rayon Tōyō Kōatsu Industries Hokkaido Colliery & Steamship Japan Steel Works	Mitsui & Co. Mitsui Warehouse Mitsui Real Estate

(Order of groups and companies at random)

Source: *Nihon Keizai Shimbun*, January 17 1967, p. 10

[22]

Chapter one: The Japanese dimensions of enterprises

Just as the identification of an enterprise is revealed chiefly by the intangibles of its business, so its organization chiefly emphasizes the aspects of its human organization rather than of its 'production' or work organization. This observation is not to deny that organization charts are known and prominently displayed in Japan, but here, as often elsewhere, they are usually given only a sort of respectful, at-a-distance attention; actual workings follow a different pattern.

The Western management levels top, middle, and lower are not found in Japanese practice, though the words are used. Generally speaking, Japanese organization has three levels[13]:

1   *Keiei* (management) corresponds pretty much to Western corporate management. This is where company policies are determined and where a great deal of time is spent on public relations (with the government and banks, as well as in horizontal and vertical associations with related firms) required by the firm's participation in the national policy of industrialization. In postwar years, most firms that did not previously have their headquarters in Tokyo have moved them there, manifesting thereby the necessity to be closer to where national policies are issued. It is at this level that retiring bureaucrats are hired by the firms with which they were formerly in contact. Officials of the Ministry of Public Health go to pharmaceutical firms; those of the Ministry of Construction to construction firms, and so on. What is expected from these former bureaucrats is not a specific management performance, but the use for the benefit of the firm of the contacts established during their service with the government.

2   *Kanri* (administration) is the level of executive management, usually in the field. Except for the plant manager, all other

13 The writer is endebted to Mr. Ichiro Hattori for most of this presentation of business organization in Japan.

posts, among which the most common are *buchō* (department head) and *kachō* (section chief), are occupied by people remunerated according to the *nenkō* (seniority) system described elsewhere in this volume. Practically all candidates for this level are university graduates who were hired at the time of graduation and have been with the firm ever since. By law, they are excluded from labor-union membership. Socially, they all belong, together with the *ippan* employees of the third level, to the postwar 'new middle class', and call themselves *sararīman* (salarymen or wage-earners). At this level, titles are most numerous, causing an undesirable swelling of management ranks more or less related to execution.

3 *Ippan* (general staff) is the operative level. Before World War II, the distinction between white-collar employees *(shokuin)* and blue-collar employees *(kōin)* was clear-cut. In postwar years, however, the distinction became greatly blurred, and a hierarchy based on formal education now prevails: graduates of middle school qualify for manual jobs, graduates of high school and university for clerical work, and university graduates may hope, further, to accede to the higher ranks of *kanri* and *keiei*. From the viewpoint of remuneration, the same *nenkō* system applies to all, except that the progression curves have different starting points and rates. All these employees are, as a rule, permanently employed *(shain)*; those temporarily employed *(rinjikō, shokutaku)* are not considered by management (or by a union!) as truly belonging to the organization.

It would be erroneous to consider these three levels, *keiei, kanri,* and *ippan,* as three distinct horizontal levels, each with its own degree of authority and responsibility. The Japanese business organization should rather be considered as an organism reacting as a whole to the pulses of life, each organ fulfilling its own function and thus contributing to the life of the entire organism. In an industrial enterprise, operational units, a section or a department, are not operational in

[24]

the sense that they are expected to contribute a specific portion of overall performance, but in the sense that somehow each section identifies itself with total performance, and thereby loses specific accountability. Consequently, authority and responsibility are altogether different from those of the West. The basic concern in the Japanese organization is not to determine clear lines of authority by which specific responsibility can be pinned on each post and its titulary. This fact is best shown in the *ringi* (decision-making) system through which most operational decisions are made.[14] Rather than authority, the over-riding principle of organization is *wa* (harmony), the delicate, ever-shifting balance between sections rivaling in their identification with the whole. Harmony is never static; it is not even ever obtained, but always striven for. Without *wa*, the organization would simply explode; but without 'sectionalism' there would only be death! It does not require, however, a referee, a man in a high position who decides who wins and who loses; such a decision would be based on authority. *Wa* requires a voice, and that is the vital function fulfilled by the next in rank in the organization. At the top of the organization, the president is this voice *par excellence;* his responsibility is not to have the far-sighted ideas that project the company into the future, but to see how the present harmony will best prevail.

In such an organization, promotion will expectedly run along a particular path. 'Promotion based on performance' is a principle valid in Japan as well as in the West if agreement is reached on the meaning of 'promotion'. In the West, promotion means greater or larger authority and responsibility for an individual, with a view to further enhancing, and benefitting from, his talents. In other words, the organization acquires a new element that will add to its total performance; the purpose of the promotion is better performance by the individual and his organization. To all this, Japan adds a new dimension, that of time, which is very like the dimension of time

---

[14] For a description of the *ringi* system, see Robert J. Ballon (ed.), *op. cit.*, pp. 164–166, 172–174.

required for 'promotion' from childhood to adulthood. In both provinces, employment and life, a minimum number of years is required for promotion. Hence it is present continuity that assures promotion rather than future, or better, performance. Such promotion is not necessarily related to economic terms (work performance), but it is related to proper organization values. This is the reason why promotions at the *ippan* and *kanri* levels of a Japanese company come almost exclusively from within and why job rotation is considered essential to the development of a promising executive.

In the organizational pyramid, vertical connections and sectionalism contract more narrowly the higher one rises in the hierarchy, until at the higher level, *keiei,* sectionalism is integrated. The president is then not an individual who carries the organization; he is *the* man of the organization. He cannot be a junior man catapulted to the top by his 'economic' talents; he can be only a senior, who enjoys the charisma of voicing *wa* for the whole.

Can it be said, then, that economic performance has only negligible importance in a Japanese industrial organization? After all, what is at stake is a business venture, not a voluntary social association. But in Japan economic performance is not so much a matter of individual employees as of an entire organization. Manpower development and executive development are primarily contributions from and to the organization; one would almost say that manpower and executive talent are not developed, but are 'processed' by the organization.

Competition

THE nature of Japanese industrial enterprise is understood not only by its internal structure, but also by its relations to other enterprises. Some of these relations operate on a basis of cooperation and determine industrial groupings, as described above. Competition determines another set of relations. In the case of Japan, however, where so much about enterprise is influenced by its appurtenance to a group, it is to be expected that competition, the relationship that pits one enterprise against another, will develop along lines that are not all plotted by the market mechanism.

As is so often the case with similar concepts expressed in Japanese and in a Western language, it would be misleading to assume that the words that denote 'competition' in Japanese and in English have the same meaning. A warning is sounded by none other than Yukichi Fukuzawa, scholar and school administrator, who did most to introduce to Japan Western Economics and Business Administration. In his autobiography, he describes how he had to coin a new word in order to translate 'competition' into Japanese, and how his new word was received.

'I was reading Chambers' book on economics. When I spoke of the book to a certain high official in the Treasury Bureau one day, he became much interested and wanted me to show him a translation . . . I began translating it . . . When I came upon the word "competition", for which there is no equivalent in Japanese, I was obliged to use an invention of my own, *kyōsō*, literally "race-fight".

'When the official saw my translation, he appeared much impressed. Then he said suddenly: "Here is the word 'fight'. What does it mean? It is such an unpeaceful word."

' "That is nothing new," I replied. "That is exactly what all Japanese merchants are doing . . . Thus all merchants 'race and fight' and this is the way money values are fixed. This process is termed *kyōsō* in the science of economics."

' "I understand. But don't you think there is too much effort in Western affairs?"

' "It isn't too much effort. It is the fundamentals of the world of commerce."

' "Yes, perhaps," went on the official. "I understand the idea, but the word 'fight' is not conducive to peace. I could not take the paper with that word to the chancellor."

'I suppose he would rather have seen some such phrase as "men being kind to each other" in a book on economics, or a man's loyalty to his lord, open generosity from a merchant in times of stress, etc. But I said to him, "If you do not agree to the word 'fight', I am afraid I shall have to erase it entirely. There is no other term that is faithful to the original."

'I did delete the offending term in black ink and let him take the papers.'[15]

Even if the Japanese language had no word for 'competition', that fact does not mean that the prosperous and less prosperous merchants of Kansai and their well developed *tonya nakama* (guilds) were only cooperating with one another. On the other hand, the small shopkeeper and the local artisan were supplying the goods and services the local community expected from them; their margin was not a problem of profit, simply one of subsistence; and everybody knew what it takes to stay alive.

Now that Fukuzawa had come up with the 'right' word, things were seemingly bound to change. In modern industrial Japan, competition has a double root, one in tradition and one in modernity. As understood and implemented from the viewpoint of tradition, the Japanese sense of 'competition' would be better described in English by 'sectionalism'. It is not the static relationship of one independent unit to another independent unit; it is the dynamic rapport of rivalry among firms within a given context. Masao Maruyama describes sectionalism in the context of the Emperor System *(Tennō sei)* as follows:

'... Sectionalism was rampant not only in the Army and the Navy, but throughout the entire structure of the Japanese government. It has often been described as "feudalistic", but that is an oversimplification. The feudalistic impulse to de-

15 Eiichi Kiyooka (trans.), *The Autobiography of Fukuzawa Yukichi,* Tokyo: The Hokuseidō Press, 1960, pp. 190–191.

fend one's own particular sphere of interests had its origins in the efforts of each unit to entrench itself in a closed, self-sufficient world. Japanese sectionalism, however, derived from a system according to its respective connection, in a direct vertical line, with the ultimate entity. This involved a constant impulse to unite one-self with that entity, and the resultant sectionalism was of a far more active and aggressive type than that associated with feudalism . . .

'The individuals who composed the various branches of the oligarchy did not regard themselves as active regulators but as men who were, on the contrary, being regulated by rules created elsewhere. None of the oligarchic forces in the country could ever become absolute, instead they all co-existed, all of them equally dependent on the ultimate entity and all of them stressing their comparative proximity to that entity.'[16]

This type of sectionalism brings us back to what was said earlier about industrial groups. It is a phenomenon not so much of an individual firm as of a group of firms within the context of 'Japan, Incorporated', that also includes the government. As seen from the description by Maruyama, it characterized the prewar government. Today also, bitter feuds arise between ministries, as, for example, when a decision had to be taken on where the authority of the Japanese delegation to the OECD originates. The Ministry of International Trade and Industry (MITI) considered itself its repository, since economic matters were involved, but the Ministry of Foreign Affairs also claimed jurisdiction, since the delegation was a representation of Japan abroad. Rivalry may also arise about basic policies, such as the one often opposing the Ministry of Finance and the Bank of Japan (as in the case of balance of payments) or the Ministry of Finance and MITI (as in the case of the reform of the industrial structure). Bureaucratic sectionalism does not differ essentially from

[16] Masao Maruyama, *Thought and Behavior in Modern Japanese Politics*, London: Oxford University Press, 1963, pp. 15, 17.

[29]

that prevailing among industrial groups. In the construction industry, for example, in an attempt to overcome the rivalries among the Big Four, some prestigious public contracts, like that for the building of the new Imperial Palace, are meted out to a consortium of all four.

But this brings us to the other root of competition in Japan, the modern one. Starting in the early 1960s, Japanese businessmen and scholars alike almost never use the term *kyōsō* (competition) without adding the qualification *katō* (excessive). All deplore this 'excessive competition' as a curse on the present-day industrial world in Japan or, more specifically, they deplore an 'excess'. An excess of what? Any economy is faced with excesses of competition; Japan is no exception. But, at the risk of pedantry, one may wonder whether there are not in Japan some important conceptual nuances between 'excesses of competition' and 'excessive competition.' *Katō kyōsō* is the effect of a set of causes that are so many sinews of the Japanese economy. Four main causes might be distinguished, though they closely overlap.

1 *Public policy*

In the expert opinion of Martin Bronfenbrenner, *katō kyōsō* is not a problem of 'too much', but 'too little' competition in the sense that so-called excesses do not result 'from the competitive market mechanism but from its opposite, the working (actual and expected) of the mechanism of public control'. He goes on to say:

'The argument . . . can be paraphrased as follows: We know there is too much output and capacity in our industry. That is the reason we call our industry excessively competitive. So why do we increase our own output and capacity? Primarily, because we expect the Government to protect our profits before very many of us fail. MITI, or some other agency, will step in, set minimum prices, allocate output, apportion imported raw materials or the foreign exchange with which to buy them, in such a way that business becomes profitable again. In such a control scheme, the larger our share of our industry's capacity or output, the larger our share of the market will be under controls, and the better off we are likely to be in the long run. This is why it is good business to expand the way we do, accepting losses at the margin to increase our share of the market.'[17]

2 *Bank policies*

Bank credit is almost exclusively channelled into large firms, and quite selectively to 'related' firms, to help them reap full advantage of the public policy described above. The result is an 'excess' in regard to all other firms that has nothing to do with the market mechanism. The main victims are the small firms; they are either 'out in the cold' financially and venture into the market at their own risk, or they depend closely on a subcontracting relationship with a large firm and then have little if anything to do with the market.

'In general, small firms cannot obtain bank credit without either a guarantee provided by a large firm or by presenting a letter of credit for exports to a foreign buyer. When credit is tight, large firms may not be willing to sponsor the loans of the small companies. This leaves only the alternative of obtaining a letter of credit for exports, which can be discounted to provide working capital for the firm. If a small company has high fixed expenses, it may be faced with the choice of producing for export at a loss or going out of business altogether. This also occasions excessive competition and distress selling.'[18]

[17] Martin Bronfenbrenner, 'Excessive Competition in Japanese Business', *Monumenta Nipponica,* Tokyo: Sophia University, XXL, 1–2, p. 124.
[18] Hollerman, *op. cit.,* pp. 162–163.

3 *Company policy*

The importance of the market share has been described earlier. This concern of the firm leads not to an excess of competition, but to a definite twist of competition itself, not reserved, however, to Japan alone. Large firms confront one another in various markets where they enjoy differing degrees of strength. One may be deterred from an advantageous cutting of prices in one market for fear of retaliation by rivals in other fields where he is weaker. What results may easily call for scrutiny by the Fair Trade Commission and be branded as 'unfair competition' rather than 'excessive competition'.

4 *Labor policy*

The nature of employment, as described elsewhere in this volume, results in labor being an overhead cost rather than a variable cost. This fact means, in blunt terms, that it is far better for the enterprise to produce for inventory than not to produce at all.

> 'Permanent staff cannot be laid off in slack times, thus so long as variable costs are met (on this point Japanese accounting practices are unreliable), the loss of producing for sale at less than full cost may be less than the loss of not producing at all. Thus firms are induced to produce for inventory if not for sale, hoping that a buyer will come along in due course. When inventories and the cost of maintaining inventories become too high, prices tumble and cutthroat selling activities ensue.'[19]

The main ingredients of *katō kyōsō* are not, therefore, those expected in a Western market mix; in Japan they have a tendency to transcend the enterprise, if not the market itself. However, evolution is the order of the day: new forces have appeared on the market.

[19] *Ibid.*, p. 162.

Chapter one: The Japanese dimensions of enterprises

The new forces

THE amazing growth rate of the Japanese economy brings to bear pressures that reveal industrial enterprises as a most dynamic institution of Japan's industrial society. One would expect that the labor movement would play a prominent role in the evolution of this society. Such is not as yet the case, however; unions are rather dragged along with the enterprises they organize, though there have been some instances, such as the proposed *gappei* (merger) between Kanebo and Toho Rayon Company in 1966, where they succeeded temporarily in stopping the move. 'Administrative guidance' by government officials plays a much more positive role, but this is little new in an economy where government and business are partners. The main factor of change—or, more accurately, of evolution—is the growth itself and its impact on society at large, the living organism of which enterprise, large or small, is but a cell.

The investment rate of Japanese enterprises would be utterly suicidal if it were not for the fact that everybody does the same thing and that financial institutions, public and private, gladly cooperate. Resulting over-capacity would spell economic collapse if exports did not keep increasing steadily and the domestic market booming at the cost, however, of rising imports. While the 'consumption revolution' snowballs, the savings rate shows no drastic decline, though the wage-price spiral is often hard to contain, and so on. The consequences of this growing affluence were predictable in advance: when international business discovered Japan to be an alluring market, domestic firms were forced to streamline operations, and employment now expands from sheer security-employment to gain-employment.[20]

---

[20] The opposition of 'subsistence employment' and 'gain employment' was proposed by Werner Sombart. (See Bert G. Hoselitz and Richard D. Lambert, 'Western Societies,' in Richard D. Lambert and Bert F. Hoselitz (eds.), *The Role of Savings and Wealth in Southern Asia and the West*, Paris: Unesco, 1963, p. 14).

C [33]

In postwar Japan, reliance on foreign capital is expressed largely in short-term loans rather than in investment. Though foreign investments are, admittedly, a trickle, that trickle is ominous, at least to the Japanese. The dimensions of capital liberalization are much more psychological than economic.[21] The reason is that foreign capital 'threatens' Japanese enterprise. Feelings are conflicting. Collectively, Japanese businessmen shudder at the inroads on such venerable mainstays of the establishment as the Mitsuis (Figure 5) or the Mitsubishis (Figure 6). But, just as collectively, they turn to the government for further liberalization. One could call it a 'double-play' if it were not for Japan, Incorporated, that acknowledges the need for technology even at the 'regrettable' cost of foreign investment, but remains determined to go at it at its own pace.

The impact of foreign investment on Japanese enterprise will be assimilated in two stages overlapping each other. The first stage implies a reform of the economic structure, of which the most obvious development has been and is the *gappei,* a form of consolidation of enterprises that has been loosely translated as 'merger'. An excellent example is given by Mitsui & Co. (Figure 7) and its progressive 'alignment' *(keiretsu)* during the 1950s. With the advent of trade and capital liberalization in the 1960s, the trend has picked up momentum and starts now to embrace more than 'related' enterprises.

But the impact of foreign investment may also hit Japanese enterprise in a more direct way, either by foreign management participation, as in the case of joint ventures, or by environmental changes such as marketing techniques disturbing outdated distribution patterns, or by personnel policies affecting the labor market, and so on. True to some ingrained outlook of 'catching up', Japan wants to bridge her technological gap with the West by acquiring its know-how. As a price for acquiring this know-how, the Japanese make no

[21] See H. Glazer, 'Capital Liberalization' in Robert J. Ballon (ed.) *Joint Ventures and Japan,* Tokyo: Sophia-Tuttle, 1967, pp. 1–20.

bones about stating that they prefer by far cold-cash royalties to management participation. On the other hand, since foreign interests are not readily permitted to have it their way by means of a fully owned subsidiary, they have to compromise and settle for a joint venture. Many such undertakings are started on the basis of such an uneasy compromise. A new enterprise is born, offspring of a mixed marriage that does not smoothly fit industrial mores. The Japanese partner will be asked to staff the new venture at the risk of getting it considered a subsidiary of the Japanese partner.[22]

In marketing, foreign interests may insist on bypassing commission agents and establish immediate contact with retailers if not end-consumers, or they may shift emphasis from rebates to cash and volume discounts.[23] The government is particularly anxious to gain time in the modernization of Japanese distribution patterns, while domestic makers form a united front, e.g., to get the Fair Trade Commission to approve 'Fair Competition Rules' that prohibit premium gifts to consumers. It may well be that commercial capital, as in chain stores, will be the last to be liberalized. Another side impact in the field of marketing is the relationship between makers and advertising agencies. In Japan, these agencies are not yet considered partners in marketing planning, but foreign interests want them to be precisely that.

Japanese personnel policies also come under fire. Starting wages are higher in foreign-controlled firms; executives, though younger, are often better paid; working hours are shorter, and so on.[24] By contrast, however, foreign personnel administration is accused of being 'dry and cold'; in other words, it values an employee according to his *individual* contribution to the firm. An often unbearable anxiety besets the Japanese employee of a foreign company; he feels that personnel can be laid off for reasons determined by the home office abroad. Justifiable or not, such anxiety remains

---

[22] See Y. Kobayashi, 'Human Aspects of Management' in *Ibid.,* pp. 78–80.
[23] *Nihon Keizai Shimbun.* Tokyo, December 5 1967, p. 10.
[24] *Ibid.,* December 12 1967, p. 10.

FIGURE 5
MITSUI GROUP: JOINT VENTURES WITH
FOREIGN FIRMS (1967)

Joint ventures	Founding	Mitsui group enterprises	Foreign partners
Kōa Oil	Nov., '50	Nippon Oil (0.8%) Others (49.2)	California Texas Oil (50%)
Tōyō Otis Elevator	June, '51	Tōkyō Shibaura Electric(Toshiba)(20)	Otis Elevator (80)
Nippon Petroleum refining	Oct., '51	Nippon Oil (50)	California Texas Oil (50)
Ray-O-Vac Co. (Japan)	June, '53	Tōshiba (56.7)	Electric Storage Battery (43.3)
Nippon Densō	Dec., '53	Toyota Motor (12.5) Others (78)	Robert Bosch GmbH (9.5)
Pine Sewing Machine Mfg.	Dec., '56	Japan Steel Works (50)	Singer (50)
Nippon Remington Univac	Mar., '54	Mitsui & Co. (50) Others (20)	Sperry Rand (30)
Shibaura United Engineering	Nov., '59	Tōshiba (51.6)	United Engineering & Foundry (48.2)
Tōyō Continental Carbon	Aug., '60	Tōyō Kōatsu Industries (66.7)	Continental Carbon (33.3)
Mitsui Polychemicals	Nov., '60	Mitsui Petrochemical (50)	E.I. Du Pont de Nemours (50)
Robertshaw Orient	Dec., '60	Tōyō Menka Kaisha(15) Others (25)	Robertshaw Controls (60)
Nippon Brunswick	Mar., '61	Mitsui & Co. (50)	Brunswick (50)
Tōshiba Musical Industries	June, '61	Tōshiba (89.8)	Capitol Records (10.2)
Beckman-Tōshiba	Mar., '62	Tōshiba (50)	Beckman Instruments (50)
Mitsui-Deuts Diesel Engine	Feb., '63	Mitsui Shipbuilding & Engineering (60)	Klöckner Humboldt Deutz (40)
Kyokuto Petroleum Industries	June, '63	Mitsui & Co. (37) Others (13)	Mobil Oil (through Mobil Sekiyu K.K.)(50)
Tōyō Products	Dec., '63	Tōyō Rayon (50)	E.I. Du Pont de Nemours (50)
Tōyō Cyanamid	July, '64	Tōyō Kōatsu Industries (51)	American Cyanamid (49)
Tōshiba Ampex	Sept., '64	Tōshiba (51)	Ampex (49)

Note: Joint ventures with capitalization exceeding ¥100 million.
Parenthesized figures indicate ratios of investment.
Source: *Nihon Keizai Shimbun*, Tokyo, March 7 1967, p. 10

Chapter one: The Japanese dimensions of enterprises

FIGURE 6

MITSUBISHI GROUP: JOINT VENTURES WITH FOREIGN FIRMS (1967)

Joint ventures	Founding	Mitsubishi group enterprises	Foreign partners
Mitsubishi Monsanto Chemical	Jan., '52	Mitsubishi Chemical Industries (50)	Monsanto Chemical (50)
Mitsubishi Petro-chemical	Apr., '56	Mitsubishi Chemical Industries (10.8) Mitsubishi Rayon (10.8) Asahi Glass (10.8) Others (35)	Shell Group (15)
Mitsubishi Acetate	July. '56	Mitsubishi Rayon (88)	Celanese (12)
Asahi Fiber Glass	Nov., '56	Asahi Glass (60)	Owens-Corning Fiberglas (40)
Nippon Clark	Dec., '61	Mitsubishi Heavy Industries (25.5) Mitsubishi Shōji Kaisha (25.5)	Dresser Industries (49)
Mitsubishi Reynolds Aluminum	Jan., '62	Mitsubishi Metal Mining (31) Mitsubishi Chemical Industries (30) Others (15)	Reynolds Metals (24)
Yuka Badische	Jan., '62	Mitsubishi Petro-chemical (51)	BASF (49)
Mitsubishi TRW	Mar., '62	Mitsubishi Electric (42) Mitsubishi Heavy Industries (10) Others (8)	TRW (20)
Mitsubishi Precision	May, '62	Mitsubishi Electric (42) Mitsubishi Heavy Industries (10) Mitsubishi Shoji Kaisha (4) Others (4)	General Precision Equipment (40)
Sanshō Plastics	Sept., '62	Mitsubishi Petro-chemical (45) Toppan Printing (10)	Shorko Investing (45)
Caterpillar Mitsubishi	July, '63	Mitsubishi Heavy Industries (50)	Caterpillar Tractor (50)
Mitsubishi COMINCO Smelting	May, '65	Mitsubishi Metal Mining (55)	Consolidated Mining & Smelting (45)

Note: Figures in parentheses indicate ratios of investment.

Source: *Nihon Keizai Shimbun*, Tokyo, February 7 1967, p. 10

[37]

FIGURE 7

MITSUI COMPANY—FROM DISSOLUTION
TO AMALGATION (1947–1959)

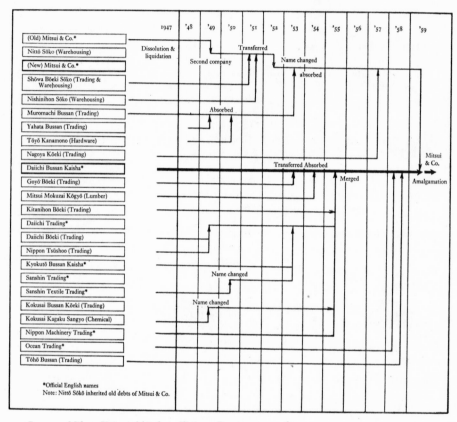

Source: *Nihon Keizai Shimban,* Tokyo, January 10 1967, p. 10

real. But what has begun to upset most Japanese employers is that foreign firms have started heavy recruiting of new school graduates, precisely at the time when labor supply is in dire shortage. They also watch with dismay and scorn the difficult progress of so-called Executives' Recruiting Agencies, so far catering mainly to foreign firms by raiding other foreign firms!

Foreign investment and its sequels are not, however, the only

[38]

new forces working away at Japanese enterprise. From within Japan herself, a new and explosive force is at work: the postwar consumer boom. The concomitant transition from security-employment to gain-employment becomes only slowly apparent, but it will probably consist in adding gain to security rather than replacing security with gain. In a country where labor was long in over-supply, economic growth has now caused a shortage, especially among the new entrants into the labor force. At least for this age bracket, as well as for some sophisticated skills, the labor market has from a seller-market become a buyer-market, and the buyer is forced to bid higher and higher prices. As will be explained in the chapter on the wage system, this development is possible only at the cost of a thorough revision of prevailing wage practices. But the economics of affluence are also affecting the outlook of the seller of labor, especially among younger male employees and female employees in general. As a result, labor-cost consciousness starts to spread: manpower reductions on the basis of work measurement, control of indirect labor costs, mechanization and automation, and the like. At the top of the industrial structure, oligopoly is advocated not only in order to rationalize production, but most explicitly, in many cases, in order also to rationalize management and pool research and development activities. At the bottom of the industrial structure, 80% of all Japanese mergers involve small firms, and the rate of bankruptcies keeps increasing, having already reached an average of thirty per day!

Some foreign observers predict (and wish?) that rising labor costs will price Japan out of international competition. If such a contingency were likely, then the United States would have lost its race many years ago. As a matter of fact, Japanese management often seems surprisingly lenient in regard to wage increases. The reason is that Japanese enterprise is explicitly and deeply part and parcel of the social fabric of Japan. The economic price of such wage increases is increases in productivity: to the Japanese employer, the reasoning is as simple as that.

And one is back at the root of Japan's economic growth, at the root of her industrialization, one hundred years ago and today. Japan's amazing drive is based on the full use of the diligence of her people, adapted to new and changing circumstances and stimulated now by the latest 'national emergency', which requires that the economy stay competitive, notwithstanding increasing labor costs. This is the type of challenge that Japan has faced in one way or another for a hundred years. And more than ever, she can count on the resilience and dedication of her enterprise, managers and managed alike.

CHAPTER TWO

Motivational forces
in
Japanese life

BY MAURICE BAIRY

The physical milieu—the social milieu—the psychological milieu

IN a previous essay about 'Japanese ways'[1], I distinguished between two degrees of motivation: one rather unconscious—total and general—and one comparatively conscious— rational and specific. Here, without excluding the second, the conscious motivation, I should like to develop the first, the unconscious motivation, which seems more illuminatingly than the other to account for a good deal of Japanese behavior.

Since no critical elaboration of the various theories of motivation that exist is relevant here, my approach cannot be strictly scientific. Rather, it will be an attempt to explicate Japanese activity according to three levels: the physical, the social, and the psychological. Through analysis of *how* the Japanese work, I may hopefully shed some light upon *why* they work.

At the outset, in order to preclude any misunderstanding, it should be noted that the dynamism of the Japanese has always taken, and continues to take, variable forms. It nevertheless seems

[1] Robert J. Ballon, (ed.) *Doing Business in Japan,* Revised Edition, Tokyo: Sophia-Tuttle, 1968, Chapter One.

that underlying that dynamism the same basic patterns never cease to exist, even though the organism that Japan has always been and continues to be is constantly reacting to the changing solicitations of a world of persons and things in an irreversible progress.

Motivation includes whatever has been and is meaningful to the constitution of an invitation to action. Accordingly, for the Japanese, motivation is a system of relationships that exists between them and the ambient world. The various levels at which the contacts of such relationships develop will be examined successively here, although they constitute a unity of influence to which the majority of Japanese react without awareness. In any case, an organism must be situated in a milieu, a place from which it can draw the various components necessary to its development.

The physical milieu

A well-known principle of Japanese life, solidarity between man and nature, is rooted in a long history of agriculture in Japan: until a century ago, the occupation involved more than 80% of the population. In fact, attachment to the soil and to the concomitant social structure has been so deeply inculcated that the Japanese industrial revolution seemed merely to shift the focus, for members of a Japanese team laboring together still feel extremely strong affective bonds with their place of work. Generally speaking, however, what has been retained is chiefly a sentiment, an appreciative sense of location, according to which, for example, Tokyo is preferred to Osaka and, in Tokyo, Marunouchi to Yotsuya. This importance of location *(ba)* in the Japanese context has somewhere been demonstrated by a Japanese anthropologist. Everywhere in the world, of course, there are places distinguished by special human affection because they have historically favored art or commerce or religion. But in Japan not only are such places regarded as national shrines or, at the very least, memorable historical spots, but also each square meter of land, wherever located, is looked

[42]

upon as a gift from above, a gift that demands active and suitable human recognition of it through dedicated work and exploitation.

Over-endowed with mountains and rivers, the land of the Rising Sun is notoriously wanting in arable soil, which consequently is as precious as it is rare. Except for a few flat areas, a great deal of the arable soil that is available must be painstakingly embanked and irrigated. In view of the country's sparsity of natural resources in general, the Japanese seem to have brought about a remarkable convergence of all pertinent potentialities for the most concentrated and effective use of them. Unfortunately, they have nothing like the great plains of the French Beauce, where the sky seems to mark the only limit and the rich soil is impatient to yield an easy harvest. Instead, on their very much restricted parcel of earth, they must still labor continually, just as an observer of the past once wrote: '... all day the peasants bent their patient backs to thrust the young rice-plants into the sloughs of the paddies, to roll spools of cotton for spinning, to flail the bearded wheat and to spread out on the straw mats the flowers of hollyhock and thistle which, when dried, could be used as crude dyer.'[2]

The historical and continuing importance to the Japanese of their location and its influence upon them would seem obvious, but a contemporary reference may reinforce the view. Recently a survey made among Japanese emigrants to South America who had become Christian revealed that they had become so not because of personal conviction but because Christianity was the religion of the country they were living in. In exactly the same way does it befit the Japanese living in Japan to be Shintoist or Buddhist.

A sensitive observer of the Japanese may notice that their feeling for location includes qualitative dimensions not always openly revealed: the dimensions of 'high-low', 'up-down', or 'above-below', for example. At the risk of some subjective interpretation of the tension these antithetical dimensions represent (since it can be proved only by hints and traces), there are yet enough indica-

[2] Patt Barr, *The Coming of the Barbarians,* London: MacMillan, Co. 1967, p. 127.

tions of the existence of such a tension in the Japanese as to warrant the surmise that it has brought about a dynamism that has long influenced both their attitudes towards and their activities among persons and things. If this hypothesis be true, it would justify an attempt to find at the physical level a series of parallel indications showing concrete Japanese intentions in their milieu and the consequent relationships motivating their actions.

The earliest social reflex instilled in the Japanese might constitute an interesting introduction into the study of this dynamism. A Japanese child seems to achieve the greatest thing on earth when he has learned how to make the bows customary in the mutual salutations of his people. Both mentally and bodily he must learn to acknowledge the scale of the varying degrees of importance of those around him: he must bow deeply to his father, less deeply to his uncles and aunts, and may simply nod to his brothers and sisters; he must bow deeply to others and very deeply to still others. Such attention to the Japanese measure of 'up-down'—or, better, the traditional training that has established and perpetuated the inherent attitude— is manifested in various actions of Japanese farmers. Given the prolonged hand-work necessary in the low and often terraced planes of their ricepaddies, they are rarely standing at their labor; there were once numbers of aged Japanese farmers, men and women alike, whose bodies, after long years of work in the paddies, were permanently ossified at right angles. Fishermen, too, must bend constantly to the pulling of ropes, the rowing of oars, the mending of nets. And in characteristic Japanese homes, where most activity goes on virtually at floor level, the necessity of bending over is almost continuous, whether in the preparation of food, in sewing, or in any other labor.

The number of actions that indicate ascent or descent in the Japanese context are so numerous that their very multiplicity might alone validate the present argument. To approach it from another direction, the Japanese especially revere height, whether in mountains or in the sources of streams. The most obvious evidence lies in the aspiration of every Japanese to ascend Mount Fuji at least once. Mountain-climbing is, of course, a fairly universal activity, but it seems to be more common and more meaningful among the Japanese than among other peoples. Indeed, the Japanese seem to have a general liking for what is tall or high. In recent years they have built a number of towers whose heights have been based on nationally and internationally competitive prestige rather than on the requirements of the instruments of communication that top them.

If the Japanese have not always left their homes by stepping downstairs or at least by stepping down from huge thresholds that exact a contrary movement upon entering, archeological findings have revealed the existence of superelevated storehouses accessible only by ladders. Although ordinary Japanese once lived on the ground, the Japanese climate forced them very soon to build their houses above the ground. In the Nara period the height of the platform of a house indicated the rank of the inhabitants. Was this shift in house-levels initiated from reasons of cleanliness or from reasons of hierarchy imported from China? Although there is no room here for an exploration of that question, it might yet be observed that the Japanese have some kind of abhorrence for what is dirty—more specifically, for what is on the earth. The sumo fighter, for instance, assures his victory by making his opponent touch the ground, and the sumo referee is not allowed to wear *geta*. Moreover, the Japanese generally consider going barefoot an indignity.

All in all, this Japanese dynamism involving the dimensions of 'updown' *(ue-shita)* might be connected with a rejection of what is unclean, impure. Consider also the Japanese living in villages located near mountain forests. As in many such villages of the world, there has always been, perhaps prototypically, a seemingly demented person associated with such Japanese villages who has singularized himself by a special affinity with nature. On the one hand, he knows all the properties of plants, and the animals are not afraid of him; on the other hand, he avoids his fellow human beings

[45]

and takes shelter higher on the mountain or in the environing woods. Sometimes, driven by hunger or a desire to see his relatives again, he comes down from his sanctuary and rewards the curiosity of the villagers by telling them fantastic tales about the beings he lives with in that region which, although it overhangs their daily lives, is for them distant and unknown. For the villagers he may be the representative of the Sacred, of the novel and mysterious that they long to know but are too busy or timid to seek out. In a similar way, Japanese hermits and monks have consciously and deliberately led secluded lives in the mountains. Suffice it to say here that the Japanese, like certain other peoples, have traditionally regarded the clean, the pure, the magic, the mysterious, the sacred, as situated above—on high, as it were—, thus determining a dynamism directed towards novelty, cleanliness, perfection. Hence their rather primitive sense grades most values according to their greater or lesser proximity to the source of all, of life itself—to what is above. In other words, to reiterate, while the strict unity that binds man and nature together manifests itself in the importance the Japanese give to location, location itself is qualitatively determined according to a scale that is graduated from low to high, from down to up.

At the same time that the Japanese are strongly motivated by what is higher and purer, by their sense of the source of life, they are also motivated by other aspects of Japanese topology as well. Since a very intense attachment exists between them and their own small holdings of the arable land that is so scarce in the entire archipelago, a parallel sense of a relationship of mutual 'give and take' between man and nature seems to have developed. Fastidious repetition of the same gestures year after year, like rote memory, generates a kind of second nature or biological habituation to the work involved. The laws of nature and the rhythm of the seasons enforce their necessities, and the irreversibility of time concomitantly inculcates the ineluctability of the work and submission to its consequences. If a crop depends, as it does, upon the human labor of seeding, cultivation, and all the various other operations required for a good harvest, the contributions of the sun and the rain are variables independent of the will of man. Nevertheless, the expectation of good results is unavoidably dependent upon a maximum of human devotion and constant attention; nature suffers no delay.

Transposed to the modern Japanese industrial setting, these observations of the importance of location and its hierarchical influence upon Japanese life are illuminating. In a recent essay on Japanese geography, the author shows the opposition of *kami* ("upper") and *shimo* ("lower") added to the names given to the cities situated along a line going from South Japan up to Kyoto, the ancient capital of Japan. Now, Tokyo is the 'top' city in which everybody would like to work and from which all directives should come. Such feelings about location have, in fact, established among Japanese workers a definite hierarchical attitude towards jobs available among the various branches of huge industrial concerns established all along the Tokaido line and foster ambitions to get as high among them as possible. At the same time that Japanese workers have great interest in the objectives of the firms that employ them, they pay comparatively little attention to specific jobs; desirous of working, they are satisfied to do what is asked of them at the places to which they are assigned. In other words, they are satisfied to have their own places in the industrial context and will contentedly concentrate on the tasks given them within that context. If specific tasks are matters of comparative indifference (job descriptions are rare in Japan), a material setting and familiarization with it are very important—an attitude reinforced, as will be pointed out later, by social milieu.

Having inherited the Japanese peasant tradition of life-time vocation, Japanese industrial workers, except at the highest level, do not yet know the typical labor mobility of the Western world. Their old habit of performing all their tasks exactly according to an agrarian cycle and their sense of grateful obligation to Mother Nature still exert a powerful though vestigial impact without negating the unavoidable necessity of working to keep alive. The rarity

[47]

and limitations of place, the nearness of workers in a restricted area, enforce the common necessity for working. One cannot remain idle when everybody else expects him to work.

So the ecology of work contributes in various ways to Japanese motivation. It would be an exaggeration, however, to say that it is typically Japanese. Locations are also appreciated in other countries, but in other countries the appreciation is usually limited to the capital city.

While these various observations have revealed a dynamism that should be confirmed later in considerations of the social and psychological aspects of Japanese life, a reader might very reasonably question their force as prerequisite to an understanding of Japan's phenomenal economic development when other reasons for it might be so easily adduced. Since a thorough treatise on Japanese psychology cannot be attempted here, it may perhaps simply be asserted as widely proved elsewhere that the perceptions of the Japanese are quite different from those of other peoples and that therefore the causes of their action cannot be blotted out so easily as are the causes of action in the West. Innumerable components *as a whole* influence and determine Japanese behavior, but such a generalization does not necessarily deny the existence of Western-minded or at least Western-educated Japanese and their very active participation in the modernization of their country; their actions are, indeed, but a natural development of those patterns whose elucidation is being attempted here.

Once again, let the argument with respect to the Japanese physical milieu be presented summarily. The household, or *ie,* situated in a definite place concretizes the Japanese sense of relationship between nature and man. It is felt that a living reciprocity of gifts binds them both in a common destiny: nature gives life and man receives it. To receive life, however, man must work, for life itself is transmitted only through his reciprocity with nature, which may, in turn, lead to mutual perfection. Witness, for example, the perfection of a Japanese garden. But the roots of the reciprocity

[48]

that exists between man and nature are centered in the localization of the *ie,* or in the place of work. In the country the peasant cultivates his field; in industry the worker fulfills the duty he has been assigned. There is a vital obligation on both sides. The field must feed the *ie,* and the *ie* must cultivate the field; the firm must take care of its workers, and its workers must serve the growth of the firm. There is mutual interdependence and constant intercommunication. Accordingly, it is not especially surprising that a Japanese labor union is the offspring of the industrial enterprise and encompasses all the workers in the firm concerned.

To put the matter another way, this Japanese dynamism, present and acting in a given place, is the dynamism of life itself, which promotes an intimate and permanent exchange with the ambient world. Moreover, it is completely undifferentiated for the Japanese; that is, it cannot be reduced merely to an enumeration of rational motives. If rice and its progression of growth through earth, water, and air have deeply impressed the Japanese, it might be said that the same phenomena are perceptible in virtually any agricultural context. What seems to be specific and determining for the Japanese, however, is that rice is the chief national food and that, again, it must be grown in the comparatively sparse and diminutive areas of the land that are arable. The Japanese have in any case become so palpably impregnated with the ideal of production, which is a frequent theme in their mythology, and so familiar with nature that they seem spontaneously, and perhaps unconsciously, to identify somewhat with the life-cycle of rice as it rises from below the ground up into the air. Hence the Japanese aspiration to climb, to overcome all the obstacles of ascent, and hence their perseverance towards the fulfillment of their actions.

Whether at the individual or at the group level, in all their contacts the Japanese regard a certain self-effacement as the guarantee of good communication. In general, also, they use their weaknesses (small stature, small pieces of land, and so on) to overcome the obstacles they meet. Like judo, many of their sports cleverly utilize inferior strength to take advantage of weaknesses discernible in superior strength and end in effects physically nil but psychologically glorious for the contestants on both sides. The Japanese seem somehow to verify that inscrutable law of nature that asks one to die in order to live.

The social milieu

Now that various Japanese values resulting from a general dynamism of geographical location based on vertical dimensions have been dealt with, the hierarchical structure of Japanese society deserves scrutiny. Numbers of studies in Japanese social psychology and cultural anthropology have attested to the existence of the phenomenon of an organic solidarity virtually peculiar to Japan that is evident among all members of aggregated units in Japan, beginning with the nation itself. The most basic unit is the *ie*, the 'household', which is an organism that must continue without breach, like a paradigm of life, irrespective of lineage or consanguinity, but very much dependent upon its location. To be successful, both agriculture and fishing require great cooperative solidarity, at least during the times of the active and concentrated labor they demand. The very structure of the Japanese household has favored the success of these two activities because it has so effectively promoted the tendency of the Japanese to work together that they spontaneously respond as a group to great incentives.

Perhaps the key relationship in the *ie* is the one that exists between a father and a son or between any two persons in the *ie* playing similar roles. Like any people living so close to nature, the Japanese are especially aware of the forces of life and death and regard each force with an almost identical reverence. If they emphasize life and its continuity, they especially revere the bearer and transmitter of life, the head of the *ie*. Although the special and privileged relationship is that between father and son, through whom the life of the family is essentially channeled, other members of the *ie* also receive both whatever they are and whatever they have from its head, the father or his surrogate. Quite apart from the fact that the social hierarchy of the Japanese makes everybody indebted to his superior, the internal relationships of the *ie* are only biological, generating no sense of superiority or inferiority. The point is that the organism remains alive through the transmission of the experience organized. Just as a Japanese family must respect its little patch of land as a gift from above and a source of food by cultivating it with devotion, so the members of an *ie* must, as their first duty, repay the head of the *ie,* the transmitter of life, for what they have received from him by keeping him alive and by assuring his subsistence until death. The obligation also extends to all issue of the *ie* who participate in maintaining the line of descendancy of the family. Thus all of them work spontaneously not only out of gratitude for the gift of life, but also out of the necessity to keep the gift living and continuous, as though they must fulfill an ideal expected of them that they dare not neglect, like an ineluctable law. If the obligation were merely a social pressure imposed by family in order to motivate work for the group or merely a facesaving measure, which is also a motivation to work, it would be only moral and somehow exterior to the individual concerned. It is, however, interior— a constitutional fulfillment. It is the individual's *raison d'être.*

Because of the 'situation' of any one of its members, satisfaction in the self-existence of the *ie* must be considered still more essential, more existential, than so far presented here. The world of a Japanese is rather limited, narrowed down to the satisfactions of in-group exigencies and needs. In the West, a child is pulled outside of his familial world by all kinds of objectives, his striving for which tends to promote a self-satisfaction quite independent of the satisfaction of his parents—except, of course, that they may be pleased to know that their offspring is standing on his own feet. In Japan, however, a child is bound fast to his familial world, in which interdependency is stressed more and more in order that each generation after generation may be indoctrinated into meeting its traditional obligations to the transmission of life. In other words, in Japan the promotion of one individual is really the affirmation of the strength and achievement of the group, whose world of concern is small, restricted, and usually undiversified. Indeed, each member of a group is entrusted only with that which his superior orders: it is not his business to evaluate or to imagine any other endeavor than that to which he is committed. His bond with authority is essential, almost existential, and it therefore exacts complete devotion.

A Japanese who flouted his situational and social obligations would be subjecting himself to unbearable loneliness. Although a supreme Japanese individualist endowed with an adamantine character and an insatiable thirst for independence can be imagined, it is unimaginable that he would be able to maintain his eccentric posture very long in the concrete context of his isolation; he would have to bow sooner or later to the general law. Very rare in any case, the material resources of Japan are possessed by groups, not individuals. Moreover, it is even pointless to consider the necessity of chastising a Japanese unwilling to work in his group, whether a school, a factory, or any other institution, for no Japanese would expose himself lightly to the social reprobation or even the fear of ostracism that such defection from duty would incur. Indifference might temporarily be tolerated in a youth not very much aware of the conditions of human existence, but it would not for a moment be tolerated in a young man who has been formally integrated into society through the job he has been given upon graduation from college. Indeed, the Japanese obligation to work for the group, for the whole, grows with age since jobs are usually given for periods of a lifetime. It is not unlikely that the prospect of working until death for one employer is itself a powerful repellent of malingering and of criticism. At any rate, employee and employer are bound together for life to realize together the fulfillment of the whole of life, the faithful achievement of the needs and exigencies of both society and nature. It is incidentally no negligible part of the strength of such bonds that they perpetuate a Japanese tradition at least fifteen centuries old.

Meanwhile, the entire Japanese industrial complex is a gigantic interpollinating living organism where everybody derives his personality from the firm—itself organically composed—in which he is working. The older the firm, the greater the prestige of the individual employed in it. The most important identification is the name of the establishment for which one works. As a matter of fact, most Japanese know others initially, if not chiefly, only by means of the badge of employment that almost every Japanese employee proudly wears in the buttonhole of his lapel. One need not be especially motivated to work for Mitsubishi or Hitachi; one is just happy to have been chosen to take part in the development of such a firm and to wear its badge. In whatever group, everybody expects one's work to be well done; that is the main condition of survival.

The hierarchy of each Japanese industrial unit usually includes a number of layers of members of the same age, often graduates of the same university, who maintain firm solidarity within their own age-groups. Shifted all through their careers from one part of Japan to another so that they might become acquainted with all branches of a firm and all other employees and officials of it wherever located, they quite understandably develop a natural spontaneity and unity of views and purposes in harmony with the entire group. The achievement of such familiarization is a strong enhancement of any firm's effective communication among its own members and with its outside associates. In short, it is a powerful incentive to pursuit of the vitality of the firm. Actually, from the top to bottom of any Japanese enterprise, all the members of the group are interested in its maximal expansion and hence sensitive to whatever could make it bigger and stronger. Given their concrete perceptions, they are aware of all potential improvements at all levels of their activity, so that it might be said that they feel deficiencies as a unit and thus report needed modifications to the responsible authorities. Even promotion by seniority does not mean progressive adaptation

[53]

to the comforts of an armchair, but rather it means greater responsibility and deeper participation in the activities of the group. Moreover, an automatic supervision of production is constantly maintained.

Communication itself includes not only the necessary transmission of information, but also, as it were, an intensive emotional 'massage'. As the constant conversational exchange within a family largely expresses its group values and determines the behavior of its members, so also the conversational exchange among members of an industrial group is essential to the most efficient functioning of the whole. Office telephones, for example, are not expected to facilitate the transmission of business information only. The long telephone conversations, sometimes predominantly social, that rather typically go on among members of a Japanese firm are thought to advance constant group readiness—that universal and general consensus so much desiderated by Japanese groups in order that whatever is presented as worthy of attainment may be immediately accepted and performed. Such a use of communication—human and social, as well as informational—is not scorned by the very largest Japanese enterprises in their relations with one another or with the government. For instance, weddings unite daughters of industrialists with promising careerists in the Ministry of Foreign Affairs or of Finance and the social gathering following the ceremony reinforces the bonds between private and public affairs. Such conscious promotion of human relations is a strong influence upon all the members of both groups. The Japanese view of the benefits of industrial communication, one might say, are like those of a fine harvest that follows upon patient, monotonous, and sometimes anonymous cooperation with the laws of nature: it is the guarantee of the perennial survival of the *ie.*

Granted the high literacy of the Japanese and the staggering number of Japanese publications, radios, and television sets, which constantly reiterate and strengthen the pressures to achieve maximal production, the Japanese motivations here presented could hardly be stronger because they involve the whole man and include all aspects of his life. Ultimately, however, the achievement and welfare of every individual Japanese is identified with the greatness of Japan itself, by comparison with which individual performance and security are secondary. Since considerations of purpose are more relevant to ends than to means, they are not the strongest conceivable incentives to efficiency. It would seem, then, that the real cause of the activity of the Japanese is to be found in their situations locational, social, and psychological.

Of course, there is always a danger that any analysis of motivation may simplify, identify, or define mistakenly under the pressure of the need for immediate and practical answers. For instance, a recent researcher among middle management personnel in the United States and in Japan purported to discover that self-actualization was the principal motivation of parallel groups in both countries—in other words, that the focus of motivation in the United States is, for all practical purposes, the same as that in Japan. But alas! self-actualization in the United States and self-actualization in Japan have very different meanings. In the States it is tantamount to the enhancement of the individual, whereas in Japan it is tantamount to the enhancement of the group. As Morimura Ichizaemon has expressed it, a Japanese should 'act in such a way as to express gratitude for the benefits *(on)'* he has received from society.[3]

The psychological milieu

THE importance of the organic group, its inner solidarity and stability, can hardly be over-emphasized in any analysis of Japanese behavior. When people have been committed for generations to working together spontaneously in a spirit of accepted necessity

[3] Quoted in Bryan K. Marshall, *Capitalism and Nationalism in Prewar Japan,* Palo Alto: Stanford U.P., 1967, p. 35.

[55]

and complete devotion, they have a very deep and strong incentive to conform, to act in the same way.

Yet the view could not be supported that the Japanese either as a whole or as circumscribed in their seemingly closed groups are not influenced by all kinds of foreign ideas and theories. An alertness to international information—most recently via the mass media of press, radio, and television—have for one hundred years kept the Japanese increasingly aware of most of the exigencies of modern life and experience, with a consequent response that has been phenomenal in the world. Yet, such gradual mutations of Japanese mentality as have ensued have chiefly followed patterns peculiar to historical Japanese methods of perception. For example, it would be an error to think that Japanese mass media today, sophisticated as they are, promulgate the same meanings as Western mass media. Although they may sell the same products, Japanese techniques are different: the signs and signals are aimed at senses conditioned only by a prolonged progression of familiarization with the outside world.

Both in their acquisition of knowledge and in their assimilation of external influences, the Japanese, consciously or unconsciously, use methods that can most illuminatingly be likened to that of biological osmosis. Rote memory, for instance, is the most frequently used technique in the Japanese educational process. Japanese children are brought up to repeat, over and over again, almost ritualistically, the same words and gestures as their mentors or models, whether familial, academic, or social, until the right reflexes become virtually embodied in their cellular structures. Perhaps Japanese patience and endurance, apparently interminable, are counterparts of such ceaseless mimicry. In any case, from childhood on, the Japanese are accustomed to serving, working, accomplishing, so that in time their bodies and minds react almost automatically to incentives to activity. Again, figuratively speaking, it is rather osmotically also that the Japanese are open to the assimilation of all kinds of new influences and techniques. In fact, the etymology of the word 'assimilation' reveals the precise applicability of its meaning to the Japanese: when they adopt an influence or technique, they 'make it similar to' their own specific tradition. Typically, they adopt very few things at their face value; rather, they take them in, transform them, and make them part of a distinctive Japanese organism.

Always active, most Japanese get up very early to go to work or school and, doing so, complain very little. Granted the fact that they work easily, they nevertheless work, generally speaking, only moderately; as a matter of fact, their best—their work done *isshōkenmei* ('with all strength')—is commonly equivalent to merely an average performance in the West. More remarkable than any flamboyance of temporary performance is their constancy; faithfully, day after day, hour after hour, they accomplish their assigned tasks with patience and perseverance. The pressures of society and their training of former years have taught them to regard work, almost unconsciously, as such a highly favored and valued component of life that their participation in it has become a completely natural and spontaneous action. Meanwhile, satisfaction in performance has a different meaning in Japan from the one it has in the West, where it equates mainly with a promotion of personality and an affirmation of independence. In Japan, however, satisfaction in performance is pleasure in having accomplished whatever was expected by the group and by Japan as a whole, and it results in relaxation and a sense of harmony. So, as they otherwise also act readily, the Japanese work readily. What is more important, they feel happy in their participation in work. *Shiawase,* the Japanese word for 'happy', signifies a convergence of all the elements requisite to the actualization of an event, and the state of satisfaction it indicates is the result of a continuous communication with the world of persons and things—in other terms, a most comforting and inspiring sentience.

Such personal rewards of psychic well-being are powerful encouragements to productivity in Japan. No Japanese can fail the expectations of those above him or the expectations of those below him, for he is the necessary and somehow irreplaceable mediator between, if not as a person, at least as an impersonal link. If he is slothful or reluctant to perform his duties, he may very soon experience a loneliness like a living death. He will feel guilty towards his parents, his younger brothers and sisters, his immediate superiors, and others who are dependent upon him. On the other hand, if he is diligent and performs well, he will be encouraged and thanked by everyone concerned. The interdependence inherent in his situation is an excellent guarantee of enthusiasm for his task. Can any motivation be stronger than such an intense participation in the expectation of all, of both men and things?

As in the physical milieu, so in the psychological milieu as well, all activity must be disposed and ordered in the service and for the realization of Japan as a whole or of some integral part of it. The limited size of a given unit of activity, however small, allows and fosters in its participants an intimate acquaintance with all the varied elements involved; the overlooking of details is hardly conceivable, and a high quality of performance is almost a necessity. In this context maximal productivity is not extraordinary. Indeed, simple negligence or a poor execution of duties, extremely harmful to the harmony of the whole, can be so far-reaching in its effects, both internal and external, that an individual must resolutely avoid any such culpability.

All things considered, then, it must be clear that the ancient Japanese habit of working hard was a valuable force in the triumph of Japanese industrialization because it provided not only minds and hands ready for whatever tasks needed to be done, but also a psychological predisposition to determined kinds of work. In other words, a monotony of labor was not introduced to the Japanese for the first time through industrialization; for generations rice-planting also had offered little by way of novelty or variety. One might almost say that, for the Japanese, the nature of work was 'standardized' long before the technical term was coined. At the same time, the much praised esthetic perception of the Japanese was not limited to their general ability to produce and respect beauty, but concretely it was an admirable ideal that fostered work well done and well finished.

Chapter two: Motivational forces in Japanese life

With reference again to the simile of osmosis, let it be said that the spontaneous reception of Japanese individuals and groups to whatever is new and potentially contributory to growth and development is an apparent condition of Japanese action and progress. One suspects that it is primarily this natural aptitude which, having made Japan great one thousand years ago, makes her great now. Thus, Japanese modernization could not have been a genuine disruption of tradition, but rather a channeling of the old dynamism into new paths. Like their Western counterparts, Japanese industrial and business groups spell out their goals clearly and logically, but the members of those groups still feel, and share the feeling, that the *ie*—from the organism that is the Japanese state down through the organisms of various big trusts to the organisms of the smallest marginal firms—must be served, nourished, and perpetuated. Nor is it correct to attribute such a feeling among contemporary Japanese to some merely nostalgic romantic love for ancient Japan; rather, it is further evidence of the fundamental dynamism that has enabled the Japanese to transform their society spontaneously from an agricultural one to an industrial one.

Finally, some word concerning the Japanese version of those decisions that are the natural terminations of motivation would seem relevant here. Descriptions of the involuted gatherings of information that support Japanese motivation illuminate also Japanese decision, which may originate anywhere and any place among the members of a group making an approach to reality. The Japanese propensity to react to any pressures of reality meets, of course, with frequent obstacles that must be removed for the sake of the efficient functioning of the whole. Because of the close and binding contacts that exist among members of a Japanese group and among the various groups inside the state, awareness of failure or deficiency is immediate, and all Japanese concerned desire a satisfactory correction of the situation. Decision usually follows and meets with immediate approval because it has already been everybody's desire. Accepting whatever the situation requires, the organism thus comes by a better

[59]

regulation or a new infusion of forces and a stronger integration. Such a process of realization may sometimes seem very aberrant, but it actually assures a desirable permeation and conditioning of a whole Japanese enterprise. In the West, most reforms are decided from above and take a long time to reach all those affected. In Japan, however, having once become aware of needed modifications by means of a management ultimately familiar with all the latest techniques of administration, the *ie* immediately and unanimously feels the necessity of adopting the advocated modifications in order to survive. Basic Japanese dynamism plays its role irrespective of the forms time and circumstances impose upon it.

Part II

EMPLOYMENT
IN JAPAN

CHAPTER THREE

Participative employment

BY ROBERT J. BALLON

Employment: the place of work, lifelong employment tenure, seniority—labor-management relations—economics of employment

THE first half-century of Japan's industrialization succeeded in establishing the main structures of industrial activity: large and integrated industrial complexes immediately surrounded by related but expendable small firms dominated while thousands and thousands of petty undertakings scattered over the traditional sector provided daily necessities. But the most essential point had been assured—the industrial commitment of a nation. A second phase could now start, and would take almost two decades to mature. It consisted in focusing the rather diffuse commitment to industrial employment on the new structures. Up to this point the relatively unsophisticated industrial processes in use had been quite easily manned by only a little skilled labor, fresh migrants from the countryside and young female workers. Then two bottlenecks appeared in the open labor market; one was the difficulty of recruiting 'industrial' skills that could no longer be expected to grow out of traditional crafts; the other was the need for employing 'administrative' talents required by the sheer size of the sprawling industrial complexes. The decision of management was apparently to bypass the labor market and to consider qualified human resources like any other resource equally hard to get. The policy was to acquire the best possible *raw* human resource and integrate it into the operational process once and for all. The dislocation and ruins of World War II ushered in a third phase. Availing itself of the pro-labor attitude of the American Occupation, labor took the initiative and established its vested right in enterprise at a time when management was still prostrated under the crush of war devastation. The prewar Japanese pattern of employment was revived and then further expanded so as to include not only white-collar employees and skilled manual workers but also ordinary blue-collar workers, yet excluding temporary workers. And to the great surprise of its foreign sponsors, Japanese labor soon appeared to be organizing not along industrial lines, as was expected, but along enterprise lines, without regard to occupation or skill.

Thus, notwithstanding a hundred years of massive assimilation of Western techniques, the key human aspect of industrialization, industrial employment in Japan has evolved its own structures and institutions.

Employment

WHEN, during World War I, Japanese industry really got on its feet, it soon became obvious that enterprise was geared more to human organization than to mere economic organization, and that employment relationships were considered accordingly. Industrial enterprise came to be regarded as an industrial family, such that the employee, rather than being hired, was adopted as a member of the family, his participation entailing grounds larger than his actual individual contribution of skill or performance, more generally, that of a human resource. Employment in Japan is not the 'give-and-take' that characterizes industrial employment elsewhere, but the 'give-and-take' that characterizes relations within a human family. For example, one's salary is felt less to be a vested liability of the firm than an active component of its working capital; essentially, salary payments are made on a deferred basis, and even one's savings are often shared with the enterprise.[1] As in the traditional family, where its own continuity guarantees subsistence, not necessarily riches, to its members, so also the industrial family offers its security. In fact, a number of sociologists have long since pointed out that the Japanese system of family kinship was, by adaptation, a major contribution to the process of Japan's industrialization.

> 'In Japan the *ie* system meant that the migrant to the city had no hope of settling in the rural area and that the elderly parents were cared for by the son who remained in the country. The rapid segmentation of the lineage in each generation meant that there was no large kinship group for a person to join when he came to the city. Kinship ties did not interfere and, if anything, worked to reinforce the ties between the employer and the employee. The common ritual kinship relationship between employer and employee became the basic tie in the city, and the migrant's original *ie* stood ready to see that that tie was maintained.'[2]

Such interpretations are usually shrugged off by the common Japanese as out-dated, but Japanese social anthropologists have to agree. A most striking statement in this context was recently made by one of them, Tadao Umesao:

> 'Japan is the "workshop-first" country. Under no circumstances does Japan give priority to families. Everybody asks himself in what way he is contributing to society. Individuals are contributing to society through their working places, aren't they? So this does not agree with the principles

---

[1] Specific consideration of the salary system has been excluded here; for a detailed analysis, see Chapter Six.

[2] Ezra F. Vogel, 'Kinship Structure, Migration to the City, and Modernization,' in R. P. Dore (ed.), *Aspects of Social Change in Modern Japan*, Princeton: Princeton University Press, 1967, pp. 99–100.

E

of regional community in which individuals are devoted to safeguarding their own families. The Japanese people are swayed by a kind of "contributionism". Even if many people today advocate the family-first principle, they cannot set themselves completely free from workshops. I believe that this "workshop-first" principle will continue to serve as the motive power to lead Japan to progress also in the future.'[3]

The traditional Japanese *ie* ('household,' as a unit of kinship) was never limited to blood relationship only, as witnessed by the widespread practice, still current, of 'adopting' a son-in-law in order to assure the physical continuity of the *ie*. The dynamics of such a social organization could, therefore, easily be transferred to the industrial environment. Enterprise thus became a sort of living organism, like a molecule. The molecule is composed of various atoms, the ingroups or the cliques *(batsu),* of which the most obvious one is the school clique *(gaku-batsu)*. These cliques seem to play a greater role in Japan than so-called informal groups in the West; though not depicted in the 'formal' organization chart, they are explicit components of the dynamics of an industrial enterprise. As such, they greatly contribute to employment relationship and to work motivation. In Japanese sociological literature, the demerits of the clique system are described at length, but a courageous exception is offered by Shinbori, who lists the following merits of the system:

'1 Human relations founded on cliques have served as a practical means of supporting the sweeping modernization of Japan.

2 A clique serves as a pier to help the individuals in a giant organization know with whom they should become acquainted.

3 The screening of qualifications of individuals eligible to join

---

[3] This statement was made as the conclusion of a round-table discussion on *Mura no Sahō, Toshi no Sahō* (Village Manners, City Manners) reported in *Energy*, Tokyo: Vol. 5, No. 2 (1968), pp. 8–17 (translation provided by the editor, the Esso Standard Sekiyu K.K.)

cliques is very strict. Even after they are admitted to their cliques, they are subject to thoroughgoing training over a long period of time. Joining the cliques, therefore, is a very effective way of training individuals.

4 As a result, cliques serve as an effective means of molding the character of groups or organizations and of maintaining it through generations.[4']

Somewhat extremely, one might say that in the West, formal (sociological) groups were discovered at work in formal (economic) organizations that are industrial enterprises; in Japan, however, formal organizations are themselves also sociological. Employment in the industrial family, or kinship-like unit, has three dimensions that, to a large extent, set it apart from what employment existentially is in other industrial societies.

1 *The place of work (shoku-ba)*

In the eyes of the Japanese, it is not the occupation *(shokugyō)* that counts, but the place of work *(shoku-ba)*. In other words, it is not *what* a man does that is the important industrial dimension, but *where* he does it. It has been pointed out that when a child is asked: 'What is your father doing?', the answer in the West is usually given in terms of the father's occupation, whereas in Japan it is given in terms of the company that employs the father.[5] In Japan, occupational pride is very slight or non-existent. Though in postwar years much talk has been heard about 'professional management,' the meaning is not that managerial skills follow a person wherever he may be employed, but that managerial skills and techniques are being improved in Japanese enterprises.

From his workplace the employee derives a sense of security

---

[4] Michiya Shinbori, '*Batsu* ('Cliques')' in *Energy, op. cit,* pp. 28–29.
[5] Arthur M. Whitehill, Jr., and Shin-ichi Takezawa, *Gimu in Transition,* University of North Carolina, School of Business Administration, Research Paper 5, 1961, p. 18.

(antei) that has often been labelled in labor lingo *oyakata hi-nomaru,* freely translated as 'Japan will provide', in the sense that Japanese enterprise (and ultimately Japan itself) will see to it that its members are somehow taken care of, whatever happens. The numerous non-cash benefits available to employees are only one expression of this all-embracing care expected by the work force.

2 *Lifelong employment tenure (shūshin koyō)*

Wherever feasible, employment in Japan is for life; i.e., an employee is hired at the time he leaves school and stays with his company until retirement. The employer will not fire him, and the employee will not leave his company. Hiring is a sort of industrial birth, and one cannot renounce his birth. Even today, moving to a more rewarding place of work is considered by middle-aged Japanese as something morally objectionable.[6] Ideally speaking, therefore, labor mobility in Japan is nil. Not all firms, however, can afford the system in its entirety, and some employees cannot stand it. As a result mobility can be sketched as follows:

large firm

↓

small firm

↓

small firm

It is possible to move from a large to a small firm (at a cost), but not from a large to another large firm, or from a small to a large firm; and it is always possible to move from a small to another small firm. Exceptions are, of course, found, but they are still explicitly considered as exceptions, i.e., confirming the rule of immobility.

6 See Soichiro Ohara, 'Labor Management in the Age of Economic Growth,' Working Paper presented at the Mont Pelerin Society, Special Meeting, Tokyo, Sept. 5–10 1966, p. 9.

Chapter three: Participative employment

3 Seniority (nenkō joretsu)

The employee of a Japanese firm or, better, the member of a Japanese industrial family will 'grow in age' with the enterprise on which he depends for his subsistence. As years go by, he acquires more and more experience of the enterprise as a human organization, experience based on his daily contact and long familiarity with all the facets of the company's activities and of the people involved. Recognition of this experience is extended in terms of promotion and the respect of fellow-employees, while the employee's own growing vital needs are acknowledged by increased remuneration.[7] Within the enterprise a human hierarchy thereby develops that is little affected by, say, nepotism or social-class consciousness. It is based on the traditional Japanese value attached to age, an essential value of the family anywhere: age is expectedly accompanied by a certain wisdom acting as a vital lubricant in any human organization. The *nenkō* concept is rooted in the devotion of oneself to his place of work as manifested by his length of service. This phenomenon is expressed in the term of *sararīman* (salaryman) that applies to a postwar middle-class consciousness pervading Japanese industrial society.

Labor-management relations

DICTIONARIES translate the term 'industrial relations' or 'labor-management relations' as *rōshi kankei,* and vice versa. The etymology of the Japanese term is, however, somewhat different: *kankei* means 'relationship'; *rō* means 'labor' or 'work'; but *shi* does not mean 'management' or 'capital', but 'use' or 'usage'. A literal translation would therefore be: 'the relationship that uses work'. Some Japanese labor economists have noticed the discrepancy

[7] See Chapter Six.

and suggested that the character now used for *shi* be replaced by another one also pronounced *shi,* but meaning 'capital'. Needless to say, such a change smacks of Marxist terminology. The fact is that the term *rōshi kankei,* as it stands now, is an adequate term for the reality it names, which has nothing to do with some ideological conflict between labor and capital. The term expresses simply some arrangement whereby work is put to use for some purpose.

Such arrangement is not expressed by a labor contract, either individual or collective. In present-day Japan, individual labor contracts are, generally speaking, used only in the case of temporary or part-time employment. For lifelong employment, such contracts do not make much sense, after all. But would it make more sense to sign collective labor agreements *(dantai keiyaku),* since enterprises that sponsor lifelong employment are mostly organized? In practice, it is the rules of employment *(shūmu kisoku)* that spell out what, in the West, would be expressed by a collective contract. Nevertheless, such agreements became popular in postwar Japan as one of the objectives of organized labor. For the most part, however, they contain only general provisions often literally transcribed from various labor laws. Their real meaning is the explicit recognition of the union by management. Let it be said that, as a consequence, 'collective bargaining' in the Japanese context has little relevance to such collective labor agreements.

The fact remains, therefore, that the relationship between an employer and his employee in Japan is not contract-oriented but rather status-oriented. Life membership in the industrial family is not a mere contractual relationship covering a certain job to be performed and the compensation to be expected. It is almost like a right secured by birth.

When Japanese management is described as paternalistic, something has been said . . . but nothing has been explained. Four or five years back, one could still hear from the lips of Japanese employers: 'I have to employ as many people as possible.' Such a statement could not be heard from a 'paternalistic' Western employer!

Chapter three: Participative employment

Immediately involved in the national policy of industrialization, the Japanese enterpreneur felt, and still feels today, shouldered with a sort of full-employment public responsibility. One could almost say that this responsibility is not so much to provide 'employment' as to provide 'subsistence' for his workers. What the employee expects is not to be employed in the sense that he must execute specific tasks for which remuneration will be forthcoming. What he most expects is security *(antei)*, which could be interpreted as subsistence—exactly, in fact, what one expects from the family he is born into, and what the traditional *ie* has been supplying for centuries.

The Western term 'paternalism' does not describe adequately such a situation. Particularly in the United States, paternalism has a bad connotation, that of management egoistically seeking its own and exclusive advantage at the minimal cost of manifesting some concern for the welfare of the workers in order to safeguard profits. This is a one-way proposition: from management to labor. But in Japan, the relationship is a two-way proposition: mutual expectations are fulfilled. Exploitation by management is, of course, not excluded; no more in Japan than anywhere else are managers angels! But this context of reciprocity remains peculiar to Japan.

And the Japanese labor union has no objection—on the contrary! It comes as a shock to foreign labor leaders that Japanese enterprise unions are not concerned about welfare. Isn't that why management exists? Indeed, the structure of Japanese unions is a reflection of the industrial *ie*. They are called enterprise or enterprise-wide unions *(kigyō-betsu kumiai)* because they organize the employees of one, and only one, particular enterprise. Relations in some industry-wide or occupation-wide federation are loose ones; generally speaking, except in the case of disputes, union members as well as their management are not too eager to bring in 'outsiders'.[8] The dimension of the work place *(shoku-ba)*, described earlier in regard to the employees, applies therefore also to their unions.

8 See Chapter Nine.

The main function of such unions is to protect lifelong employment. They organize mostly only the regular or permanent employees of an enterprise, white-collar and blue-collar alike, without consideration for skill or occupation. For example, the labor union in a university organizes professors, laboratory assistants, countergirls, electricians, and drivers all in the same union. And all Japanese unions are most willing to pay the concomitant price: the exclusion from membership, sometimes *de jure*, practically always *de facto*, of all temporary employees.

The unions also strongly back the *nenkō joretsu* system as a safeguard of the internal harmony *(wa)* so essential to the industrial *ie*. Since differentials in wage, in promotion, and so on have little relation to performance, *nenkō* provides the basis for most differentials in a manner that suits Japanese mores. Even monetary differentials are thereby diffused over the group, where they achieve, and very well indeed, their expected motivational impact.

As a result, one may wonder legitimately whether Japanese employees are company-conscious or union-conscious. This is a moot problem. They are not 'hired' in the Western sense; as members of the industrial *ie*, they are enterprise-conscious, whether as members of the enterprise or as members of the enterprise union! This is the reason the phrase 'labor-management relations' is translated into Japanese as *rōshi kankei*, 'the relationship that uses work'!

Economics of employment

THE economic feasibility of such an employment relationship remains, however, fairly restricted. Though permanency of employment is considered ideal, it presupposes, of course, permanency of the enterprise. And some enterprises go bankrupt. Here again the socio-economic workings of the dual structure offer an explanation. Large firms are not permitted to go bankrupt; even if one failed in Western economic terms the entire establishment would move to the rescue.[9] Even the upper bracket of medium firms should not be allowed to go under.[10] But all other firms, the small and petty enterprises, especially those in the non-modern sector, are on their own and take the grim brunt of any business fluctuations.

The economics of Japanese enterprise, therefore, experience their supreme test in labor costs—not, however, in the sense that these costs are variable and therefore subject to manipulation according to business fluctuations. Lifelong employment means that labor costs should be considered as fixed costs! Even if prices should decrease below average total costs, Japanese enterprise will continue to produce as long as prices remain higher than average variable cost.[11] Flexibility is obtained by the employment of temporary workers and by the subcontracting system.

> 'The reliance of large companies on subcontracting from medium-sized enterprises rose from 20% in 1957 to 50% in 1960, and was approaching 65% in 1962 (measured by number of working hours devoted to specific manufactures in parent and offspring factories). In the average large enterprise in 1961, 2.5 times as many workers as in the parent plant were employed in the subcontractor factories.'[12]

As a matter of fact, payrolls should be considered as a social overhead of Japanese enterprise. If this is the price to pay for life-

[9] A recent and well-known illustration is the case of the Yamaichi Securities Co., one of the Big Four in the Securities industry, that in 1965 was rescued by the government.

[10] The dismay caused by the failure of the Sanyō Special Steel Co. in 1965 was typical in this regard. All commentators on the case agreed that this should not have happened, meaning that the size of the company was such that it would have been rescued if proper accounting had revealed the crucial nature of the emergency.

[11] See Leon Hollerman, *Japan's Dependence on the World Economy,* Princeton: Princeton University Press, 1967, p. 48.

[12] John W. Bennett, 'Japanese Economic Growth: Background for Social Change,' in R.P. Dore, *op. cit.,* p. 423, footnote.

long employment, what do the firms gain from it? Expectedly, jobs are assigned to employees rather than employees to jobs; whatever authority and responsibility are attached to a position, their degree will essentially be a function of some 'human', rather than professional, qualities of the titulary, especially of *nenkō joretsu*. Nor is this system all negative.

Recruitment standards have to be much higher than elsewhere since hiring is for life, not for specific jobs. The procedure centralized in personnel departments is an elaborate system of checks:

selected channels of recruiting (e.g., requests to some schools to submit candidates selected by teachers);
company entrance examinations with objective marking;
investigations of family backgrounds and evaluations of recommendations and references;
individual interviews conducted by senior officers of the company, if not by the president himself.

Given such high-caliber human material to work with, Japanese enterprise embarks on equally elaborate training programs. Training for what? The right question should be: Training what? In a family, who wonders what children are educated for? The problem in Japan is to educate them in becoming honorable members of the family. Thus in enterprise also, training is first of all a schooling in company consciousness and loyalty, and very positive results are obtained: great flexibility in regard to technological change. Where there are no mental blocks of professional pride, and where conformity to the common objectives of an enterprise has been instilled, its work force turns out to be most malleable. A particular point to watch, however, is that such devotion does not necessarily mean readiness to do whatever is requested by management. The managers are not the enterprise; they are *for* the enterprise, no less and no more than the work force. As mentioned above, authority does not rest with individual qualities, but reacts to the dynamics of the entire industrial group. Again the image of the family may help the understanding: the father has authority over the children, but he does not have that authority when there are no children: in fact, he would not even be a father if there were no children. It is almost as if the children make him a father!

Technological innovation, such as automation or computing, is no labor problem in Japan as far as it means simply 'another' job. The management and the union will carefully watch job or location transfers, but the psychological problems that would be caused by some exacerbated professional consciousness do not exist in Japan. Rapid economic expansion makes this evolution possible without leading to the recourse of lay-offs. But what if the rate of growth should slow down? The aging of the work force would be a dreadful prospect if it were not for the average young age of the population. Meanwhile, other forces like gain-employment are at work in the economy. But every so often, there is an enterprise that finds itself off base . . . If it is a small one, it is permitted to go bankrupt, and labor mobility among small firms takes care of the employment problem involved. If it is large enterprise, however, a merger might be arranged, and lifelong employment will continue for better or worse.

Technological change is, however, one of the factors that undermine the institution of lifelong employment. Too many specialists are in demand, and training within a given company cannot possibly satisfy the demand. A new Japanese labor market is therefore in the making, and firms are beginning to scout talent in short supply. This revolution is only postponed when companies give as reasons for their mergers the better use of managerial skills and the pooling of research and development.

The greatest positive value of the Japanese style of employment is the kind of motivation that it fosters. Is it, however, sound motivation? It looks much more like devotion, devotion to a place of work where a familial harmony prevails, devotion to an industrial family where subsistence is guaranteed and companionship with others equally devoted is available, all sharing the inner satisfaction of doing whatever is expected for a common purpose: the continuity of the industrial *ie*.

In summary, not 'employment', but 'membership' in the industrial family has brought about in Japan a participative type of employment that is not contract-oriented, but status-oriented. This participation has, however, nothing to do with a participation in management rights or the like. The Western gap between management and labor does not exist in Japan, where management and labor are the two faces of the same coin, the enterprise. The first requisite of such an industrial status for labor is subsistence or security *(antei)* provided by lifelong employment tenure wherever possible and expected by employees and enterprise unions alike. Some individuals may rebel, but by and large the Japanese working population is satisfied by the contribution of its work to the industrial *ie*. In former ages, this end was accomplished by wresting from nature its products; today it is done by producing industrial goods and services. True to Japanese mores, human collective considerations take precedence over mere economic individual considerations, as so aptly expressed by the *nenkō* system. And since man is primarily motivated by the realization of where his main stake is, the Japanese employee is highly motivated by the realization that his main stake is in the enterprise of which he is a member and thereby, also, in the national economy of which his enterprise is but a partial component.

CHAPTER FOUR

The Japanese executive

BY HERBERT GLAZER

Company organization—the ringi management system—the generation gap—the future

SINCE a Japanese employee may be an executive, it is important, here, to begin with the Japanese concept of an executive. The title *jūyaku,* which means 'big business executive', has the connotation in Japanese that 'V.I.P.' once had in the United States, and it still implies some of the feeling of position, power, and influence formerly associated with the executives of the prewar *zaibatsu* firms of Japan. The awe this title once conveyed to a Japanese is comparable to that which an average American might feel with respect to the president of General Motors. Naturally enough, just as Japanese companies have proliferated since the war, *jūyaku* have also proliferated until now the title has become quite common. Generally speaking, titles are as important in Japan as, say, a Doctor of Philosophy degree is among scientists in the United States, where, if a scientist does not have the degree he counts for very little among his colleagues, whereas if he does have it, even though he may not be another Einstein, he commands a minimum of respect among them. Accordingly, when a foreign businessman hands his *meishi* ('business card') to a Japanese businessman, the first thing the Japanese will look at is the designated title to determine whether the foreigner commands a requisite minimum of respect. If the foreigner's title

[77]

is *torishimariyaku* ('director'), then the Japanese proceeds on the assumption that he is dealing with a person who is important in his company. This high evaluation of titles applies not only to foreigners, but to Japanese as well. If a Japanese title is only that of *kachō* ('section head'), then its holder is not considered very important and may be treated accordingly. Occasionally an important foreign businessman on a first visit to Japan may be snubbed solely on the basis of the fact that the Japanese translation of his title makes him appear unimportant in Japanese eyes.

Granted such title-consciousness, it is not surprising that the Japanese actively seek titles that convey an aura of importance and that they value them even more highly than salaries. Advertising agencies in particular abound in titles like *buchō* ('division head'), *kachō*, and *kakarichō* ('assistant section head'), and they have created many other titles for assistant heads in order to satisfy the demand for titular prestige. In fact, the majority of men working in such agencies have titles ending in *chō* ('head'). Often, therefore, employees who appear to be heads of something in Japan would be ordinary personnel in the West.

In this context it is an especially revealing fact that the Japanese Foreign Office *(Gaimushō)* recently decided that the English translations of Japanese titles gave an inferior impression and hence decided to upgrade the English titles. As a result *kachō* has been changed from 'section head' to 'division head and bureau deputy director-general' and *kyokuchō* from 'bureau chief' to 'bureau director-general'. *Buchō* has been changed from 'department chief' to 'department director-general', *kyoku-jichō* from 'deputy bureau chief' to 'bureau assistant director-general', and *shuseki jimukan* from 'assistant section chief' to 'division deputy head'.[1] Surely such name changing must be considered a classic example of overskill.

---

[1] 'What's in a Name', *The Yomiuri,* 5 July 1968.

Company Organization

THE STOCKHOLDERS

IT has been popular in Japan in recent years to note that in Japan as in the United States diffusion of stock ownership has led to a separation of ownership from control of an enterprise.[2] In America today only a handful of stockholders may attend stockholders' meetings of giant corporations. *The Wall Street Journal* recently reported that a number of large corporations are toying with the idea of eliminating such meetings altogether. Nevertheless, in form if not in substance, the average American stockholder considers himself part owner of any enterprise in which he owns stock, and occasionally a vocal owner of a few shares of stock will attend a stockholders' meeting and not hesitate openly to grill or condemn the corporate management concerned.

In Japan, however, it is doubtful whether a small shareholder has ever considered himself part owner of an enterprise. The fact that most companies pay fixed dividends at fixed periods implies that management does not expect its shareholders to share in the vagaries of company successes and failures. It is more likely that the typical Japanese small shareholder considers his investment to be more like a postal-savings account or a savings-bank account where his money is safe and fixed interest is paid. This small shareholder would no more question the manner in which management uses his funds than he would question the manner in which the Post Office Department or his bank uses his savings.

To circumvent the vocal participation of small shareholders in Japanese stockholders' meetings, there exists in Japan a special

---

[2] See A. A. Berle and G. C. Means, *The Modern Corporation and Private Property*, New York: The MacMillan Co., 1932.

species of 'stockholders' meeting men' called *sōkaiya*.[3] Paid professional shills whose job it is to move a meeting along without protest, they fill the room where a meeting is held with shouts of 'Approve!', 'No objection!', and 'Move on with the meeting!' Since other stockholders are too timid to object to such harassment, *sōkaiya* are able to insure that no questions arise during a meeting. Most meetings are therefore over in less than ten minutes, having elicited no objections from those in attendance.

The *sōkaiya* are themselves stockholders, of course, but they are stockholders only in so far as holding stock is a means to their particular ends. Specifically, they are underworld characters who use their power to blackmail management into buying off their threats of interfering with meetings. When properly bought off, allowing no dissenting voices to be heard in the din they create, they see to it that meetings move briskly along and end rapidly. Thus the role of the average shareholder in Japanese company management is nil, and the *sōkaiya* phenomenon guarantees that it remains so. *Nihon Keizai Shimbun* (evening edition) of 24 June 1968 indicated that the 1968 payoff of 250 companies registered in the Chuo Ward of Tokyo for one year's services to *sōkaiya* was ¥196 million ($544,000), euphemistically referred to as *tsukiai ryō* ('friendship fee').

ORGANIZATION CHARTS

ALTHOUGH company organization charts vary considerably in Japan as in the West, the one selected for illustration here (Figure 1) is indicative of a highly developed management structure and was, in fact, chosen for that very reason. The Kajima Construction Company is Japan's largest construction firm[4]; in 1967 it was capitalized at ¥10.88 billion ($30.2 million) and had approximately

---

3 Kazuo Noda, *Nihon no Jūyaku* ('Big Business Executives in Japan'), Tokyo: Diamond Press, 1960, p. 55.

4 *Kaisha Nenkan 1968* ('Company Yearbook'), Tokyo: Nihon Keizai Shimbunsha, 1968, pp. 36–37.

9500 employees. Its total organization is not known, but in addition to the twenty-three divisions that are shown, the company has eight other subdivisions and one hundred and eleven sections, not to mention subsections.

The horizontal elaboration of Japanese management structures is thus clearly illustrated. Streamlining this structure is an attractive idea to a foreign management consultant, but the *nenkō joretsu* (the Japanese seniority system of lifetime employment) makes it all but impossible if reduction in rank, transfers, layoffs, or firing of employees would result. One can only remark on the efficiency with which such a system operates in Japan and how inefficient it would be outside of Japan.

Some special note should be taken of *torishimariyakkai* ('board of directors'), *kansayaku* ('the auditor'), *jōmukai* ('managing directors' board'), and *shachōshitsu* ('the office of the president'). These are interesting aspects of Japanese management that need some explaining.

Meanwhile, considerable interest is being shown in Japan in attempting to overlay the top, middle, and lower management concepts of the West upon the Japanese management structure and thereby more accurately defining Japanese management responsibilities. Nevertheless, while theoretically interesting, such attempts do more to obscure than to elucidate the nature of Japanese management.[5]

THE BOARD OF DIRECTORS

As mentioned earlier, the title of Director in a Japanese company is a prestigious one, and every Japanese *sararīman* (white-collar worker) aspires to this exalted position. The postwar situation in Japan is such that most Japanese companies select almost all their directors from inside the company. They are individuals who hold

5 See Hiroshi Gōhara, *Nihon no Keiei Soshiki* ('Japanese Management Organization'), Tokyo: Tōyō Keizai Shimposha, 1968, pp. 218–9.

line positions, such as president, vice-president, executive director, managing director, and manager (division head). This system places the board in the strange (to an American) position that the hierarchy of the company organization is reproduced in the board of directors. It is reasonable to assume therefore that the members of the board have little to do that they are not already doing in their line positions in the company. If one were to construct an American company with a similar board of directors, one could conceive of the board meeting serving as an opportunity for top and lower management levels to communicate outside of normal channels. But in the rigid vertical structure of Japanese society, such a consequence is not conceivable. Thus the board of directors in Japan is really a ceremonial body concerned with matters of form, and the title of *tori-shimariyaku* is really a symbol of social rank. One Japanese top executive has said, 'A meeting of the board of directors is as formal as the stockholders' meeting but it is less thrilling'.[6]

THE AUDITOR

THE title of *kansayaku* ('auditor') is one that is modelled on the German *Aufsichsrat,* but the function serves the Japanese purpose rather than the original German purpose.

In Germany the authority of an *Aufsichsrat* is very strong, and he exercises considerable supervision over all phases of company operation and the personal performance and activities of top management as well as those of lower management. In America no equivalent position to that of *Aufsichsrat* exists, and the audit function is performed by independent public accounting-firms. In Japan the *kansayaku* follows German organization in form, but in reality the title is more or less honorary, and the individual holding it need have no accounting or financial background. Formally, the *kansayaku* is responsible for insuring the upright conduct of top management, but in fact, as a member and a director of top manage-

---

6 Noda, *op. cit.,* p. 82.

ment, he is in no position to do so. In reality, this position merely involves another honorary top-management title to which a *sarariman* may aspire.[7] As T. W. M. Teraoka has pointed out, too often auditing by outside accounting firms in Japan has been more formal than real.[8]

THE MANAGING DIRECTORS' BOARD

HAVING disposed of the ceremonial board of directors as a policy-making body for the Japanese company, we come to a board which does, actually, run the company; that is, the *jōmukai*. This managing directors' board is usually made up of *buchō* (with the president as chairman), who carry along with their title of *buchō* the additional title of *jōmu torishimariyaku* ('managing director'). If one must find a sure locus of top-management decision-making authority in a Japanese firm, it must be here in the *jōmukai*. Here too, however, we must distinguish form from reality. The managing directors are in reality operating heads of their divisions or plants. In the *tateshakai* ('vertically structured society') of Japan,[9] horizontal coordination is very weak, and yet, despite the fact that it is itself composed of individuals whose primary concern is the performance of their own vertical divisions, the *jōmukai* is supposed to effect just such horizontal coordination. As individuals concerned with their own divisions, these men naturally have strong divisional prejudices that are difficult to overcome, and the problem is compounded by the fact that none of them has had any training in the performance of top-management decision-making functions.[10] The net result in such an organization is that more often than not the strong overcome the weak so that, given a production-oriented economy,

---

[7] *Ibid.*, p. 75.

[8] Robert J. Ballon (ed.), *Doing Business in Japan*, Revised Edition, Tokyo: Sophia-Tuttle, 1968, Chapter Eight.

[9] Chie Nakane, *Tateshakai no Ningen Kankei* ('Human Relations in a Vertical Society'), Tokyo: Kōdansha, 1967.

[10] Noda, *op. cit.*, p. 106.

production overrules marketing, and company policy is set along the lines recommended by the production *buchō*. The differing seniorities of the members of the *jōmukai* strengthen this tendency by forcing junior members into subservience. In fact, the president, who has the highest seniority, may use the *jōmukai* as a means of personal control of the enterprise. Meanwhile, not to overlook staff function for emphasis upon line responsibility, it ought to be pointed out that, although it might be expected that the *jōmukai*, since it has such extensive responsibility, would be able to depend on extensive staff support, such support is extremely limited and, in any case, not qualitatively adequate.

THE STAFF FUNCTION

ALTHOUGH the staff function is highly underdeveloped in Japanese companies, some changes are being made. The vertical structure and the seniority system leave little room for an influential horizontal staff appendage. When a man is going to be with the same company twenty to thirty years and is promoted on the basis of seniority only, a staff position presents a problem. A move from staff to line is difficult, because all higher line positions are filled from subordinate line positions. The staff man therefore has nowhere to go. As the organizational pyramid narrows near the top, senior line people may be moved into senior staff positions, just to be allowed formal promotion while being removed from the line organization. This procedure means that young dynamic people with new ideas and training in modern management techniques (i.e., operations research, computers, and so on) are unlikely to be found advising senior line executives, but rather are to be found in lower line positions where they cannot apply their special knowledge. Their positions are determined by age and seniority. Alternatively they may be found in research groups, many of which are so theoretically oriented that their existence in the company is an expensive luxury justified more on the basis of prestige than of any practical contribution made to the development of the firm. Consequently,

Chapter four: The Japanese executive

Japanese management's view of the staff function of Operations Research, for example, is like that of econometrics: O. R. is a highly theoretical field and of little practical value in individual firms. The Japanese are surprised to learn that the majority of O. R. practitioners in the United States are concerned with very practical problems and expect to see the results of their work applied in practice in their firms. Unfortunately in the United States, practical O. R. applications are not published often enough because of company security, and the impression left by the published theoretical work is that O. R. is a highly impractical field.

It is not that the staff function does not appear in Japanese company organization charts; it does appear frequently in most major firms. But the reality of the situation is that it is more formal than real and in many cases may be providing administrative support rather than managerial know-how. There is staff work done in Japan by staff groups at high levels such as the *shachōshitsu*, but in most cases people in the line positions do their own staff work as a part of the *ringi* system, which will be described later.

Mention should be made here of the *i-inkai* ('committees') which provide staff support for the *jōmukai*. Asahi Chemical, for example, has four committees under the *jōmukai*: *yosan* ('budget'), *gijutsu* ('technical know-how'), *kikō* ('organization'), and *senden* ('publicity'). The budget committee also exercises a long-range planning function, as the *chōkikeikaku i-inkai* ('long-range planning committee').[11] One must question, however, the nature of this support, for, although it is provided at a high level, it may be more administrative than advisory in effect.

Another staff organizational form is exhibited by the Tokyo Automatic Machinery Works *(Tōkyō Jidō Kikai Seisaku Sho)*. It has a number of staff *kaigi* ('councils') under the *jōmukai*; they are *keikaku*-('planning'), *gyōmu*-('business'), and *kachō*-('section

[11] *Nihon Keiei no Kaimei* ('Elucidation of Japanese Management'), Tokyo: Tōyō Keizai Shimpōsha, 1961, p. 84.

[85]

chief') *kaigi*. A number of other committees are also subsumed under these councils.[12]

THE OFFICE OF THE PRESIDENT

THE *shachōshitsu*, a staff function attached directly to the President of the company, is an interesting development of postwar Japan. A number of large companies in different fields have adopted this function—for example, Hitachi Manufacturing, Japan Petroleum (Nippon Sekiyū), Hitachi Shipbuilding, and Marubeni-Iida Trading.[13]

Nippon Sekiyū established its *shachōshitsu* in 1953 as a support function for the *jōmukai*, to carry out, among other things, studies in planning and budgeting. Later, in 1958, the *shachōshitsu* added electronic data-processing equipment for record keeping and handling of orders. The measure of the influence of this function is revealed in the facts that it is attached to the central locus of decision-making authority in a company, the *jōmukai*, and that the *shachō* ('president'), as chairman of the *jōmukai*, has direct authority over the function, whose very title, *shachōshitsu*, literally means 'president's room'.[14]

Today the *shachōshitsu* is also concerned with long-range planning and the introduction of Management Information Systems (MIS). In fact, one reads in Japan today that the present age is the MIS-*jidai* ('the era of MIS'), and the subject itself is very popular in management circles. It is asserted that about one-fourth of computer time in Japan today is devoted to MIS. Although one cannot doubt the sincerity of such an assertion, most of the research on what Japanese management is doing is based on the results of inter-

---

[12] *Bessatsu Chuō Kōron (Keiei Mondai)*, Spring Edition, 1968, p. 146. A comprehensive discussion of the staff function and its development in Japan can be found in Susumu Takamiya, *Keiei Soshiki Ron* ('Theory of Management Organization'), Tokyo: Diamond Press, 1968 (a reprint).

[13] *Nihon no Hyakusha, op. cit.*

[14] *Nihon Keiei no Kaimei, op. cit.*, p. 82; and Noda, *op. cit.*, p. 128.

views or questionnaires, which are not entirely reliable. There is little doubt that long-range planning models have been developed and that computers are being used to provide information for management.[15] But it is difficult to determine the extent to which MIS and long-range planning models have been integrated into the top-management decision-making process. It is one thing for a company to say, in reply to a questionnaire, that it is using MIS at the top-management level and quite another thing for a professional management scientist to verify to his own satisfaction that what is being called an MIS is not in fact an open-loop reporting system providing computerized data and information to management.

Although one can find companies organized with various staff functions, councils, committees, and so on, the basic problem of Japanese organization remains the fact that, in order to perform the type of service exemplified by the U. S. Defense Department's 'whiz kids' under former Secretary Robert McNamara and in order to equal the so-called 'think tanks' assembled by the Rand Corporation, a staff group must contain highly talented, dynamic individuals who are aware of the most modern thought and techniques in all fields relating to their firm. Although the *shachōshitsu* in the Japanese firm is certainly well placed in the Japanese company organization, the seniority system and the vertical structure of Japanese enterprise work against the likelihood of the staff function's being performed by the people who should be performing it.

One solution to this problem that will most likely develop in the future is an extensive vertical elaboration of the *shachōshitsu* so that it becomes in form another *bu* of the company, allowing for vertical advancement on the basis of seniority from *sha-in* ('employee') to *kakarichō* to *kachō* to *buchō* and so on, all within the *shachōshitsu*. The alternative possibility, that not just the form, but the reality of Western staff management will eventually appear in Japan,

---

15 Hiroshi Gōhara, *Nihon no Keiei Keikaku* ('Management Planning in Japan'), Tokyo: Tōyō Keizai Shimpōsha, 1968, p. 211.

would require such radical changes in Japanese society that it could become common for younger and older men to work together on a basis of equality in salary and rank.

Under the title *Senmonshoku* (Professional Occupations), *Nihon Keizai Shimbun* of 8 July 1968 (morning edition) described how 'specialists' and 'experts' in technical areas of Honda Motors and Hitachi Shipbuilding were being given recognition through promotion to executive titles outside of regular line positions. A cartoon accompanying the article illustrated the general Japanese quandary that resulted from such developments. Entitled *Ekisupāto wa ippiki ōkami* ('The expert is emperor of a one animal kingdom'), the cartoon showed a *senmonbuchō* ('professionally skilled division head') sitting atop a chair high up on a pole with nobody under him. Next to him sat another *buchō* at the same height, but atop several rows of chairs extending out horizontally below him. The quandary results, of course, from the use of hierarchical titles for technical experts who have no hierarchy beneath them. It seems to be anomalous to the thinking of Japanese management to promote staff people to titles that are so inherently associated with line responsibility.

The *ringi* management system

THE *ringi* system[16] always attracts the attention of foreign businessmen in that it has characteristics that are useful in illustrating the group nature of the Japanese management decision-making process and, in general, the group nature of Japanese society. Yet one can also speak of the *ringi* system in terms of staff planning in a hierarchcal system where the highest line authority gives rubber-stamp approval to the staff work done for it. In essence, the system involves any subject at issue on which staff work is to be done. Noda gives five characteristics of it:

---

[16] Noda, *op. cit.,* p. 109; Hiroshi Gōhara, *Ringiteki Keiei to Ringi Seido* ('The Ringi System and Management'), Tokyo: Tōyō Keizai Shimpōsha, 1966; and Ballon, *op. cit.,* p. 177.

1 A proposal written up by middle management
2 Cautious horizontal consideration of the proposal
3 Cautious vertical consideration of the proposal
4 Formal affixture of the necessary seals to the *ringisho* document, which contains the proposal
5 Deliberate final ambiguity with respect to authority and responsibility for the proposal.[17]

Noda goes on to say:

'The *ringi* system is uniquely Japanese not only in its treatment of the management decision-making process, but it also exhibits the characteristics of the social nexus within the body corporate which spawned it. The *ringi* system blurs individual responsibility because the human personalities using the system consciously and unconsciously prefer that individual responsibility remain indistinct.

'We have found that basically the *ringi* system allows the middle management levels to perform the detailed planning, programming, and execution of almost all management actions. Top management's authority is similar to that of a rubberstamp general who delegates it formally to his subordinate officers. When top management is not too talented, the appearance of authority remains in the form of *ringi* approval, but in fact talented middle management is the power behind the throne, so long as it maintains appearances and does not embarrass the man at the top. This sort of arrangement offends Western rationalism which is the backbone of modern business, but from the point of view of the Japanese family system, it is a beautiful custom which is at the heart of the structure of Japanese society.'[18]

As mentioned earlier, the *ringi* system in essence involves the line

17 *Op.cit.*, p. 109.
18 *Ibid.*, p. 119.

functions in staff work. Whether the *ringisho* document originates at the *kakari* or *ka* level is of less importance than the fact that its originator and his subordinates do considerable study and research on it and that discussions of the proposal involve many horizontal and vertical levels. A *ringisho* document may reach a president's desk with tens of official seals on it that indicate the approval of all levels concerned.

Thus the *ringi* system not only illustrates the nature of the Japanese management decision-making process, but it also explains why the organization charts of Japanese companies show such limited staff functions. The system insures that all line elements concerned with a problem not only do the necessary staff work themselves, but also combine and coordinate their staff work before sending the *ringisho* to the president for final approval.

THE LADDER OF SUCCESS

SINCE the early part of the Meiji Period (1868–1912) in Japan, there has been a close connection between the former imperial universities, expecially the Law Faculties of Tokyo and Kyoto on the one hand and the Japanese Civil Service on the other. The Law Faculty of Tokyo University in particular has been the most prestigious of all university faculties in Japan. By the end of the Meiji Period, university graduates were routinely seeking employment in industry as well as in government, and a type of industrial civil-service system had developed whereby certain prestigious universities sent their graduates to prestigious companies. Today, also, most Japanese companies look to selected universities for their new *sarariman*, require company entrance examinations and personal interviews, and may even conduct background investigations on candidates. In any case, the university has become a key rung on the ladder of Japanese executive success.

Given the limited number of prestigious universities in Japan and an excessive demand for the available openings in freshman classes, competition for entrance has, of course, become very severe. The competition extends also to high school admissions, especially into those prestigious high schools that have a good record of placing their graduates in prestigious universities. In fact, the situation is reflected all the way down to lower school levels, where there is even severe competition for entrance into the prestigious *shōgakkō* ('elementary schools').

Thus at every educational level the Japanese executive has faced competition that he has had to overcome in order to reach even the *sararīman* level. The strain of the competition is considerably relieved once the student enters the university, where he may, if he chooses, relax for four years and merely devote himself to club activities. Thereafter the strain of competition for company jobs is not as great as one might think, for the student is pretty sure of getting a job, and the university he graduates from largely determines the companies that might hire him. At any rate, the shortage of white-collar labor in Japan today insures the university graduate a reasonably good job. It was not always so, however, for during the depression of the mid-1920s even graduates of the highest ranking imperial universities were lucky to find jobs as policemen and other low-level government workers.[19]

Today, the parent who is planning his child's future can plan it with considerable accuracy by carefully selecting his schools. In fact, he can even determine the dozen or so companies the student might enter, based on their preference for the graduates of certain universities. The companies that need the talents of science and engineering graduates are, of course, limited; but, as far as other companies are concerned, whether a young man has studied French Literature or Anglo-Saxon Law, he will still begin his *sararīman* career as a junior clerk.

Literally, *nenkō joretsu* means 'long-service rank' and connotes both lifetime employment and seniority based on years of service. Because of this system, the Japanese university graduate is assured

[19] *Ibid.,* p. 152.

[91]

of automatically moving up the ladder to *kakari, ka,* and *bu* levels within the same company. Below these levels, mobility between or among companies is almost non-existent. In any event, according to the system, the *sarariman* should have reached the *bu* level by his late forties. Then he has only a few years left until the age of fifty-five, which is the usual age of Japanese retirement. If he is lucky he may be made a *torishimariyaku* ('director') of the company by fifty, and then by fifty-five a *jōmutorishimariyaku* ('managing director'). With health, ability, luck, and good personal relations both inside and outside the company, he may even become *senmutorishimariyaku* ('executive director') and by sixty the *shachō* ('president') of his firm. As president, a Japanese may keep his position indefinitely, for he must retire only voluntarily. When he has decided to retire and has selected his successor, he can then move up to the honorary and ceremonial position of *kaichō* ('chairman of the board'), where he can remain as long as his health and determination allow.[20]

THE EXECUTIVE SELECTION PROCESS

OBVIOUSLY, as the organizational pyramid narrows, not all *sarariman* are able to reach the limited executive positions near the top. In the rapidly expanding economy of Japan, expansion of old plants, building of new plants, new branch offices, overseas assignments, joint ventures, and the like have enabled firms to avoid discharging or demoting managers, while at the same time such activities have enabled them to remove managers from immediate organizations. Those who have been removed, *shukkō sha-in* ('transferred employees') are often found, for example in Japanese-foreign joint ventures.[21]

But what is it that leads to their being weeded out? One survey that probed this question listed six factors as important in promotion: seniority, chance, personality, ability, school background, and

[20] *Ibid.,* p. 179.
[21] *High Adventure in Joint Ventures,* Tokyo: The American Chamber of Commerce in Japan, 1966.

personal connections.[22] The first three in order of major importance were school background, ability, and seniority.

One reason that school background came to be of such major importance in Japanese firms is that during the postwar Allied occupation of Japan SCAP (Supreme Commander, Allied Powers) 'democratized' the elite Japanese university-system by permitting many high schools to promote themselves into universities. Although today some of these new universities are great academic institutions (e.g., Yokohama National University), the older prewar institutions were considered to have superior reputations when compared to the new *ekiben daigaku* ('railroad-station lunch-box universities'), which seemed to proliferate so rapidly in the postwar period that they were thought to be as common as the *bentō* ('lunch-boxes') sold at railroad stations.

In the Japanese system, seniority is, of course, an obvious prerequisite for promotion, and no one can argue with the fact that ability is also important. It is not, however, clear what criteria the Japanese use to measure ability. In Japan, as in the West, higher levels evaluate performance at managerial levels with a ponderably subjective bias.

Chance, needless to say, may result in accidents, poor general health, specific illness, and death—universal elements in all human systems. Personality traits can be defined in psychological terms and can be measured, although here, again, as with ability, the higher levels tend towards judgments more quantitative than qualitative.

As for personal connections, called *kone,* they refer to the advantages that certain managers derive from family or school ties and the like—generally, whatever can be used as 'pull' in influencing promotion in a favorable direction. Here, again, because the phenomenon is universal, it needs no elucidation for a Western reader.

---

[22] Noda, *op. cit.,* p. 179.

The generation gap

HAVING risen from the ashes of defeat in World War II to such great heights, the phoenix-like resurrection of Japanese industry has been extensively analyzed in an attempt to determine the role that management played in its rebirth and growth to give Japan the already realized status of the world's third greatest industrial power, following upon only the United States and the Soviet Republic. It is tempting to seek as a cause some new entrepreneurial type born in the chaos of the postwar period and thereby endowed with some special qualities which, when applied to industry, produced economic miracles. Whether some special breed of talent was responsible or not, the search for the answers does cause one to look more carefully at postwar Japanese executives and, in attempting to analyze their characteristics, to find some method of categorizing the individuals concerned. In a sense, this is not unlike the parallel attempt scholars made in their study of the governing elite of the Meiji period to discern the role of entrepreneurship in the earliest manifestations of Japanese industrialization.

Noda considers that there are four types of executives in Japan today: (1) the founder type, (2) the second-generation type, (3) the *supā sarariman* ('super-salaryman') type, and (4) the professional manager type.[23]

THE FOUNDER TYPE

THE founder type is thought to be endowed with great innovational ability, for he has been able to overcome enormous financial and other obstacles to establish his enterprise and guide it to the front rank of the companies of Japan. For this type, school background played an insignificant role in success. Armed with a strong drive for innovation, the fortunate assistance of able collaborators, and an in-

[23] *Ibid.*, p. 141 ff.

domitable fighting spirit, the founder type made it to the top.

Foremost among this type of founder-executive is Sōichirō Honda, president and founder of the world-renowned Honda Motors. A poor student who hated studying and quit school at primary-school level, Mr. Honda loved machines and, in lieu of additional schooling, entered a machine shop as an apprentice. By the age of twenty-six he was running a small shop of his own. His enterprise flourished so fast that during the war he reached a point where he ran a piston-ring factory that employed several hundred workers.

Another famous founder type is Kōnosuke Matsushita, head of Matsushita Electric. He also quit primary school, then went to work as an apprentice in a *hibachi* shop at the age of twelve. Later he became a wiring technician in the Osaka Electric Light Company, and by the age of twenty-two he was an inspection supervisor. Because his superior was not interested in a design for a socket that he had developed, he quit and, in the spring of 1918 at the age of twenty-five, he set out on his own with some borrowed capital and some friends in a small shack to begin what was to become the great Matsushita Electric enterprise of today.

THE SECOND-GENERATION TYPE

BROUGHT up in the shadows of their famous fathers, managers of this type are thought to be introverted, but the best of them reach both a high intellectual level and high managerial skills, particularly with respect to their management of personnel and their reception of new and modern techniques and ideas. To be successful, having inherited large established enterprises, these men must win the confidence of the men their fathers led. They must adapt their enterprises to current conditions at the same time that they avoid alienating older company officials whose allegiance was to their fathers. Although most of these men are very conscious of the generation-gap between themselves and their famous fathers, there are exceptions who follow closely in their fathers' footsteps.

In any case, such are the characteristics of the second-generation type according to its Japanese image or caricature. As a matter of fact, the Japanese expression *nidaime* ('second generation') has a very definitely ironic or cynical connotation, such that it would be unfair to characterize all second-generation executives alike.

THE SUPER-SALARYMAN TYPE

THIS type of executives, super-salarymen, is thought to be composed of individuals who have reached the top because of their ability rather than family connection. Of course, there are many executives who reach their positions by *yoko-suberi* (literally, 'side-slipping'); that is to say, they move from government, bank, or parent corporations to company-executive status, but super-salarymen are the rare birds who make it on ability alone. Such men are supposed to be characterized by self-confidence, charm, strong leadership, and administrative ability, all derived from years of personality development and successful achievement. Perhaps the best example of this type is the great Taizō Ishizaka, retired head of *Keidanren* ('The Federation of Economic Organizations').

THE PROFESSIONAL MANAGER TYPE

WHAT we have left, then, are the troops of Japanese management: organization men who comprise the majority of Japanese executives today. The best of these men are truly professional in the best sense of the word: experience alone has developed in them the skills and abilities required to run a complex organization. It is thought that this professional-manager class carried Japanese industry through its traumatic postwar period when top managers were purged by SCAP and the control of enterprises was in the hands of middle management. They are, at any rate, the backbone of modern Japanese industry. They are thought to be men with amicable personalities, deep intelligence, and an up-to-date philosophy of management.

A special category of these professional managers is the class of engineer executives who have created such spectacular successes in postwar Japanese industry. Best known among them in the West is Masaru Ibuka of Sony Industries, Inc.

The future

THE spectacular success of Japanese executives in creating the economic miracle that is Japan today suggests that the system which fostered their rise will not see many radical changes in the near future. A most noteworthy postwar development is the engineer executive through whom much of what is new in the science of management will most likely pervade the Japanese hierarchy of management in the years to come. University graduates in law and literature will probably continue to make up the bulk of the professional manager class, and it is likely that they will continue to think of themselves and their future in terms of their being lifetime employee-executives of the same firm.

As Professor Susumu Takamiya has pointed out, the staff system, which was a new, postwar development in Japan, has been widely adopted organizationally in the country, although he questions whether it is an effective part of organization.[24] As mentioned earlier, the seniority system is an obstacle to the rational use of ability within an organization, whether in a staff or in a line position. Thus, in any look at the future, all prognostication should be hedged on the eventual modification of the seniority system.

[24] Ballon, *op. cit.*, Chapter Ten.

FIGURE I

KAJIMA CONSTRUCTION CO.: ORGANIZATION CHART (1965)

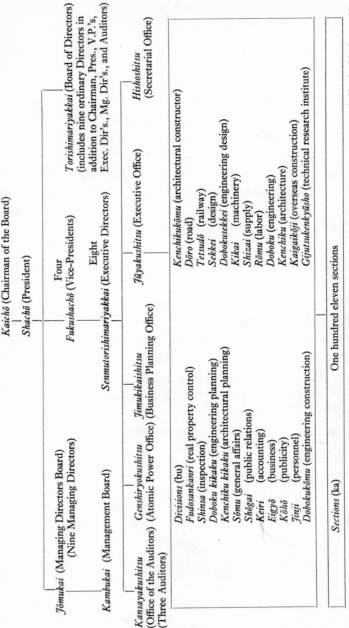

Kaichō (Chairman of the Board)

Shachō (President)

Torishimariyakkai (Board of Directors) (includes nine ordinary Directors in addition to Chairman, Pres., V.P.'s, Exec. Dir's., Mg. Dir's., and Auditors)

Four *Fukushachō* (Vice-Presidents)

Eight *Senmutorishimariyakkai* (Executive Directors)

Jōmukai (Managing Directors Board) (Nine Managing Directors)

Kambukai (Management Board)

Kansayakushitsu (Office of the Auditors) (Three Auditors)

Genshiryokushitsu (Atomic Power Office)

Jimukikaishitsu (Business Planning Office)

Fuyakushitsu (Executive Office)

Hishoshitsu (Secretarial Office)

Divisions (*bu*)

Fudosankanri (real property control)
Shinsa (inspection)
Doboku kikaku (engineering planning)
Kenchiku kikaku (architectural planning)
Sōmu (general affairs)
Shōgai (public relations)
Keiri (accounting)
Eigyō (business)
Kōhō (publicity)
Jinji (personnel)
Dobokukōmu (engineering construction)

Kenchikukōmu (architectural constructor)
Dōro (road)
Tetsudō (railway)
Sekkei (design)
Dobokusekkei (engineering design)
Kikai (machinery)
Shizai (supply)
Rōmu (labor)
Doboku (engineering)
Kenchiku (architecture)
Kaigaikōji (overseas construction)
Gijutsukenkyūsho (technical research institute)

Sections (*ka*)   One hundred eleven sections

Sources: *Nihon no Hyakusha* (100 Japanese Companies), Tokyo, Japan Productivity Center, 1965, pp. 154–5, and *Kaisha Nenkan 1968*, *op. cit.*, p. 36

[98]

CHAPTER FIVE

Organizational change[1]

BY JAMES C. ABEGGLEN

Companies in this study—recruiting the work force—education of the work force—compensation of employees—fringe benefits and allowances—leaving the Japanese company—some conclusions

THE organizations of any society, to the extent that they are to be effective and viable in the long run, must be built on the value systems and styles of interpersonal relations that are predominant in that society. American society, with its emphasis on individualism, high rates of social and geographic mobility, money as a principle basis of compensation and status, and impersonalization of work relations, has evolved an approach to industrial organization that is both distinctive and effective. As a way of fitting Americans together in a work situation, and for motivating and disciplining them, American methods of organization have achieved outstanding results. It does not follow, however, that these methods will be equally productive in other societies.

Japanese society has evolved an approach to the organization of its industries that is distinctive and effective; it is at the same time quite different in important respects from American organization methods. Japanese value systems and styles of interpersonal relations differ

---

[1] All rights to this article are strictly reserved by the author.

from those in the United States. It is inevitable, then, that industrial organization in Japan has followed a different course from that of the United States; yet it has also achieved outstanding results. Indeed, it seems likely that it is as a consequence of having developed a different, Japanese approach to organization that Japan has accomplished the industrial success that it has.

The approach to business organization developed in Japan, necessarily derived from that country's unique history and social system, has a characteristic pattern different in important respects from organization methods of industry in the West.[2] Normal practice for a large company includes the following:

Recruitment of employees directly from school at their terminal levels of education;

Retention of employees for their entire careers, without recourse to layoffs or discharges;

Compensation based on age-length of service, with starting compensation low and a function of levels of education;

Paternalistic fringe compensation including provisions for housing and allowances for size of family;

Compulsory retirement at an early age, usually 55 years, excepting only top management, and lump-sum retirement allowances.

These and related elements of Japanese organization methods have often been seen by both Western and Japanese observers as sources of inefficiency and competitive weakness. It has been pointed out that the labor force of a Japanese company cannot quickly be ad-

---

[2] The organization of large Japanese companies was intensively studied by the author in 1955–56. The results of that research are reported in *The Japanese Factory* (Glencoe: The Free Press, 1958), which examines in some detail the pattern of organization and personnel relations observed at that time. This article is a reexamination, ten years later, of some of the conclusions reached in that earlier report. This study, like the earlier one, deals with very large organizations. Differences in organization that may exist in smaller companies compared with large ones are not discussed.

justed to changing business conditions: differential compensation is not available as a motivating device; inefficient employees are retained in the organization; and the company takes on a range of social obligations on behalf of its employees in such areas as housing that are costly and not directly profitable.

Countering this view, it can be noted that this approach to organization is entirely congruent with Japanese social organization, which is generally less individualistic, more personalized, and more group-centered than Western societies. Loyalty to and identification with the work group and company seem to substitute well in Japan for compensation techniques as a motivational base. And it is not at all self-evident that Japan's lifetime employment system is more costly than the costs and losses involved in the high rates of job mobility in U. S. organizations.

In any event, there has been a rather general expectation that as Japan's economy grew, as Japanese companies expanded in scale, and as they entered into broad international competition, Japanese organization methods would move towards the Western model. It has been assumed that job mobility would increase sharply, that compensation would become tied to output and efficiency, and that personnel would be treated in a more impersonal and 'rational' way. There is a considerable cultural arrogance in this assumption that Western methods of handling men in work situations are inevitable and intrinsically more efficient than any other. Still, this has been a widespread expectation, shared rather generally in Japan and the West.

To test the view that Japanese business organizations, as they grow and are successful, must change and are changing towards the American pattern, the period from 1956 to 1966 is useful. Both years were relatively prosperous ones for Japan, and the intervening decade was a period of industrial growth in Japan seldom if ever equalled in any other economy. Japan's gross national product increased, on average, about 10% annually during the decade, and industrial production more than tripled. Exports increased 15% annually during the decade, or about double the increase in world trade.

This has been, therefore, a period of very rapid change in size and technology for Japanese companies, and a period in which they have been fully competitive in world markets. A comparison of elements of organizational methods over the decade provides a measure of the extent to which these methods are changing under stress and the degree to which they may be moving towards Western methods.

Companies in this study

THE Boston Consulting Group obtained from twenty-five large Japanese companies a summary of their employment, compensation, and recruitment and exit practices as of year-end 1956 and year-end 1966. The companies included in this study are listed below. Each is a leader in its product area of field of activity. The range of business is broad, including a long-term bank, two commercial banks, a trading company, and manufacturing companies

FIGURE I
COMPANIES IN THE STUDY

Ajinomoto Co., Inc.	Mitsubishi Shoji Kaisha, Ltd.
Asahi Glass Co., Ltd.	Mitsui Bank, Ltd.
Asahi Optical Co., Ltd.	Nichiro Gyogyo Kaisha, Ltd.
Fuji Iron and Steel Co., Ltd.	Nippon Electric Co., Ltd.
Fuji Photo Film Co., Ltd.	Nippon Reizo K. K.
Hokkai Can Co., Ltd.	Oji Paper Co., Ltd.
Industrial Bank of Japan, Ltd.	Shinetsu Chemical Industry Co., Ltd.
Jujo Paper Mfg. Co., Ltd.	Shiseido Co., Ltd.
Kubota Iron and Machinery Works,	Showa Denko K. K.
Ltd.	Sumitomo Chemical Co., Ltd.
Lion Dentrifice Co., Ltd.	Sumitomo Electric Industries, Ltd.
Mitsubishi Bank, Ltd.	Toyo Rayon Co., Ltd.
Mitsubishi Oil Co., Ltd.	Yawata Iron and Steel Co., Ltd.

in product areas from consumer items to heavy industry. The sample is not systematic; rather, it includes companies with which members of the Boston Consulting Group have relations such that cooperation with the request for data was likely. No systematic bias in selection is believed to have occurred, however.

The twenty-five organizations represent a significant share of the total Japanese economy. Their combined labor force totaled over 176 thousand in 1956 and over 269 thousand in 1966. This is about 1% of Japan's entire 1966 industrial labor force. The sales of the twenty-two non-banking firms totaled over \$2,261 million in 1956 and \$9,569 million in 1966, or about 10% of Japan's 1966 gross national product. Finally, the three banks represented are among Japan's most important. It seems likely, therefore, that any substantial changes in the organizational methods of Japanese companies would be reflected by these firms; they certainly represent an important segment of the total economy.

FIGURE 2

COMPANY SIZE AND WORK FORCE, 1956 and 1966
(Average, 25 companies)

	1956	1966
Annual sales, excluding three banks ($ million)	$102.8	$435.0
Capitalization ($ million)	$10.5	$57.7
Total employees, of which	7,048	10,415
Top management	0.2%	0.2%
Middle management	2.4	5.2
Male employees	70.2	64.4
Female employees	18.0	23.9
Temporary workers	9.2	6.3
Total	100.0	100.0

The impact of a decade of very rapid change and economic growth on the size and work force of these companies is shown in Figure 2. Sales have increased for the non-banking firms by an average of more than four times in the ten-year period, from about \$100 million to about $435 million. Capitalization of the twenty-five companies has increased nearly five and one half times from 1956 to 1966, reflecting both the gradual improvement of financial positions of Japanese companies and the very high rate of investment in new facilities during the period. The effects of capital investment on productivity have been dramatic. Against an increase in sales per company of about 325% in 1966 over 1956, the average work force of these companies increased less than 50% over 1956 levels. As a result, sales per employee totaled over $40 thousand in 1966 compared with about $15 thousand ten years earlier.

There have been some substantial shifts in the composition of the average work force in this period.[3] While the proportion of the work force in top management positions has not changed during the decade (the increase is from about fifteen, on average, to about twenty), there has been a sharp increase in the proportion of the work force in middle management positions. From a ratio of top to middle management of about 1:10 in 1956, there has been a shift to a ratio of about 1:25 in 1966, suggesting that increased size of companies, and presumably increased sophistication of technology, has caused a proliferation of staff and supervisory functions. The suggestion of increased administrative and staff functions is reinforced by the increase in the proportion of female employees in the total work force; females now make up nearly a quarter of total employees. On the other hand, male employees and temporary employees

---

[3] To provide data meaningful in terms of Japanese company practice, and at the same time not make unreasonable demands on responding companies, this study used the following categories for employees: 1) top management *(yakuin)*, which includes all executives at the executive or director level; 2) middle management *(bukachō),* including division and section chiefs, and assistant and vice-chiefs; 3) male employees *(jūgyōin-danshi),* all male employees below the section-leader level, whether in white-collar or blue-collar jobs; 4) female employees *(jūgyōin-joshi),* similarly non-titled and combining clerical and production employees; and 5) temporary employees *(rinjikō),* a special Japanese category for employees who are outside the system of lifetime employment, are non-union members, and who provide some flexibility regarding total work force size, since they can readily be laid off on relatively short notice.

(presumably largely male) have decreased—again suggesting very substantial increases in output by directly productive workers.

Recruiting the work force

THE pattern of employment for large Japanese companies has been to recruit all personnel directly from schools. They are, as a result, not employed for a particular skill nor for a particular job opening. Rather, they are employed because their personal background and characteristics, and their general education, make them appear to be desirable and useful persons to bring into the company for their careers. Similarly, the new employee makes his choice of job offers not in terms of the attractiveness of a particular position and its compensation, but rather because the organization as a whole appears to be a desirable group with which to identify oneself.

Therefore, a first test of the degree and direction of change in organization practices is the issue of amount and source of recruitment of new personnel to the company. Figure 3 shows the total recruitment into the work force for 1956 and 1966 and the sources

FIGURE 3

WORK FORCE RECRUITMENT, 1956 and 1966
(average, 25 companies)

	Top management		Middle management		Male employees		Female employees	
	1956	1966	1956	1966	1956	1966	1956	1966
Total recruitment, as percent of work force	0%	0%	0%	0.3%	7%	3%	8%	14%
Of which,								
recruited from schools	0%	0%	0%	0%	53%	77%	74%	91%
recruited from related companies	0%	0%	0%	67%	0%	2%	0%	0%
recruited from labor market	0%	0%	0%	33%	47%	21%	26%	9%

of recruitment. The three sources of recruitment examined were:

... directly from school
... from affiliated or subsidiary companies *(keiretsu kaisha)*
... from the outside job market.

On balance, the practice of recruiting directly from school is substantially more marked in 1966 than a decade earlier. For both periods, top management was drawn from within, with no mobility between companies in either period. There was only a single case not conforming to this rule—the fastest growing company in the group of twenty-five reported that one of its top executives in 1966 was recruited from outside the company. At the level of general employees, recruitment directly from school now accounts for virtually all female employees and more than three-quarters of male employees.

A partial exception to this general pattern of continuing the unique recruiting system of Japan was the middle management group. While there had been no recruitment either from related companies or from the general labor market of middle management personnel in 1956, in 1966 a few cases were reported, still well under 1% of the total group. Eight of the twenty-five companies reported cases of bringing in middle management from outside the company. However, six of these cases involved sourcing middle management personnel from related companies. Of the few cases of outside recruitment of middle management reported, nearly all were by a single company. This company, the same one that reported recruiting one of its top executives from outside, was, as noted, the fastest growing company of the twenty-five. In fact, its sales increased more than ten times in the ten-year period, and the company was a substantial one in 1956.

The suggestion here, then, is that the Japanese practice of recruiting directly from school, and not recruiting from an open labor market, remains very much in effect. Indeed, at the lower levels of the corporate structure this practice is substantially more widespread than a decade ago. However, there is some indication that at the middle management level, and under extreme stress, the large Japanese company can and does recruit from outside. There is little or no indication of any trend towards the free flow of personnel between companies that is held to characterize U. S. management practice.

Education of the work force

RELATED to the issue of recruitment, and to that of compensation patterns and changes, is the educational level of the Japanese work force. As the recruitment pattern suggests, education in Japan almost totally determines career chances. Point of entry into the company hierarchy, compensation for the career, and chances for a high-status position in the career are substantially determined by the amount of education the employee obtains before joining the company and thus the status level at which he enters. Table 4 indicates how education and position in the company interrelate. Virtually all the members of top management of the companies studied have university educations. This is generally true of Japa-

FIGURE 4

EDUCATION AND COMPANY POSITION, 1956 and 1966
(average of 25 companies in %)

| | 1956 | | | | 1966 | | | |
	College or university	Higher school	Middle school	Total	College or university	Higher school	Middle school	Total
Top management	91%	5%	4%	100%	94%	5%	1%	100%
Middle management	75	21	4	100	74	23	3	100
Male employees	10	23	67	100	10	37	53	100
Female employees	1	41	58	100	2	57	41	100
Temporary workers	0	0	100	100	0	1	99	100

[107]

nese management, which has a level of formal education well beyond that of management in the United States and far beyond that of such European countries as the United Kingdom.

In general, the Japanese work force at all levels is a well-educated one. The high level of formal education of the entire Japanese work force in 1956 is further reinforced by developments over the last decade. The proportion of workers with at least a higher school education has sharply increased in the entire work force. Indeed, it must be concluded that the emphasis on formal education in Japanese business, with its implications for discipline, technical knowledge, and work force adaptabllity, is a major factor in Japan's successful industrialization and present economic achievements.

Looking at recruitment by education, the shift in emphasis has been, over the decade, dramatic. In 1956 over half of the male entrants to the work force of the companies studied were recruited from middle school graduates, while in 1966 over a third were university graduates and more than half were graduates of high schools. In addition to the implications for improved quality of the work force suggested by this shift in recruiting, it should be noted that when Japanese companies complain of a 'shortage of labor' they usually are in fact complaining that middle school graduates— the least costly in terms of wages and most accommodating in terms of starting jobs—are diminishing sharply in numbers as the educational level of the whole society moves sharply upward.

In terms of female recruits to the work force, the proportion recruited from universities remains low—4% in 1956 and only 3% in 1966. This reflects the inability of the Japanese company to use women in jobs of any significance and the unattractiveness of corporate employment to well educated women in Japan. It is extremely difficult to integrate a college trained woman into a system in which she is no more than a drawer of tea and hewer of paper. Even female recruits, however, reflect the steadily increasing emphasis on education, in that more than three-quarters of the

new female entrants to these work forces in 1966 were higher
school graduates compared with 56% in 1956.

Compensation of employees

A further test of change in Japanese organization methods is that of
compensation. As generally practiced, Japanese compensation has
three main components. The first is wage or salary, the second a
bonus paid semi-annually and, to a degree, dependent on corporate
results, and the third a wide range of fringe benefits and perquisites.
The reports of the twenty-five companies studied regarding compensation in 1956 and 1966 are summarized in Figure 5.

FIGURE 5

ANNUAL COMPENSATION, PER INDIVIDUAL 1956 and 1966
(average in $ equivalent)

	1956			1966			Increase 1966 over 1956
	Salary or wages	Bonus	Total	Salary or wages	Bonus	Total	
Top management	$5,328	$2,694	$8,022	$11,496	$6,994	$18,490	130%
Middle management	2,088	1,188	3,276	3,408	2,466	5,874	79
Male employees	804	302	1,106	1,524	646	2,170	96
Female employees	425	142	567	840	320	1,160	106
Temporary workers	396	70	466	756	262	1,018	118

The average cash compensation in 1966 of the twenty or so men
who direct each of these large companies is reported to be about
$18,500 annually. Slightly more than a third of this is in the form of
bonus payments, with base salaries averaging slightly less than
$1,000 monthly. Executive compensation is up substantially from
the $8,000 a year level of 1956, but is still very low indeed by U.S.

standards. This group includes, of course, the board chairmen, presidents, and managing directors of large companies. Even at the $18,500 level, executive compensation had increased more rapidly over the decade than was the case with other categories of company employees.

Overall, compensation for employees of these companies has roughly doubled in the decade. Within each of the employee groups, there would be, of course, wide variation in compensation depending on length of service and level of schooling. The level of starting compensation is a function of educational background, and base compensation increases in direct relation to length of service. These two factors combine in the case of female and temporary employees whose educational level and length of service are low to make for very low levels of compensation, only slightly above $1,000 annually. Average annual compensation for male employees is about twice that of female employess, $2,170. The average compensation of middle management personnel has increased less rapidly than that of the other groups, and is now just under $6,000 per year. This is no doubt due to the buildup in size of the middle management group, with the result that average length of service is likely to have decreased over the decade for the group.

Fringe benefits and allowances

IN addition to base salary or wages and bonus payments, employees of Japanese companies receive a variety of fringe benefits and perquisites. For senior officers of a publicly held company, these may include car and driver, company-owned housing, and substantial expense accounts. For clerical employees and laborers, a range of special allowances are paid: housing or housing allowances may be provided, and the company may provide such perquisites as company stores for discount purchases and mountain and seaside vacation facilities. The foreign observer of Japan, taken aback at low salary levels and impressed by the company hospitality offered him, is apt to exaggerate considerably the magnitude of these fringe benefits and their impact on the individual employee's income. Putting closely-held or family owned companies to one side as a special case (as indeed they are also in the West), the increment of these benefits to income of the employee of a large company and to his family is minor except in the case of housing.

In this survey, two elements of these fringe benefits were examined: company-owned housing and special allowances. The proportion of employees provided company-owned housing in 1966 was 21% for top management, 44% for middle management, 34% for male employees, and 8% for female employees. In sum, perhaps one-third of company employees, on average, are provided company housing. The proportion in company housing is down slightly for all categories of employees from 1956.

This housing is rented to the employee at nominal rental amounts, and its quality depends on rank in the company. As a man is promoted, he will successively move to larger and more attractive housing. The quality is often not high. In one discussion comparing U.S. and Japanese salaries, a young Japanese executive was reminded that he paid virtually nothing for his housing and replied that he was paying precisely what it was worth. However, in housing-short Japan where rentals can be very high indeed, provision of company housing is a substantial increment to real income.

The low proportion of senior executives in company housing probably does not entirely reflect their real housing benefits. Several companies included in this study, anxious to reduce their capital commitments in housing, have made it possible for executives to buy company houses at book value (well below market value) and finance the purchases by loans from the company against their retirement allowances. The capital gain to the individual under this arrangement would be considerable.

The range of allowances paid to employees below the management level is shown in Figure 6. The seventeen allowances listed are not exhaustive, but are those most commonly offered employees. Five allowances are paid by virtually every company included in this study. Three of these are normal international practice—special pay for holiday, overtime, or night work. One company only does not pay a special allowance for overtime or night work; this is a manufacturer that put its entire work force on a salary basis in 1965. Two of these generally paid allowances are more special to Japan: the payment of part or all of commutation expenses, which is a tax deductible item for Japanese companies, and the payment of a family allowance, intended to compensate the employee partly for the additional costs of maintaining a family (these payments are small).

Among the other allowances listed in Figure 6, a shift in emphasis should be noted. Allowances for age and length of service have declined in frequency from 1956 to 1966, while allowances for position, job classification *(shokumukyū)*, and 'special work' have increased in incidence. This reflects an effort on the part of many

FIGURE 6

COMPANIES PAYING SPECIAL WORKER ALLOWANCES,
1956 and 1966

Allowance	Number of companies 1966	Number of companies 1956
Commutation	25	22
Holiday work	25	24
Family	24	23
Overtime	24	24
Night work	24	22
Position	19	17
Job classification	17	9
Dangerous work	14	12
Housing allowance	13	8
Cold district	13	11
Length of service	11	15
Age	10	12
Vacation	10	11
Area	9	10
Attendance	7	9
Efficiency	6	8
Remote area	4	3

companies to move toward compensation based on job and output and away from compensation based on age and education. Eight companies reported introducing a job classification allowance in the decade, so that by 1966 most of these companies included a job classification allowance in total compensation. This change should be reviewed with some caution, however. In at least some of these companies the job classifications established to date are little more than seniority categories under another name.

To put this matter of extensive allowances in perspective, the sums involved need to be noted. They are small. Average allowance payments in 1956 for male employees were about a 20% increment to base wages or $160 for the year. In 1966 the ratio to base wages had declined to about 18%, or a total allowance payment of about $276 for the year. This represented a 12 to 13% increase in total cash compensation (wages plus bonus). For female employees, allowances represented an increment to base wages in both 1956 and 1966 of about 10%, or an addition to cash compensation of 7 to 8%. In sum, then, a wide variety of types of allowances, many paternalistic, continue to be paid, and to be paid in about the same proportions at the end of the ten-year period as in 1956.

Leaving the Japanese company

A critical test of the degree and kind of change in organization methods in Japan is the movement of employees out of companies. The lifetime employment concept assumes that the individual employee will not quit the company and that the company will not lay off or discharge the employee. While such a system could hardly exist in its pure form, it has been an accurate way to describe the normative behavior of employers and employees in Japan. Indeed, this concept is a key to Japanese employment practices since many of the paternalistic features of employment are directly derived from this principle of an exchange of social obligation on the part of employee and employer.

H

The question of whether this basic principle is changing has been the subject of some controversy over the past few years. Figure 7 summarizes the results of a comparison of exit rates and causes for the twenty-five companies in this study for 1956 and 1966. It appears that the exit rate from companies, as a component of labor turnover rate, has not changed appreciably in the decade, with the exception of female employees whose exit rate has increased rather sharply. The proportion of management and of male employees who have left the company in the year is substantially the same. The proportion of female employees leaving these companies in the year has increased from 9% to 15%, parallel to the increase in percentage recruited in these two years from 8% to 14% (see Figure 3).

FIGURE 7
LEAVING THE COMPANY, 1956 and 1966
(average, 25 companies)

	Top management		Middle management		Male employees		Female employees	
	1956	1966	1956	1966	1956	1966	1956	1966
Exits from work force as % of total	2	2	5	3	3	4	9	15
Of which, Retirement for age	100	100	67	56	40	36	1	2
Voluntary retirement	0	0	27	25	56	54	99	97
Move to related company	0	0	6	7	2	5	0	0
Discharge	0	0	0	13	2	5	0	1

Looking at the causes for leaving the work force, with the exception of discharge from these companies, which is discussed further below, the pattern of causes has changed little. Most management personnel retire for reasons of age. Some middle management personnel, and over half of male employees, retire for reasons of health, family needs (such as returning to agricultural work), and other personal reasons. (This category may include employees who leave for other work. To the extent that it does, the proportion seems not to have changed over the decade.) Almost all female employees leave for personal reasons, and in almost all cases the main reason is marriage. By company rule earlier, and by continuing custom, women leave the industrial work force at or soon after marriage.

The category of 'related companies' requires some comment. The retirement age in Japan for all but top management is usually 55 years. Since new employment at that age is difficult to obtain, retirement payments small, and social security benefits much smaller, retirement at so early an age works a real hardship in many cases. One form of fringe benefit available to a favored employee is to place him in a senior position in a subsidiary or affiliated company where he can continue in fulltime and fully compensated employment for some additional years. It is likely that most cases of exit to related companies are of this type.

Thus, the rate and causes of leaving the work force appear to have changed very little over the past decade of rapid economic change—with one exception, and a critical one, discharge. From almost no cases of firings in 1956, discharge from the company appears in 1966 as a significant cause of exits from these compannies. Of the 3% of middle management who left their companies in 1966, about 13% were fired. Similarly, of the 4% of male employees who left their companies, 5% were fired.

To put the proportions in perspective, these discharges totalled less than two-tenths of 1% of the 1966 work force. The numbers are tiny, by any measure. Yet, the question remains, does this indicate the beginnings of a real and basic change in the way in which the Japanese business organization operates? The answer is not entirely clear, but closer examination of the data suggests that a basic change has not yet taken place.

Of the discharges reported, totalling about 450 out of a total work force of 260,000, the majority were discharges from a single company.

Almost all of the middle management and of the female employee cases, and most of the male employee cases, occurred in this one company. This company states,

> 'The cases of discharge are the result of a rationalization of management, and while these employees were discharged, they were given assistance in finding other employment.'

The company in question is a leader in an industry that has been under severe pressure in Japan due to raw materials sourcing problems and uneconomic size of production units. As a result, this company was by a considerable margin the slowest growing of the twenty-five companies included in the study. Against an average increase in sales of more than four times of other companies studied, its sales increased in dollar value only about 70% in the ten years. What is referred to by this company as 'rationalization of management' in justifying its dismissal of employees in 1966 was rather clearly drastic surgery aimed at saving an organization that was in trouble.

This case suggests that the basic rules of lifetime commitment remain in force to about the same extent as a decade ago in Japan, but that under extreme stress a kind of spasm-reaction can take place in a company during which the rule is temporarily waived to deal with severe crisis. It is, of course, implicit in the explanation given by the company in question that these cases of discharge were temporary deviations from the norm of corporate policy.

It will be recalled that one of these twenty-five companies deviated from normal practice and recruited a number of middle management personnel from the outside labor market. This was, by a good margin, the fastest growing company in this group. Again, in terms of discharge—the other extreme form of deviation from normal practice—it is the slowest growing company that provides the instance of exceptional behavior.

Chapter five: Organizational change

Some conclusions

'. . . in spite of the phenomenal character and the rapidity of the transformation of Japan, it has not been accompanied by such a revolutionary break with the traditions and customs of the past as was caused by the development of industry in some Western countries. Here it is only necessary to emphasize once more the importance of taking the family system into account in examining the problems of industrial Japan . . . Out of this influence arises a fundamental problem for the future of industrial organization in Japan.

'This problem may be stated as being whether the future industrial organization of Japan is to be evolved in conflict between the traditional influences and ideas—especially the family system—and the new ideas and institutions which in Japan as in most other countries have accompanied the growth of industry, or whether means can be developed of integrating the new institutions in the traditional Japanese social organization.'

This statement of the question of degree and rate of change in Japanese organizations was published over a generation ago, in 1933.[4] Its startling relevance to current conditions indicates that the issue is a long-term and continuing one. Business organizations, as integral parts of their society, must reflect in their organization methods the same values and sets of relations that exist in the family, schools, religions, and other elements of that society. Otherwise they will fail to be effective units in keeping together their members in efficient combination.

The problem, then, has not changed in over a generation. Japa-

[4] *Industrial Labour in Japan,* Studies and Reports, Series A (Industrial Relations), No. 37, Geneva: International Labour Office, 1933, p. 370.

nese methods of organization, when different from those in the United States, are not necessarily less effective or less rational. Both systems are adapted to the people that make them up. The hazards of rapid adaptation of U. S. methods by Japanese companies are rather clear—they may, in so doing, destroy the very basis of their strength. By the same token, U. S. companies operating in Japan must adapt their methods in order to be really effective.

This study of the 1956–1966 period indicates something of the fundamental nature and durability of Japan's approach to industrial organization. The companies studied have been by any reasonable measure successful organizations. In fact, it is a considerable tribute to the skill of their management and the capability of the organizations that they have succeeded in keeping pace with the rate of economic growth and change of Japan's last decade. It is also quite clear that they have done so within the customary framework of Japanese organization, with only minor deviations from the norms of Japanese methods. There is little indication that these companies are moving towards the American, or Western, model in the ways in which they recruit, reward, and punish personnel. The conclusion must be that successful industrial organization is not an absolute and single model to be pursued in every case. Rather, organizational methods can and must vary as the values and interpersonal relations of the members of the organization vary.

There has been, as noted, a general tendency to assume that Japanese companies are changing in their methods of organization. These data do not encourage that view. No doubt Japanese society, like any other, is changing and will continue to change, and no doubt its institutions—companies, schools, families, and the like—will be components of that change. But it seems quite clear that the change will be slow and continuous and little evident in so short a period as ten years. Societies do not change so quickly as that in their fundamentals, however much the surface may reflect change.

As the 1933 study concluded,

Chapter five: Organizational change

'It would be hazardous to attempt to forecast the probable lines of development of Japanese industrial organization.'[5]

It is by no means clear as yet in the Japanese case that change, as it occurs, will move towards the Western model.

[5] *Ibid.*, p. 371.

Part III

REMUNERATION
OF THE
JAPANESE EMPLOYEE

CHAPTER SIX

Lifelong remuneration system

BY ROBERT J. BALLON

Lifelong remuneration structure—cash earnings—efficiency remuneration—age limit and thereafter—when employment is not for life—trends

THE salary system anywhere in the world is influenced by the nature of the employment relationship. In Japan, this relationship is ideally a lifelong one. Employers and employees alike consider that employment by the same firm should start at the time one leaves school and last until the age limit is reached. Such a practice can be followed economically only by larger firms, where it is applied to the majority of the labor force, the so-called 'regular' or 'permanent' employees, but even where the lifelong relationship cannot be carried out for economic reasons, as in smaller firms, it remains valid largely as an ideal to be striven for. Where not in force, exception is consciously taken.

This institution of lifetime employment, though so much akin to Japanese social psychology, has developed in fairly recent times. It appeared in the interwar period, but became entrenched only after World War II. It is related to the role Japanese society expects industrial enterprises to play: besides a productive function, they must also fulfill a social one. The economic problems of the thirties, combined with population pressure, imposed on enterprises responsibilities far beyond their role of producers of goods and

[123]

services; in the forties, the war and its aftermath engrained this feature, on which the postwar labor movement capitalized.

Organized labor had much to do with the institutionalization of lifelong employment by being heavily concentrated in the larger firms and by pretty much limiting its membership to 'permanent' workers, those blessed with a lifelong commitment. It is now facing the inevitability of a change in viewpoint with regard to enterprise. Because of its growing involvement in international economics, Japanese society is being pushed in a new direction, where a clearer distinction must be made between the economic imperatives enterprise faces and the social needs that, more and more, government faces.

Meanwhile, the managers of larger firms, now increasingly professional, find themselves shackled with lifelong employment as the pattern for their salary systems. As a consequence, they make frantic efforts to gain vital freedom of action and get around the obstructions of organized labor. For all we know, the odds are against labor; at any rate, management hopes to hit the mark before lifelong employment has completed the full circle of a generation.

In order to convey an easier understanding of the lifelong salary system, many references will be made to the system in use for national government employees for two main reasons. First, when Japan started to industrialize under the promptings of the Meiji government, it had at hand a 'modern' system of employment and remuneration, namely, the system introduced in 1872 for the new bureaucracy, which may have been the seed of what, decades later, would become standard in the private sector. Secondly, Western countries apply to their government employees a sort of lifelong remuneration system, since employment with the government is usually accompanied by tenure. The Japanese system may, therefore, look somewhat familiar to the Western reader.

Chapter six: Lifelong remuneration system

Lifelong remuneration structure

A CASH REMUNERATION

BUILDING on a 'participative' type of employment, postwar Japan has, with the help of organized labor, institutionalized lifelong employment tenure and concomitantly evolved a lifetime remuneration system with a wage structure and methods of payment quite different from the Western wage-rate approach. Such a development was possible for two special reasons. Up until 1964, larger Japanese firms annually hired new employees who had just left school, as as well as additional females by the thousands, so that the average length of service for all employees in each firm was always pulled back. For all industries, in 1962 the average length of service was 7.8 years for male and 3.9 for female employees; in 1966 it was 8.0 for male and 4.0 for female employees. In large firms with one thousand or more employees, the average was substantially higher; in 1966 it stood at 11.4 years for male and 5.1 for female employees.[1] A labor-cost conscious manager therefore watches carefully the average length of service in his enterprise. He must also reckon with labor turnover. The large steel firms of Japan, for example, lose up to one-third of their newly hired employees during the first year of employment.[2] The nearly universal Japanese practice of almost exclusively hiring fresh graduates determines a particular age structure that delays the full impact of the increasing length of service. It postulates a rapidly expanding economy.

Another reason for the possibility of the postwar lifelong remuneration system is that a lifetime employment span would cover about thirty years, but the practice got rooted only fifteen years ago.

[1] See *Year Book of Labour Statistics 1962*, Tokyo: The Ministry of Labor, 1963, p. 124, and *Id.*, 1966–67, p. 118.
[2] *Shūkan Rōdō Nyūsu* ('Weekly Labor News'), Tokyo: Nihon Rōdō Kyōkai, 15 April 1968, p. 1.

This fact means that the salary system has not yet compassed the full swing of one generation of employees; it is especially significant that the total weight of retirement allowances for a steady work force has not yet been experienced.

In the context of participative and lifelong employment, cash remuneration is not meant to pay off services just rendered. Rather, a 'cost-of-living' approach is adopted, in the sense that a member of the family receives the cash that an enterprise, as a unit in the global society, knows to be necessary for his subsistence. Wages therefore follow norms primarily set by society, while rates are set by each enterprise. The financial or capitalization aspect of the salary is, by and large, shared with the family, i.e., the enterprise.

It is remarkable, for example, that most wages are paid by the month. Since in Japan as well as anywhere else a monthly family budget is a near impossibility, the employee is very much aware of his dependence on employment in his daily purchase of necessities.

FIGURE I

LIFELONG REMUNERATION STRUCTURE

  I Basic salary (monthly)
 II Allowances:
    1 Monthly allowances
       Such as overtime, position, family, transportation, attendance, cost-of-living, etc.
    2 Seasonal allowances
       Usually at mid-summer and year-end.
    3 Retirement allowance
    4 Non-work allowances
       Such as sick leave, paid vacations, etc.
III Statutory welfare costs (monthly)
       Health insurance
       Welfare pension insurance
       Unemployment compensation insurance
       Workmen's accident compensation insurance, etc.
 IV Non-statutory welfare costs (monthly)
  V Non-cash benefits and other benefits like intra-company saving schemes.

Chapter six: Lifelong remuneration system

With more detailed explanations reserved for the next section, the wage structure in the lifelong remuneration system is as given in Figure 1. The concept of 'wage' (*chingin*)—or, more specifically, *gekkyū* ('monthly salary')—includes both basic salary and monthly allowances; official statistics use the terms 'regular earnings' or 'monthly contract cash earnings'. Generally speaking, labor unions have so far respected such a wage structure because it expresses the lifelong employment institution they defend. Wage problems for Japan's organized labor are problems of amounts, not of structure.

B NON-CASH BENEFITS

JAPANESE non-cash benefits are nowadays often lumped together as 'non-statutory welfare costs', a phrase that misleads in as much as the word 'costs' implies precise accounting. Until recently few Japanese enterprises really cared to account precisely for non-cash benefits, even if they could, considering them less 'cost' than a kind of 'social overhead' of enterprise. The many tax advantages such costs carry, though exacting somewhat more precise accounting, tend at the same time to strengthen such a view. Certainly

FIGURE 2

WELFARE FACILITIES IN TOTAL ASSETS,
BY SIZE OF ESTABLISHMENT (1966)

	Total	5000 or more	1000–4999	300–999	100–299	(%) 30–99
Total fixed assets	100.0	100.0	100.0	100.0	100.0	100.0
Welfare facilities	7.1	8.7	6.3	5.8	6.8	5.7
Housing facilities	5.7	6.8	5.2	4.9	5.4	4.7
Other welfare facilities	1.2	1.5	1.0	.8	1.3	1.0
Training facilities	.2	.4	.1	.1	.1	.0

Source: *Rōdō Hiyō* 41 *Nenban* (Labor Costs, 1966), Tokyo: The Ministry of Labor, 1967, p. 34

Japanese unions manifest little interest in sharing welfare responsibilities with management, seemingly not wishing to shoulder them. Thus they are left in the hands of the employer—or, more exactly, they are one of the functions of the industrial family, for which the employer is traditionally held responsible. (Figure 2)

Where employment is participative and lifelong, almost anything can qualify as a non-cash benefit, outbidding by far the most sophisticated paternalistic devices of the West, ranging from birth-control clinics through marriage brokerage to funeral arrangements—truly a family affair, through which the entire range of familial services becomes available. The enterprise is not a second home; yet, for all practical purposes except the procreation of children, it looks like *the* fundamental home. (Figure 3)

FIGURE 3

WELFARE FACILITIES ASSETS PER EMPLOYEE (1966)

	Total	Housing facilities	Other welfare facilities	(¥ thousand) Training facilities
Total	87.9	70.6	14.8	2.5
5000 or more employees	149.0(100.0)	115.6(100.0)	25.9(100.0)	7.5(100.0)
1000–4000	114.9(77.1)	94.7(81.9)	18.9(72.9)	1.3(17.3)
300–999	72.1(48.4)	60.6(52.4)	10.4(40.3)	1.1(14.4)
100–299	48.7(32.3)	39.0(33.7)	9.3(35.7)	.5(6.6)
30–99	30.6(20.5)	25.0(21.6)	5.3(20.5)	.0(3.2)

Source: *Rōdō Hiyō 41 Nenban* (Labor Costs, 1966), Tokyo: The Ministry of Labor, 1967, pp. 34, 164–169

Living-in has long been a feature of employment in small Japanese firms, made up for in large firms by factory dormitories for girls, for 'bachelors' *(dokushin ryō),* and individual company housing at a nominal rent for married couples. In the last few

Chapter six: Lifelong remuneration system

years, chiefly because of the increasing cost of maintenance work and the shortage of such skills, large companies have started to curtail their housing facilities in more populated areas and to provide their employees with financial stipends, instead, for affording their own dwellings. On the other hand, the rapid development of industrial sites away from congested areas has forced large firms to provide more and more housing if they want to cope with the

FIGURE 4

RISE OF LAND PRICES IN URBAN AREAS, (1955–1967)

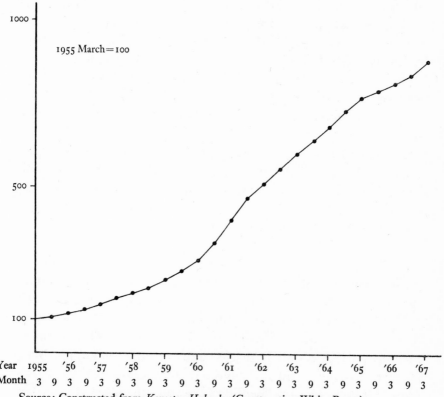

Source: Constructed from *Kensetsu Hakusho* (Construction White Paper),
Tokyo: The Ministry of Construction, 1967, p. 213

tightening labor shortage. In postwar years the appalling lack of housing has done much to reinforce this non-cash benefit.

Together with shelter, food and clothing are, of course, major considerations. Company stores or privileged purchasing arrangements, by which their own goods can be obtained at substantial rebates, are provided by most larger Japanese firms. It is also quite common for them to offer the products of related firms at considerably reduced prices and thereby to settle some outstanding accounts, bypassing the stringencies of cash. Up to a certain percentage of the seasonal allowance, in fact, company goods are often given instead of cash. Company dining rooms, as well as medical and sanitary services are common, and all at a nominal cost.

Recreational facilities are a very substantial non-cash benefit for Japanese employees. Mountain and sea resorts are dotted with company villas *(bessō)*, where employees and their families can spend several days at nominal charges. Command relaxations are also common, as when an entire section of a firm spends a weekend in one of these villas or when everybody takes off on a company outing.

For large firms, the substantial investment in these non-cash welfare services is facilitated by generous government and bank loans, especially in the form of real estate, a favorable investment in view of the postwar inflationary trend that has sky-rocketed Japanese land prices. (Figure 4)

C OTHER BENEFITS

JAPAN is a paradise of company expense accounts. For one thing, the sky is the limit when it comes to entertaining a visiting VIP from abroad; his main concern, the contract he came to sign, seems forgotten in the whirl of social life. As for Japanese businessmen themselves, they regularly discuss and conclude important deals, and even less important ones, in the friendly atmosphere of restaurants and golf courses. The difference from the West is probably that expense accounts are not looked upon as a sales gimmick easily abused, but are an acknowledged means of maintaining in the business world and in society at large an expected standing that cannot be defrayed out of earnings.[3]

Private automobile ownership has barely started in Japan, but many passenger automobiles are driven at company expense. Membership in golf clubs is mostly also a company expense, which starts to be validated at the level of chief of section *(kachō)*.

A much more significant benefit in the context of lifelong employment commitment with an industrial family is the long-standing practice of intracompany saving and financing schemes. It is reported that even relatives of employees may, in some companies, join the schemes. According to the Labor Standards Law, forced employees' saving schemes are prohibited (Act. 18); the law does not, however, exclude the many cases when, for lack of cash, companies put into savings part of the seasonal allowances of their employees. As for financing, especially of housing, retirement allowances often serve as handy collateral. The scope of these

FIGURE 5

AMOUNT OF DEPOSITS AND NUMBER OF
DEPOSITORS BY TYPE OF DEPOSIT (1966)

	Amount of deposits		Number of depositors	
	Amount (million yen)	Distribution	Number (person)	Distribution
Total	924,002	100.0%	5,508,036	100.0%
Ordinary deposit	566,895	61.4	3,741,428	67.9
Time deposit	228,112	24.7	852.416	15.5
Installment saving for house	62,621	6.8	407,670	7.4
Other installment saving	41,334	4.5	364,861	6.6
Other deposits	25,040	2.7	141,661	2.6

Source: *Shōwa 41 nendo, Yokinkamei Tokyō Hōkoku no Gaiyō,* ('Summary of Deposits Administration Report, 1966'), Tokyo: The Ministry of Labor, 1967, p. 3.

[3] For an explanation of the sociological background of these expense accounts, see Ralph Hewins, *The Japanese Miracle Men,* London: Secker & Warburg, 1967, pp. 39–49.

intracompany saving and financing schemes was described in a recent survey.[4] In 1966, 65.5% of all firms with three hundred or more employees sponsored such schemes, and the amount of their deposits totalled ¥900 billion, an increase of 7.5% over 1965. The number of depositors stood at over 5.5 million, with an average per capita deposit of ¥167,775. (Figure 5) The interest rate on ordinary deposits (over 60% of the deposits and of the depositors) varied between 6.00 and 7.37%, but reached more than 9.8% in over 20% of the firms. The interest rate on installment savings for housing purposes was over 9.8% in more than half of the firms.

Cash earnings

As mentioned earlier, most Japanese salaries are paid once a month. For the employee, this is the income from which daily expenditures are paid; for the enterprise, the monthly payment means that a substantial expenditure has to be faced only once a month, thereby considerably easing the flow of working capital. But at least twice a year seasonal allowances are paid. For the employee, this income defrays the purchase of durable consumer goods and feeds savings; for the firm, it means, again, a payroll cost delayed for six months and some elbow-room, since the amount of such allowances is still partly determined by business conditions. Lastly, at the end of the employment period, a retirement allowance is paid. For the employee, this income represents finally a capital meant to buttress further security; for the enterprise, however, it is a deferred wage payment which all through the employment period has depressed actual salary, but which, again, has greatly helped the flow of funds. As a matter of fact, throughout his employment career with a firm, the Japanese employee has because of the wage system invested heavily in the enterprise on a short-term as well as a long-term basis. The system costs the employer fairly little—specifically, a relative

4 *Showa 41 Nendo, Yokinkanri Jōkyō Hōkoku no Gaiyō* ('Summarized Report on Deposits Administration'), 1966, Tokyo: The Ministry of Labor, 1967.

impossibility of firing the employee, but the gain in terms of working capital and steadiness of the labor force is considerable.

Let us now examine more closely each component of the lifelong salary structure.

A MONTHLY SALARY

IN Japan, monthly salary cannot convey an adequate idea of salary level because it is only one part of the system of lifelong remuneration. The matter is easily overlooked even by foreign firms operating in Japan, and to their detriment! To hire a new employee at 'so much per month' is probably to the liking of the home office, but the price is heavy; the Japanese employee will not see the 'point' of his salary, and his employer will sooner or later discover that he has neglected the expected annual increase as well as the implicit long-term liability of the retirement allowance.

In Japan, hourly rates, besides their misleading use for international comparisons, are, generally speaking, used only for the calculation of overtime allowances. Daily rates apply, of course, to day workers; they may also quite often determine the income of temporary employees. They are prevalent in some outdoor industries, if technology has not thoroughly changed the nature of those industries, and in traditional crafts such as carpentry, gardening, and the like.

A monthly salary is the common Japanese form of compensation for work and even for non-work. In order, however, to safeguard regular attendance at the place of work, a daily rate discount *(nikkyū gekkyū)* is commonly used. It consists in subtracting 1/25th of the basic salary for each day of absence up to a certain limit. Another common practice is the 'allowance to encourage attendance'.

The composition of all the various components of monthly contract cash earnings is illuminating. (Figure 6) Besides the basic salary that amounts to about 70% of the total cash earnings including overtime, 30% or so is given as allowances, some of which—like the incentive wage, the attendance allowance, and the important overtime allowance—is meant to promote group conformity and aimed at encouraging total group performance. Most other allowances are, in one way or another, related to the cost of living. At the bargaining table, they offer a great advantage to management, which thereby can grant increases in 'salary' without necessarily increasing basic salary and all the charges it determines. These allowances, in Japan and abroad, are often referred to as 'fringe benefits.' Contrary to Western use, however, 'fringe benefits' as used by the Japanese is a term that almost exclusively covers statutory and

FIGURE 6

COMPOSITION OF MONTHLY CONTRACT CASH
EARNINGS AND RATIO OF COMPONENTS, ALL INDUSTRIES
(1966)

Components	Ratio
Monthly contract cash earnings	100.0%
1 Cash earnings	88.5
Basic wage	82.8
Incentive wage	5.9
Duty allowances	3.5
Supervisory position allowance	–
Special work conditions allowance	–
Skill allowance	–
Cost-of-living allowances	6.0
Family allowance	–
Regional allowance	–
Commuting allowance	–
Housing allowance	–
Other cost-of-living allowances	–
Allowance for encouraging attendance	1.4
Other allowances	0.4
2 Overtime allowance	10.7
3 Miscellaneous allowances	0.8
Allowance for extra work	–
Allowance for non-work, etc.	–

Source: *Year Book of Labour Statistics, 1966,* Tokyo: The Ministry of Labor, 1967, pp. 349–350 and 171.

non-statutory welfare costs that are entirely borne by, or shared with, employers. Other allowances, like the mid-summer and year-end bonuses, paid holidays, paid vacations, and family and housing allowances, are all considered parts of salary. Recently, the Supreme Court made the decision that the retirement allowance also is to be regarded as a part of salary.[5]

B BASIC SALARY

BASIC Japanese salaries follow a group-oriented norm that has little to do with the technical qualifications of employees. At least in an individual capacity, employees do not argue over the amount, nor do firms have any recourse, short of bankruptcy, against it. The norm seems to result from an implicit understanding by society at large of what daily living costs its members. Even a change in amounts requires group action on a society-wide basis: at the enterprise level, unions bargain for a *base-up*[6] with management, much less out of immediate consideration for the needs of their members than out of a wide-spread need felt throughout society for an adjustment of the wage level. The labor movement voices this feeling year after year in its Spring Wage Offensive, hammering home the increasing costs of living and setting the 'mood'[7] favorable to the *base-up*.

Basic salaries embody a salary progression *(teiki shōkyū),* the meaning of which is often translated into English as 'seniority'. The Japanese word *nenkō* (as in *nenkō chingin seido,* the so-called 'seniority wage system') combines the two key factors of wage progression: 'years' *(nen)* and 'merit' *(kō).*

---

[5] *Hanrei Jihō* ('Court Cases Journal'), No. 511 (April 1968), Tokyo: Hanrei Jihō Sha.

[6] The expression *base-up* is used as such in Japanese labor lingo. Usually it means a wage increase, hopefully expressed in the basic wage, but practically only to a certain extent, in the form of either a flat amount or a uniform percentage, or a combination of both, applicable as a rule to all regular employees.

[7] The word 'mood' is transliterated in Japanese as *mūdo,* and means a psychological climate which will practically force a given decision or attitude. In recent years the expression has often been used in the context of the Spring Wage Offensive, in which instance the climate involves employees as well as managers.

1 Years *(nen)*

Wage progression is determined by years of service, which practically coincide with the age of an employee, because lifelong employment means precisely, at least theoretically, that there is no labor mobility. The current principle is that every twelve months basic salaries will be increased fairly automatically. The method is best illustrated in the salary tables of national government employees: in each vertical column, the next amount is granted every year. (Figure 7) The increase is not fully automatic, for it is sub-

FIGURE 7

BASIC SALARY FOR NATIONAL GOVERNMENT
EMPLOYEES: OFFICE EMPLOYEES (1968)

Grade	Classes							
	1	2	3	4	5	6	7	8
1	89,200	65,200	—	—	—	27,900	23,900	17,600
2	93,700	68,600	56,600	46,100	36,100	29,600	25,200	18,400
3	98,200	72,000	59,300	48,600	38,400	31,400	26,500	19,200
4	102,700	75,400	62,000	51,100	40,700	33,400	27,900	20,000
5	107,200	78,800	64,700	53,600	43,000	35,400	29,400	20,900
6	111,700	82,300	67,400	56,100	45,400	37,500	31,000	21,900
7	116,200	85,800	70,100	58,600	47,800	39,600	32,800	22,900
8	120,700	89,300	72,800	61,100	50,200	41,700	34,600	23,900
9	125,200	92,800	75,500	63,600	52,600	43,800	36,300	24,900
10	129,500	96,100	78,200	66,100	55,000	45,900	38,000	25,900
11	133,100	98,900	80,700	68,500	57,100	48,000	39,700	27,000
12	135,700	101,700	83,200	70,900	59,200	50,000	41,300	28,100
13	138,300	103,700	85,700	73,200	61,300	52,000	42,900	29,200
14	140,500	105,700	88,200	75,500	62,900	53,900	43,900	30,300
15	142,700	107,700	90,100	77,600	64,300	55,300	44,900	31,200
16			92,000	79,700	65,500	56,500		32,000
17				81,500	66,600	57,600		32,800
18				83,300	67,700	58,600		
19					68,800	59,600		
20						60,600		

Source: *Kyūyo Shōroppō* ('Summary of the Six Laws Related to Salaries'), Tokyo: Gakuyō Shobō, 1968, Appendix p. 2.

[136]

mitted to review. The penalty may be a delay of three, six, nine, or twelve months; a promotion may consist in jumping one grade, depending upon how the employee is appraised.

2 Merit *(kō)*

Since lifelong employment starts when a Japanese graduates from school, the level of education is the first merit considered, and it decides an employee's starting salary *(shonin-kyū)*. For example, for national government employees, in 1968 a university graduate started with a basic salary of ¥23,900 per month; a two-year college graduate at ¥20,900; a high-school graduate at ¥18,400, and a middle-school graduate at ¥15,100.[8] It is from this point on that the semi-automatic wage progression sets in, differing according to differences in starting salaries. (Figure 8)

FIGURE 8

EDUCATION LEVEL AND WAGE DIFFERENTIAL AT
THE SAME AGE, MALE (1967)

									(%)
Age	22	25	27	30	35	40	45	50	55
University graduate	100.0	100.0	100.0	100.0	100.0	100.0	100.0	100.0	100.0
High school graduate	95.6	96.3	93.7	91.4	88.6	87.3	87.3	85.5	88.1
Middle school graduate	93.8	90.7	87.0	82.5	76.0	70.3	62.4	65.8	62.3

Source: *43 Nendoban Chingin Jittai Chōsashū* ('Report on the Survey of Wage Situation, 1968'), Tokyō: Seikei Kenkyūsho, 1968, p. 45.
Note: The survey covered 326 companies.

At the time of hiring, a candidate is not considered as having any particular qualification. He is to be employed for life and, therefore, is not hired for some particular job; it is understood that the

[8] *Kyūyo Shōroppō* ('Summary of the Six Laws Related to Salaries'), Tokyo: Gakuyō Shobō, 1968.

enterprise will train him. Except for science graduates, little attention, if any, is given, for example, to the university department from which the new employee graduated: graduates of a Department of Literature are hired by banks and those of a Department of Law by trading firms. Meanwhile, starting salaries are fairly uniform among large firms. (Figure 9) The amounts are

FIGURE 9

STARTING SALARY BY SCHOOL GRADUATION AND
CLASS OF EMPLOYMENT, SIZE OF ESTABLISHMENT:
500 OR MORE EMPLOYEES (JUNE 1966—MAY 1967)

School graduation	Class of employment	Starting salary Male	Female
2-year post-graduate	Office employee	¥34,532	—
	Technician	34,381	—
4-year university graduate	Office employee	28.890	—
	Technician	29.190	—
2-year college graduate	Office employee	—	¥22,702
Technical school graduate	Technician	25,142	—
High-school graduate	Office employee	21.072	20,289
	Technician	21,298	—
	Manual worker	21,470	—
Middle-school graduate	Manual worker	17,335	17.201

Source: *Shōkyū Base-up Jisshi Jōkyō Chōsakekka* ('Results of the Wage Increase and Base-up Survey'), Tokyo: Kantō Keieisha Kyōkai, 1967, p. 16.
Note: 225 firms with 500 or more employees were surveyed.

close to subsistence level for a young bachelor with no social obligations; but he knows that under normal circumstances this amount will be raised annually for thirty-odd years to come. Because of the labor shortage, however, starting salaries have recently had to be increased; from the viewpoint of the long-term liability of salaries, this development dangerously tips the lifelong curve.

From the time of hiring forward, wage progression is largely based

FIGURE 10

LIFE-TIME SALARY CURVE FOR REGULAR EMPLOYEES
IN ESTABLISHMENTS WITH 1,000 OR MORE, AND
30 TO 99 EMPLOYEES, AND CORRESPONDING SALARY
LEVEL OF TEMPORARY EMPLOYEES AND DAILY WORKERS
(1965)

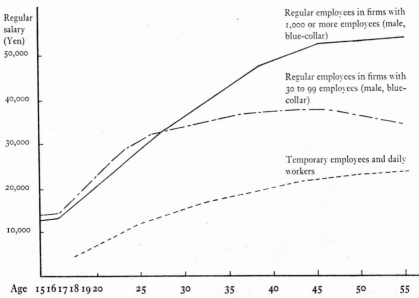

Source: Based on *Shōwa 40 Nen Rōdō Keizai Bunseki* (Analysis of the Labor Economy, 1965), Tokyo; The Ministry of Labor, 1966, *passim.*

on length of service, a criterion practically parallel with age, as manifested in Figure 10. The amounts increase, usually yearly, in a fairly automatic fashion somehow related to the evaluation of performance. The curve is always positive, but the rate of increase fluctuates. In the initial years of employment, the increase is rather slow; this is the time when the enterprise provides training and the employee is still a bachelor. Then the slope becomes steeper as family obligations begin to burden the employee and his contribution to the firm increases. Later on, the rate of increase slows down again

[139]

as some stability in social obligations is hopefully arrived at and his involvement in the enterprise is complete. Still, the most striking feature of such wage progression should be stressed again: it is not directly related to performance or promotion of the beneficiary, nor, for that matter, is it directly related to the performance of the enterprise; it follows a pattern given to both. Thus, for example, in the early 1960s, the rate of increase was generally accelerated at about the age of thirty, whereas now it is more typically accelerated at about the age of forty in order to help employees shoulder the burden of their children's longer schooling that has followed upon the postwar rise in the Japanese educational level.

As for amounts involved in the *nenkō* system, the salary tables of national government employees are typical; basic-salary yearly increases average about 5%. (See Figure 7)

The same principles apply by and large to the *base-up*, granted now several years in succession, after negotiations with the unions. The final settlement combines *nenkō* increase and *base-up*, but management, with the tacit understanding of the unions, maintains a practical distinction between the two increases in order to avoid letting the *base-up* be totally reflected in the life-income curve. Thus, according to a recent survey, between June 1966 and May 1967 in 225 firms with five hundred or more employees the average increase was ¥4,436, or 12.5% of the basic salary, of which 5.2% went to the *nenkō* increase and the rest, 7.3%, to the *base-up* proper.[9]

A major function of basic salaries is to determine the amount of some allowances, among them expensive seasonal allowances and retirement allowances. This is the main reason why management avoids as much as possible tampering with basic salaries when skill, performance, or promotion come into question; such considerations are better made independent variables in the form of specific allowances.

---

[9] *Shōkyū Base-up Jisshi Jōkyō Chōsakekka* ('Results of the Survey on Wage Increase and Base-up'), Tokyo: Kantō Keieisha Kyōkai, 1967, p. 3.

Chapter six: Lifelong remuneration system

C MONTHLY ALLOWANCES

CONTRARY to the group orientation of basic salaries, allowances make for personalization of salaries; they introduce a personal touch. They come under numerous titles. Some are specific and almost universal, like overtime, family, and transportation allowances, and leave little leeway to the employer; others are vaguer and more flexible, like cost-of-living allowances. At one time or another, a union will bring up one or the other allowance for reconsideration of amount; but, as mentioned in connection with basic salaries, it will not go so far as to question the structure itself.

Two groups of monthly allowances can be distinguished. Some are somehow related to the amount of a basic salary: overtime allowances, location and various other cost-of-living allowances, attendance allowances, and so on. Still others are independent of a basic salary: family allowances (usually flat amounts for each dependent)[10], transportation allowances (usually full costs of daily commuting by public facilities regardless of distances), housing allowances, position allowances, and so on.

D SEASONAL ALLOWANCES *(kimatsu teate)*

SEASONAL allowances in Japan are still called 'bonuses', but organized labor prefers the expression *kimatsu teate* ('seasonal allowances') that clearly expresses the notion that they are a part of salary. Theoretically, they should be a reward for profits earned and therefore not submitted to bargaining with employees. Such is the feeling of management in 16.7% of 233 companies surveyed in 1967, at any rate. (Figure 11) But by and large most firms have come to consider them as deferred wage payments, as they are in reality. The practice started in the interwar period and was considered as an expression of an employer's generosity; it spread during the war as a means of adding to frozen wages. In postwar years, however, it has come to be

---

10 In 1968 the monthly family allowance for government employees was ¥1,000 for the wife and ¥600 for the first child, ¥400 each for the others.

FIGURE II

COLLECTIVE AGREEMENT REGARDING THE BONUS (1967)

	Number of companies surveyed	Agreement					No agreement				Agreement cancelled
		Total	Duration		Agreement on		Total	But positive attitude[1]	And negative attitude[2]	Others	
			1 year	Others	Flat amounts	Formula					
Manufacturing	233 (100.0)	65 (27.9)	57	8	38	27	162 (69.5)	81 (34.8)	39 (16.7)	42 (18.0)	6 (2.6)
All industries	168 (100.0)	41 (24.4)	35	6	23	18	123 (73.2)	67 (39.9)	29 (17.3)	27 (16.1)	4 (2.4)

Source: *Shōyo Ichijikin Seido no Jittai* (Bonus and Temporary Payment System), Tokyo: Kanto Keieisha Kyōkai 1968, p. 5

Notes: 1 By "positive attitude" is meant that the companies wish to conclude, or will soon conclude such an agreement, and that such an agreement was proposed by management, but no definite prospect exists as yet.

2 By "negative attitude" is meant that such an agreement is irrelevant to the nature of the bonus.

regarded no longer as a gift, but as a right over which unions keep watch.

Seasonal allowances are usually paid twice a year, at mid-summer and year-end. Their calculation is directly related to basic salary. As a result, their amounts increase every year, at least by the amount of automatic annual increase incorporated into the basic salary; to this may be added the *base-up*. Some of the monthly allowances, like family and cost-of-living allowances, may also be part of the computation formula. For a number of years, the annual average was two or three times the monthly salary, in some cases going as high as six to eight times and, in unfortunate cases, as low as one. In 1966 the national annual average was 3.38 times, an increase of 13.9% over 1965.[11] Where this allowance is paid twice a year, the mid-summer

FIGURE 12

BONUS BY SCHOOL GRADUATION AND YEARS
OF SERVICE, MALE (1967)

School graduation	Age	Years of service	Amounts	Times monthly salary
College graduate	25	3	¥103,754	3.0
(White collar)	35	13	219,886	3.3
	50	27	453,095	3.8
High-school graduate	25	7	38,284	3.0
(White collar)	35	17	183,823	3.1
	50	33	369,249	3.6
Middle-school graduate	25	10	88,400	2.7
(Blue collar)	35	21	135,403	2.7
	50	36	202,921	2.9

Source: *Shōwa 42 nen Shimoki Shōyo Ichijikin Chōsakekka Hōkoku* ('Survey on Bonus and Temporary Payments, Second Half of 1967'), Tokyo: Kanto Keieisha Kyōkai, 1968, p. 8.

Note: This survey covered bonuses and temporary payments, from October 1967 to March 1968, in 245 companies with more than 500 employees, in all industries.

[11] *Shōwa 42 Nenkan Rōdō Hakusho* ('Labor White Paper 1967'), Tokyo: The Ministry of Labor, 1967, p. 250.

amount is usually lower than the year-end amount. In regard to seasonal allowances also, *nenkō* plays a definite role; i.e., school graduation and years of service, though already affecting the monthly salary on which the bonus is based, also affect the formula of bonus calculation. (Figure 12)

To settle the amount of a bonus is a very active issue for organized labor. Since most unions are enterprise unions, however, they are aware of an enterprise's ability to pay. Where financial plight warrants it, they may agree to a reduction or will not object too strongly to a certain percentage's being turned into intracompany savings or given in the form of company products. But one thing remains sure: a seasonal allowance must be paid.

Though the high personal savings rate of the Japanese people remains a mystery to many experts, they agree that the custom of seasonal allowances accounts for a great deal of that extraordinary rate, which was 18.4% in 1966.[12] At about the time bonuses are paid, all financial institutions throughout the country go on a wild spree of advertising their interest rates on deposits; many families consider the purchase of durable consumer goods; welfare institutions intensify their appeals to public generosity; and, recently, airlines sell tickets for trips abroad.

E RETIREMENT ALLOWANCE *(taishoku teate)*

A Japanese retirement allowance is, in fact, a wage payment delayed until an employee quits or reaches the age limit. It is usually paid out in the form of a lump sum arrived at by multiplying the last basic salary by the number of years of service according to some progressive formula. The regulations for national government employees are typical in this regard. (Figure 13) The meaning is thus that, every year, at least one monthly salary is not paid to the employee; that much can remain in the company as part of the working capital—at a heavy cost, however. The amount on which the computation

[12] *Annual Report in National Income Statistics, 1968,* Tokyo: Economic Planning Agency, 1968, p. 33.

Chapter six: Lifelong remuneration system

FIGURE 13

RETIREMENT ALLOWANCE FORMULA FOR NATIONAL GOVERNMENT EMPLOYEES (1968)

Base:
The monthly basic salary at the day of retirement

Percentage:

Two possibilities:

A Retirement before the age limit and less than 25 years of service:

1st to 10th year	100 percent
11th to 20th year	110 percent
21st to 24th year	120 percent

B Retirement at the age limit and 25 or more years of service:

1st to 10th year	125 percent
11th to 20th year	137.5 percent
21st to 30th year	150 percent
31st year and more	137.5 percent

Formula:
The base multiplied by the proper percentage for each lapse of time multiplied by the number of years in each lapse of time.

Source: See *Kyūyo Shōroppō* ('Summary of the Six Laws Related to Salaries'), Tokyo; Gakuyō Shobō, 1968, pp. 913, 914

is based, namely, the basic salary, has meanwhile been increasing on two scores: one is the automatic annual increase and the other the *base-up*. Even today, retirement allowances run easily into several hundred thousands of yen and may reach several millions for employees with twenty or thirty years of service. A recent survey revealed that in June 1968 lump-sum retirement allowances for university graduates with 32 years of service were as high as ¥6,392,555; for (prewar) middle-school graduates in clerical jobs and 38 years of service, ¥6,093,060; and for male blue-collar workers with 41 years of service, ¥4,453,226.[13]

The lump-sum retirement allowance in Japan is a practice that dates back to the early 1900s, when large employers got anxious

[13] *Taishoku Ichijikin Chōsa Kekka Hōkoku* ('Survey Report on Lump-sum Retirement Allowance'), Tokyo: Nikkeiren, June 1968, p. 4. See also *Year Book of Labour Statistics 1966, op. cit.*, p. 189; and Chapter Eight in this volume.

about attracting skilled workers and keeping them. Today all enter-prises that employ twenty or more employees have a section in their employment regulations that establishes a retirement-allowance system. It always makes a distinction between voluntary retirement, i.e., for reasons personal to the employee, and involuntary retirement i.e., for company reasons, like layoff or bankruptcy or age limit. In the latter case, a more generous formula of calculation applies. Unions are now of the view that it is natural for management to guarantee economic security after retirement to an employee who dedicated the best part of his life to the enterprise. When they assess amounts of the allowance, unions contend that living expenses of the employee and his dependents should be taken into consideration.

The retirement allowance is not compulsory according to Japanese labor legislation, but in this context custom is stronger than law! Cost is totally borne by management. The necessary funds, ac-cumulated in a retirement fund *(taishoku-kikin),* are unilaterally managed by the employer, who at best sets them aside as a loss account. Recent improvements in accounting techniques are helping considerably towards better provisions for this long-term liability, making management more than ever aware of its substantial cost.

This custom is responsible for the lag in the development of a pension system *(nenkin-seido).* But things are changing. Since unions have kept clamoring for higher retirement allowances and the public at large has been quite dissatisfied with the public pension system, management has started to consider the payment of a portion of the allowance in the form of annuities, to be combined with social security benefits. To this end employees and unions have been generally in agreement, and the government has followed suit: since the early 1960s, several new laws have been enacted granting relevant tax advantages and possibilities for combining private and public pension schemes.

F WELFARE ALLOWANCES

WELFARE allowances represent about 14% of an employee's total

FIGURE 14

WELFARE ALLOWANCES BY AMOUNTS AND PERCENTAGE
(1966)

	Per employee, per month	Ratio		Ratio of monthly wage
Welfare allowances	¥7,698	100.0%		
Statutory				
Total	3,382	43.9	100.0%	6.1%
Health insurance	1,675		49.5	3.0
Welfare pension insurance	999		29.5	1.8
Unemployment insurance	391		11.6	0.7
Workmen's compensation insurance	306		9.1	0.6
Seamen's insurance	3		0.1	0.1 (less than)
Others	8		0.2	id
Non-statutory				
Total	¥4,316	56.1	100.0	7.8
Housing	1,701		39.4	3.1
Medical care	435		10.1	0.8
Payments in kind	1,399		32.4	2.5
Mutual aid	220		5.1	0.4
Cultural, recreational services	391		9.1	0.7
Others	170		3.9	0.3

Source: *Dai 11-kai Fukurikōseihi Chōsakekka Hōkoku* ('Report on the 11th Welfare Expense Investigation'), Tokyo: Nikkeiren, 1967, p. 13

monthly cash earning; more than half are non-statutory. (Figure 14) As noticed in all previous instances, large firms differ considerably from smaller firms in welfare allowances.[14]

There are four major social security plans for Japanese workers. One is health insurance *(kenkō hoken),* which requires a monthly premium of 7% of an employee's basic salary, of which one-half (in small and medium firms) or more (in most large firms) is paid by the employer and the rest by the employee. As a result the insured

[14] See *Dai 11-kai Fukurikōseihi Chōsakekka Hōkoku* ('Report on the 11th Welfare Expenses Investigation'), Tokyo: Nikkeiren, 1967, pp. 22–23.

receives medical treatment, medicine, and hospitalization at a nominal cost, and his dependents receive the same services at one-half actual cost. Furthermore, those unable to work because of injury or illness may receive 60% of their monthly salary for six months, or for eighteen months in the case of tuberculosis. A second social security plan is unemployment insurance *(shitsugyō hoken)*, the monthly premium for which amounts to 1.4% of an employee's basic salary, borne equally by employer and employee. Unemployment benefits may amount to 60% of a monthly salary for ninety to two hundred seventy days, according to length of employment. A third plan is welfare pension insurance *(kōsei nenkin hoken)*, for which the monthly premium amounts to 5.5% of an employee's basic salary, borne equally by employer and employee. Those who have paid premiums for over twenty years can receive a pension of about ¥10,000 per month after the age of sixty. Moreover, a law enacted in 1966 permits some companies to combine certain additional private pension plans with the national pension plan. Finally, there is workmen's compensation insurance *(rōdōsha saigai hoken)*, which applies to factory workers only and the cost of which is borne by the employer and the government. According to this plan, all of a factory worker's medical expenses exceeding ¥1,000 are to be compensated, and a worker absent from work because of illness is entitled to 60% of his average salary. Special provisions are made for accidents. The scheme includes survivors' compensation, funeral-expense compensation, and incapacitation compensation.

In the meantime, voluntary welfare schemes are numerous in Japan. The most important is company housing and dormitories. In manufacturing, about 40% of married employees live in company apartments or houses, and about 50% of the unmarried live in company dormitories. The rental is usually only about 10 to 20% of the market price.[15] Some larger companies also offer company-owned land at discount prices to their employees and, as mentioned earlier,

[15] *JFEA News*, Tokyo: Japanese Federation of Employers' Associations, No. 32 (March 1968), p. 7.

sponsor special savings schemes for building purposes. Other voluntary welfare allowances include medical care, lump-sum allowances insurance, financial aid to education, and so on and on.

Efficiency remuneration

A EFFICIENCY AND ALLOWANCES

IT is quite obvious that the Japanese salary system, as described so far, is not geared specifically to rewarding performance, at least individual performance, which is somehow felt to be alien to the principle of lifelong employment. Efficiency plays, however, a definite role in the system, but at the group level, as it is reflected in the efficient performance of an enterprise as a whole. For the individual, therefore, there is little differentiation, if any, between efficiency and loyalty to his enterprise. When bonuses started to be given in the interwar period, they were essentially a sharing of benefits accrued by the performance of all, i.e., of the entire enterprise. This is not to say that monetary incentive for individual efficiency is not to be found in Japan. Commissions to salesmen, piece rates for production workers, performance-incentive programs, and the like are in wide use; but all share a common characteristic: they are regarded as adjuncts to lifelong salary, if, for all practical purposes, they are not actually a part of it.

The stimulation of better performance, in so far as it enters the view of lifelong salary, takes subtle forms that are still minimal compared to the maximal weight of basic salary in total monthly-contract cash earnings.

1 A so-called incentive wage is in wide use in Japan. In 1966 it amounted to only 5.9% of the cash earnings, themselves 88.5% of total monthly-contract cash earnings.[16] In order to determine its amount a formula is usually used whereby the monthly

16 *Year Book of Labour Statistics 1966, op. cit.,* p. 171.

amount does not fluctuate much, if at all, and a certain uniformity within the group is respected. The same amount is, for example, valid for the duration of an 'efficiency drive', or from one seasonal allowance to another, or for an entire fiscal year. Basic salary is the one important component of the formula, allowing individual differentials remotely related to performance.

2 Attendance is considered as one aspect of the 'total' performance of a section or of an enterprise. It presents the great advantage of resting on the mechanical record of a time-clock. It is rewarded by a monthly attendance allowance *(shōrei teate)* that in 1966 amounted to 1.4% of the cash earnings.

3 Quite unexpectedly for the Western mind, another method of efficency remuneration in Japan is overtime allowance. Generally speaking, the Japanese are not yet too anxious to punch a time-clock at the immediate end of their working hours. It is, for example, still considered rude by many employees to quit before their section chief quits. Such an attitude is now under heavy fire: the unions clamor for shorter hours; labor legislation gets more severe; and younger employees are not so keen on traditional etiquette. The custom, however, reaches deep into the Japanese sociological context. Male employees (as well as unmarried female employees) are not impatient to return home, which is usually much less comfortable than the office, and where it is almost impossible to meet friends. After all, the place of work is not just where one works; it is also where one lives. It may go as far as providing recreational activities and facilities in downtown offices for hours after work. Besides, Japanese management looks favorably upon overtime that has no effect on the long-term wage level, and most employees welcome the additional income that bolsters their monthly earnings, which are otherwise depressed by built-in forced savings such as seasonal and retirement allowances. Expectedly, the lifelong employment system does not lend itself to a 'second'

job at some other place of work. To put in overtime willingly is regarded as a manifestation of loyalty to the enterprise; it is interpreted as a sign that one is eager to contribute to overall performance. In order to calculate the overtime allowance, hourly rates are used; they are, however, derived from monthly salary, not *vice versa*, by dividing the basic salary by the official number of monthly working hours, usually multiplied by the minimum legal overtime rate of 125%. (Figure 15)

FIGURE 15

INDEX OF HOURS WORKED BY REGULAR
EMPLOYEES, SIZE OF ESTABLISHMENT: 30 OR MORE
EMPLOYEES (1965=100)

	Total hours worked	Scheduled hours	Non-scheduled hours
1960	105.6	102.9	135.2
1963	101.7	100.9	110.8
1965	100.0	100.0	100.0
1966	100.0	99.6	105.0

Source: *Year Book of Labour Statistics, 1966,* Tokyo: The Ministry of Labor, 1967, p. 206

4 A given percentage of the seasonal allowance is often set aside as performance remuneration. Let us say that the amount of a seasonal allowance is set at 200%, meaning twice the basic salary plus whatever monthly allowance enters into the calculation. On top of this uniform 200% given to all permanent employees, a certain percentage is pooled and made available for remuneration of efficiency and better performance, according to evaluations of individual and group performances prepared by section chiefs and discussed by higher management. All in all, such evaluations are left entirely to the discretion of management, which usually gives great weight to attendance records (an objective measure), smoothness of individual social relations with co-workers, and sense of loyalty to the firm (subjective measure, indeed!).

[151]

B PROMOTION AND SALARY

PROMOTION and its expression in monetary terms is regarded in the West as a strong incentive for the better performance it hopes to elicit. In the Japanese system of lifelong employment, however, promotion is also, if not primarily, based on considerations that have little, if anything, to do with individual performance. As far as monetary compensation is concerned, promotion is mainly expressed by a specific allowance, the supervisory position allowance *(kanrishoku teate),* or any similar denomination. This means that promotion does not directly affect basic salary, although indirectly a relationship exists because years of service are almost always a decisive consideration for promotion, and years of service determine the root of basic salary. For example, at the factory of a large watch manufacturer, seven years of service are required in order for an employee to qualify for the position of sub-section chief *(kakarichō),* six more years for section chief *(kachō),* and seven more years for head of department *(buchō).* Furthermore, the position allowance is sometimes calculated as a percentage of basic salary, as in the case of government employees: a position allowance is 18 to 25% of basic salary, starting from the level of section chief and up. Private industry, however, seems to prefer a flat amount to the percentage of basic salary. The rationale commonly given by employers and employees alike for this practice is interesting: supervisory and middle-management staff are expected to work overtime, and overtime is customarily not paid to section chiefs and higher personnel.

Promotion may also be reflected, however, in the progression of basic salary. If so, an employer should not overlook the fact that, until retirement because of age limit, such promotion means not only higher salary, but also higher bonuses and higher retirement allowance, since the rate of progression, though based on higher amounts, is not affected. In Japan, two methods are chiefly in use. The first depends entirely on managerial evaluation of performance.

Chapter six: Lifelong remuneration system

Where the normal automatic increase is expected every twelve months, the increase may be granted, say, after six months, or the salary may be raised by two grades instead of the normal one. The second method is more mechanical. It is best understood by looking again at Figure 7. Instead of an increase in one of the vertical columns, i.e., an automatic increase every twelve months, a change of column is now considered. Government employment regulations are most explicit in this regard. For example, suppose that Mr. Suzuki, who has just graduated from a two-year college, enters governmemt employment; his starting salary will be Class 8, Grade 5, or (8–5) ¥21,900. One year later, his basic salary rating will be (8–6); after two years, (8–7); and so on. With respect to salary, promotion for Mr. Suzuki will mean his moving from Class 8 into Class 7 at a corresponding rate of increase in basic salary. Say, then, that after seven years of employment promotion is considered for Mr. Suzuki; his salary is first increased to the next amount, from (8–12) ¥28,100 to (8–13) ¥29,200, and then to the same or next higher amount in the next Class (7–5), ¥29,400. To qualify for the next rank, Class 7, however, Mr. Suzuki must have been at least

FIGURE 16

YEARS REQUIRED TO QUALIFY FOR SALARY
PROMOTION, NATIONAL GOVERNMENT EMPLOYEES:
OFFICE EMPLOYEES

Graduate of	Starting rate	8	7	6	5	4	3
University	(7–1)ᵃ	–	–	3	4	4	4
Two-year college	(8–5)	–	3	3	4	4	4
High school	(8–2)	–	6	3	4	4	4
Middle school	3ᵇ	3	7	3	4	4	4

Source: *Kyūyo Shōroppō, 1968* (Summary of the Six Laws Related to Salaries), Tokyo: Gakuyō Shobō, p. 208.

Notes: a Figures in parentheses indicate the class and the rank in the class. (See Figure 7).

b A middle-school graduate needs 3 years of experience in some other employment status (e.g. manual worker) before qualifying for 8–1.

three years in Class 8; to qualify for Class 6 at least three years in Class 8; to qualify for Class 6 at least three years in Class 7; to qualify for Class 5 at least four years in Class 6, and so on. (Figure 16)

C EFFICIENCY SALARY *(nōritsu-kyū)*

IN recent years there has been much talk in Japanese management circles about efficiency salary *(nōritsu-kyū)*, sometimes presented as an outright efficiency wage ringing the deathknell of the *nenkō* remuneration system. Many different formulas and names are used for it; the oldest probably the 'grade system' *(shikaku seido)* pioneered by the Jujo Paper Company in 1952. The truth of the matter, however, is that such attempts are not yet what one could call revolutionary. Most of them result, in one way or another, in a modification of the prevailing system, whereby *more* explicit consideration is granted to ability, not only through special allowances, but also through augmentation of basic salary. A fixed percentage of the salary goes to straight length of service, while the bulk is determined by 'grades' for which a major criterion is, besides length of service, ability as determined by job evaluation *(shokumu)*. The main role of this consideration of ability is to speed up or slow down the rate of salary increase, which usually remains positive if based on length of service only.

D REMUNERATION OF EXECUTIVES

A recent survey has revealed some interesting data concerning the remuneration of company officers.[17] Two principles are here respected: 1) their remuneration is outside the scope of the lifelong remuneration system since they are expected to stay on beyond the mandatory age limit and 2) age plays an important role.[18] Graphi-

[17] *42 Nenban Yakuin no Hōshū to Shōyo* ('Salary and Bonus of Executives, 1967'), Tokyo: Seikei Kenkyūjo, 1967. In all, 143 companies were surveyed. According to the size of capitalization, the members were: 36 with a capital of over ¥1,000 million, 36 with ¥300 to 1,000 million, 28 with ¥100 to 300 million, and 43 with less than ¥100 million.

[18] See William Brown, 'Japanese Management—The Cultural Background', *Monumenta Nipponica*, Tokyo: Sophia University, Vol. XXI, Nos. 1–2 (1966), pp. 46–60.

cally, the matter can be presented as in Figure 17. As a rule, at about the age of fifty, eligible executives in the company staff are harnessed for higher functions and are segregated according to salary. Others come from the outside, mostly from government services and banks,

FIGURE 17

MONTHLY SALARY CURVE BY AGE AND POSITION (1967)

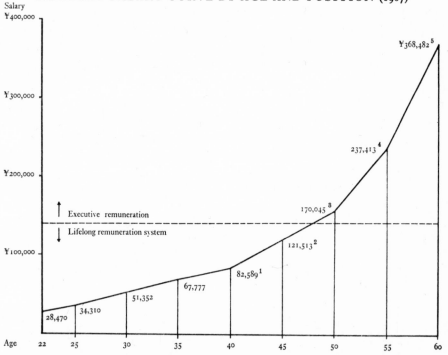

Sources: Constructed from *42 Nenban Yakuin no Hōshū to Shōyo* ('Salary and Bonus of Executives, 1967'), Tokyo, Seikei Kenkyūjo, 1967, pp. 17, 63 and *43 Nenban Chingin Jittai Chōsashū* ('Survey on the Wage Situation, 1968'), Tokyo; Kenkyūjo, 1968, pp. 45, 514

Notes: 1 Section chief *(kachō)*
 2 Department head *(buchō)*
 3 Executive *(torishimariyaku)*
 4 Executive director *(jōmu)*
 5 President *(shachō)*

FIGURE 18

EXECUTIVES: PERCENTAGE DISTRIBUTION BY ORIGIN, MONTHLY SALARY, SALARY DIFFERENTIAL, AND SHARE HOLDING BY CAPITALIZATION OF FIRM (1967)

	Chairman (kaichō)	President (shachō)	Vice president (fuku shachō)	Executive manager (semmu)	Executive director (jōmu)	Executive (torishimariyaku)	Auditor (kansayaku)
Origin							%
From among employees	100.0(1)	43.4	33.4(2)	45.2	70.1	79.4	69.2
From outside the company	0.0	47.8	44.4	45.2	27.7	18.2	30.8
From affiliated company	0.0	8.8	22.2	9.6	2.2	2.2	0.0
Total	100.0	100.0	100.0	100.0	100.0	100.0	100.0
Monthly salary							
Average	¥285,150	368,482	353,905	276,552	237,413	170,045	134,151
Ratio president =100	(77.4)	(100.0)	(97.4)	(75.1)	(64.4)	(46.1)	(36.4)
Salary differential per capitalization							%
Over ¥1,000 million	100.0 (¥327,143)	100.0 (¥473,379)	100.0 (¥370,417)	100.0 (¥350,765)	100.0 (¥283,611)	100.0 (¥213,276)	100.0 (¥158,438)
¥300 to 1,000 million	106.0	82.1	100.6	79.2	85.5	81.0	89.5
¥100 to 300 million	52.0	58.9	75.6	67.6	72.4	72.2	61.9
Less than ¥100 million	78.6	69.2	88.7	69.0	70.1	65.6	74.1
Share holding per capitalization			(Number of shares per capita) (3)				
Over ¥1,000 million	143,633	512,098	112,122	266,021	82,808	24,354	30,292
¥300 to 1,000 million	338,938	686,604	115,500	82,502	57,187	28,798	37,098
¥100 to 300 million	170,000	225,174	180,000	47,820	45,120	24,717	49,100
Less than 100 million	179,653	255,524	—	104,756	64,745	54,481	10,000
Average	204,760	452,579	123,085	164,621	69,524	23,096	33,639

Source: *42 Nenban, Yakuin no Hōshu to Shōyo* ('Salary and Bonus of Executives, 1967'), Tokyo: Seikei Kenkyūjo, 1967, pp. 19, 28, 29, 32, 57, 66-70.

Notes: 1 Only one case   2 Nine cases only   3 Par value per share=¥50

some in smaller number from related companies. The highest paid officer in the company is the president *(shachō)*, averaging ¥360,000 per month. Percentally the chairman *(kaichō)* receives about 75% of this amount, the vice-president *(fuku-shachō)* 95%, the executive manager *(senmu)* 75%, the executive director *(jōmu)* 65%, and the executive *(torishimariyaku)* about 50%.[19] All these remunerations are, of course, determined by the size of the company. Besides their regular monthly remuneration, these officers will be offered some shares of the company. The average number of shares held by the chairman is 200,000, by the president 450,000, by the vice-president 125,000, by the executive manager 160,000, and by the executive director 70,000. (Figure 18)[20]

Age limit and thereafter

FOREIGN observers easily express dismay when told that the age limit for employment in Japan is still commonly set at fifty-five years of age when life expectancy is more than sixty-seven for men and seventy-two for women.[21] In July 1964, through a survey conducted by the Ministry of Labor throughout 3,011 enterprises with thirty or more employees all over the country, it was learned that more than 75% of the enterprises enforced the age limit of fifty-five, although the rate of application per size of enterprise was very different: 90% and more in enterprises of three hundred or more employees, but only 40% in those of thirty to ninety-nine employees.[22] This fact does not mean that fifty-five is considered the termination of productive life in Japan, but essentially and foremost means that lifelong employment (and the commitment thereby expressed)

[19] *42 Nenban Yakuin, op. cit.,* p. 19.
[20] *Ibid.,* pp. 66–70.
[21] *Kōsei Hakusho 1965* ('Welfare White Paper'), Tokyo: The Ministry of Health and Welfare, 1966, p. 384.
[22] *Teinensei Chōsakekka Gaiyō* ('Summary Report of the Survey on the Age-Limit System'), Tokyo: The Ministry of Labor, 1964, p. 9.

is then terminated; actual employment, though usually in less favorable conditions, may go on.

But things are changing. The Tokyo Chamber of Commerce conducted a survey of 879 firms in order to determine the current

FIGURE 19

CHANGE IN AGE LIMIT AFTER 1960

	Extension of age limit	Extension of age limit and establishment of re-employment system	No change	(%) Total
All firms	14.1	28.3	57.5	100.0
Manufacturing	14.1	32.6	53.3	100.0
Non-manufacturing	14.2	20.0	65.8	100.0
Size of firm 1,000 and more employees	16.7	32.9	50.5	100.0
300–999	11.6	28.2	60.2	100.0
100–299	15.5	28.5	56.0	100.0
99 and less	12.8	23.1	64.0	100.0

Source: *Kigyō ni okeru Teinensei no Jittai to Teinen Enchō ni kansuru Ikenchōsa* ('Survey of the Age-Limit System in Enterprises and of Opinions on the Extension of the Age Limit'), Tokyo: Tokyo Shōkō Kaigisho, 1967, p. 18

FIGURE 20

EXTENSION OF THE AGE LIMIT (1967)

	Request of union	Management initiative	Both	Total
All firms	7.0	37.0	56.0	100.0%
Industry				
Manufacturing	9.0	40.7	50.3	100.0
Non-manufacturing	2.5	28.4	69.1	100.0
Size				
1,000 and more employees	16.9	57.1	26.0	100.0
300–999 employees	5.7	36.6	57.7	100.0
100–299 employees	2.8	31.9	65.3	100.0
Less than 100 employees	—	14.0	86.0	100.0

Source: *Kigyo ni . . .op. cit.,* p. 22

FIGURE 21

RETIREMENT AGE (1967)

(%)

Age	54 or less	55	56	57	58	59	60	60 or more	Total
All firms	.5	61.2	3.5	7.0	7.0	.5	19.9	.5	100.0
Manufacturing	.7	62.3	3.4	6.8	6.2	–	20.0	.7	100.0
Non-manufacturing	–	58.2	3.6	7.3	9.1	1.8	20.0	–	100.0
Size of firm									
1,000 and more	2.6	65.8	7.9	13.2	2.6	2.6	5.3	–	100.0
300–000	–	61.8	5.5	3.6	7.3	–	20.0	1.8	100.0
100–299	–	56.4	1.8	7.3	10.9	–	23.6	–	100.0
99 and less	–	62.8	–	5.7	5.7	–	26.4	–	100.0

Source: *Kigyō ni . . .op. cit.*, p. 7

trend of the age-limit system as of the end of April 1967.[23] (Figure 19) Because of the pressure of unions and the labor shortage (Figure 20), firms are now extending the age limit by two or three years, in some cases even up to the age of sixty. (Figure 21) This extension does not, however, necessarily mean that the lifelong remuneration system is extended by so many years; in many cases, extension simply means a certain formal establishment of the re-employment system, i.e., that so-called temporary employment *(shokutaku)* is applied to more employees who have reached the age limit, if not to all the regular employees.

The general lines of *shokutaku* status are as follows. When, at the age of fifty-five, an employee receives his retirement allowance, his lifelong employment is discontinued and, with it, his lifetime remuneration stops. If an employer judges, however, that the services of a particular employee are still needed, he may keep him on the payroll at a fixed salary, e.g., at 20% less than his last regular salary, without periodical progression and without many of the normal allowances. (Figure 22) This new employment status is

[23] *Kigyō ni Okeru Teinensei no Jittai to Teinen Enchō ni kansuru Ikenchōsa* ('Survey of the Age-Limit Systems in Enterprises and of Opinions on the Extension of the Age Limit'), Tokyo: Tokyo Shōkō Kaigisho, 1967,

FIGURE 22

RE-EMPLOYMENT AND CHANGE IN WAGE,
MANUFACTURING (1966)

Size of enterprise	Possibility for re-employment	Continuation of wage progression	Unfavorable conditions for wage progression	% No increase in wage
5,000 employees	97.0	4.1	32.0	63.8
1,000–4,999	98.9	4.9	52.3	42.8
500–999	96.7	5.2	60.9	33.9
100–499	84.4	14.0	64.5	21.5

Source: Calculated from *Year Book of Labour Statistics, 1966*, Tokyo; The Ministry of Labor, 1967, pp. 188, 189.

valid for one year and is renewable, but it entails no new retirement allowance. The line position formerly occupied usually changes to one of mere staff capacity. The *shokutaku* has functioned for many years in Japan as a status of temporary employment that is fairly common for middle and lower management and for technical staff after retirement at fifty-five. Trying now to make it an institution applicable to all regular employees, the unions are concentrating their efforts even more forcefully upon the extension of the retirement age.

To be sure, as pointed out before, age limit does not apply to corporate management. In larger firms, when a department head *(buchō)* has risen to the position of director at about the age of fifty-two or fifty-three, he knows that the deadline of fifty-five will not apply to him. In such cases, the amount of salary is increased, but the basic lines of the system remain, and it is often continued until the individual concerned reaches almost total incapacity.

What happens when the *shokutaku* does not continue employment in the same enterprise? Custom expects an employer to show concern for his retiring employees. Most large firms have for them a special 'Placement Service', which fosters introductions to other business contacts; all too easily, however, retiring employees are merely unloaded on smaller, related firms. This is an especially dreadful experience for international joint ventures.[24]

When employment is not for life

NOT all wage-earners in Japan are permanent employees—far from it! And this anomaly is but one more manifestation of the dual-structure problem that plagues Japan. It would, however, be wrong to regard the lifetime salary system as restricted to larger firms, where it applies explicitly to permanent employees. The matter requires further elaboration.

Most female employees, in large as well as in small firms, are not considered as *really* employed for life; it is understood that they will retire when they get married, or at least when they bear a first child. Yet their salaries, except when they are explicitly hired on a temporary basis, follow the lifelong remuneration system, though the level of their basic salaries and of their allowances may be lower than average. Yet like male employees, they receive a retirement allowance based on their usually shorter lengths of service.

Larger firms employ besides their permanent work force two other types of labor, one on a subcontractual basis, whereby the salary system is the problem of the small firm subcontracted, and the other on a temporary basis.[25] For temporary employees, the forms of payment vary; at one extreme the *nenkō* wage system holds, but without tenure and without full allowances; at the other extreme a system of day-labor wages or hour-rates prevails. A fairly common form of payment is that described under the *shokutaku* status just discussed. As a rule, these temporary employees do not qualify for membership in enterprise unions. The implicit assumption is that

[24] See T. W. M. Teraoka, 'Technical Procedures', in Robert J. Ballon (ed.), *Joint Ventures and Japan*, Tokyo: Sophia-Tuttle, 1967, pp. 78–97.

[25] In large firms, the percentage of temporary to regular employees seems to hover around twenty, at least in the fairly prosperous years of 1959–1961. See T. Miyashita, *et al.*, *A Survey on Management Decision Process, IV*, Tokyo: Center for Economic Research, 1963, p. 56 (in Japanese).

they work in the enterprise only to make lifelong employment possible for the others! It is through this exception that the rule is confirmed.

Whatever statistical measure is used, smaller firms are the overwhelming majority in terms of sheer number in Japan; their contribution to the national economy in terms of production and employment is substantial. And all of them share two broad characteristics relevant to our purpose: very little, if any, labor organization and outright labor mobility. The fact that organized labor has so far bypassed small firms leaves them free from union pressure to implement the lifelong salary system. The second characteristic is, however, even more significant. Is the impracticability of the lifelong salary system for small firms the cause or the effect of their labor mobility? The question in these terms is probably more academic than real.

For many years in Japan, the best of the employment candidates who have left school have been hired, according to their wishes, by large firms. The others, the majority, have been either less successful or less ambitious. They are now employed at the lower level of the dual structure, where changes are not less rapid than at the upper level, but are less technological and organizational than economic and sociological. This is the 'floating world' *(uki-yo)* of smaller enterprises.

As far as the average employee in a small firm is concerned, his employment history may be considered as having two stages. The first lasts from ten to fifteen years (Figure 10), during which period his salary follows closely the general wage progression of the lifelong salary curve. At about the age of thirty-five, however, a second stage sets in: the employee now faces his firm's inability to pay, and from this point on until the age of forty-five to fifty, his salary remains static, then starts to decline. It is during this second stage that labor mobility prevails. Some employees of thirty-five start still other independent small businesses, while others drift from one small employer to another.

Chapter six: Lifelong remuneration system

A similar uncertainty besets the small employer; today he is in business; tomorrow—who knows? All too often one of the reasons for his going out of business is that seniority is piling up among his employees and has come to be too much for him. This development does not mean, however, that so long as the progression of seniority obtains it offers all the advantages of larger firms in addition to lifelong commitment. When, as he often does, a small employer hires middle-aged employees, the assumption is that it is not for too long, for he must avoid the snowballing of payroll obligations. Yet the fact remains that, for the time of his employment, the employee involved is considered a member of the industrial family, this time a shaky and much harsher one, to be sure. It is understood that his earnings are substantially less than before, but that they will last as long as conditions permit.

But the situation is far from remaining at *status quo*. The shortage of young workers that has appeared in Japan in recent years is cutting smaller firms off from a life-line of cheap labor. It could be argued whether the one-time advantage of these smaller firms in this respect was due to a deliberately depressed wage level or, rather, to the fact that they never actually reached the take-off level of the lifetime remuneration system. Of necessity, smaller firms have now to offer higher starting wages, sometimes even higher than those of larger firms, but such a measure does not alone attract young job-seekers. Consequently, smaller firms operating under subcontracting systems are drawing closer to their parent firms and are starting to advertise salary conditions similar to those of their sponsors, including retirement allowances. Some independent small firms have in fact organized in their lines of activity a sort of employment cooperative in order to pool resources required for offering salaries closer to those of large firms and to foster joint training programs, common welfare facilities, and joint retirement funds. Their main advantage, however, seems to be a guarantee of mobility within an organization without loss of seniority.

The system of lifelong employment and concomitant lifelong remuneration is of recent origin in Japan. Before World War II, it was reserved to some selected groups of white-collar employees; after the war, primarily because of the pressure of enterprise unions, it became the privilege of all permanent white-collar and blue-collar employees in large firms. Its pervasiveness, however, results from its correspondence to the deeper sociological trait of Japan's industrial society, namely, the fact of considering the industrial enterprise an industrial 'family'.

But the pressures on the system are getting stronger and stronger, some for, some against.

Organized labor is dead set against any lay-offs, not so much because of the plight of the unemployed (they are not members of the enterprise union any longer!) as because of the threat to lifelong employment, its *raison d'être*.

Management sees many advantages in pinning down a work force in which it has invested substantial amounts in training; on the other hand, it dreads the *base-up* that, year after year, increases the present and, even more, the future burden of the system. Employers have been successful, however, on two scores: 1. the lifelong salary curve is not as steep as before and 2. the weight of seniority is more and more counterbalanced by considerations of efficiency.

Younger workers are beginning to manifest a growing interest in cash on hand, rather than a guaranteed income over a lifetime. They are also becoming aware that they are often better qualified than older employees to meet the rapidly shifting demands of new technology.

Older employees have so much at stake in their deprived past that they are adamantly against any change and force their no-compromise attitude on the unions.

The Japanese business world at large is growing leery; it feels that it is getting close to the point of no-return, and yet it needs more flexibility than ever to face the international imperatives of productivity.

It is agreed that Japanese labor mobility, even for so-called permanent employees in large firms, will increase substantially in the future. It will be fostered by governmental policies concerning industry location, the ever-widening coverage of social security, the rapidity of technological change, and so on. As a result, it will be easier than ever before for management to be explicit in its attention to efficiency. Another factor of mutation will be the shortage of labor, especially of younger workers and of more specialized skills.

It is not likely, however, that the guaranteed life-income approach to the remuneration of industrial work will be abandoned altogether in Japan. Indeed, the economic miracle of Japan has rested most precisely on those very industrial sectors where the lifetime system has become most deeply entrenched and is now standard practice. What it required from Japanese managers, and from their foreign counterparts in Japan, was to consider the use of human resources as an overhead cost rather than a variable one!

CHAPTER SEVEN

Labor cost accounting

BY IWAO TOMITA

Payroll forecasting—accounting for deferred salary payments— income tax on payrolls—accounting for the salaries of foreigners—legal benefits or social security taxes—voluntary fringe benefits—a model calculation of total labor costs

Payroll forecasting

FORECASTING of payroll liability is especially important in Japan because of the lifetime employment commitment assumed by both employers and employees. This liability must, therefore, be accounted for specifically. Yet only in recent years has Japanese management started to give it proper attention, as it has been forced to do by annual increases of the wage level that have dreadfully swelled long-term liabilities. Although most Japanese employees have recently been expecting annual salary increases in the range of 10 to 12%, such increases are not at all related to increases in productivity; companies must absorb them as an inevitable consequence of the seniority system and of increases in the cost of living. If a company has followed the usual Japanese policy of hiring new graduates directly from school, starting salaries will have increased by 5 to 8% year after year. As a result, the salaries of *sempai* ('senior graduates') having been affected, average salary increases for an entire company will have become even higher than would otherwise be the case.

Japanese seasonal allowances (so-called 'bonuses') are usually estimated on the basis of such increases. A total of three to four months' salary a year is customary. Moreover, the employers' portions of social security taxes (health insurance, welfare-pension insurance, unemployment insurance, and workmen's accident-compensation insurance) should also be estimated on the basis of salary increases.

Accounting for deferred salary payments

BONUSES and retirement allowances are, in fact, deferred salary payments and must be accounted for as such.

Bonuses are accrued on the basis of estimates only and should not be recorded on a cash basis by force of the fact that they are deferred salary payments and are not of a profit-sharing nature. From the point of view of accounting, the entire accrued amount of bonuses should be recorded each month or at the time of the closing of accounts. Opposition to this method may be expected from two sources: one from labor-relations departments and the other from tax authorities. For their part, labor-relations managers often complain that by accruing the estimated full amount of bonuses room for bargaining with company labor unions would automatically be precluded or substantially reduced. As for tax authorities, they accept only the actual of 'bonus reserves' based on the figures of prior years. (Figure 1)

Retirement benefits should also be accrued on the basis of estimates, the full amount ranging between the basis for voluntary retirement (i.e., when the employee quits for personal reasons) and the basis for involuntary retirement (i.e., when the employee retires for company reasons, e.g., age limit). Because accounting for tax purposes predominates in Japanese companies, most of them accrue only the 50% or less of the voluntary basis, but this practice is not

Chapter seven: Labor cost accounting

FIGURE I

BONUS RESERVE ACCOUNTING

The maximum amount deductible is
either of the following amounts:

1. $\left(\text{Total of bonuses per employee paid in the previous calendar year} \times \dfrac{\text{Number of months of the current calendar year until the end of the accounting period}}{12} \right) - \left(\text{Bonuses per employee paid in the current calendar year until the end of the accounting period} \times \text{Number of employees at the end of the accounting period} \right)$

2. $\left(\text{Total of bonuses per employee paid in the previous year} \times \dfrac{\text{Number of months of the accounting period}}{12} \right) - \left(\dfrac{\text{Amount of bonuses paid as applicable to the period included in the accounting period}}{\text{Number of employees at the end of the accounting period}} \times \text{Number of employees at the end of the accounting period} \right)$

The amount credited to the reserve in an accounting period is added back in
full to income in the following accounting period.

Source: *Outline of Japanese Taxes,* Tokyo: The Ministry of Finance, 1967, p. 83

acceptable from the point of view of sound accounting principles.
'Automatic' annual increases of salaries raise retirement benefits not
only with respect to their current portions, but also with respect to
accruals recorded in prior years. Furthermore, prepaid taxes should
be considered in all accruals of retirement benefits because, under
certain conditions, 50% of the ending balance is ordinarily deductible for tax purposes; the remaining 50% becomes deductible
when paid.

Recently, the concept of present value has been introduced into
Japanese accounting practices. Thus retirement benefits may be

discounted to their present value by use of the current interest rate applied to those portions of the benefits that are payable each year. If concepts of both prepaid tax and present value are adopted, the net amount would ordinarily be 50 to 75% of the full balance. It should be noted, however, that retirement benefits in Japan are, as a rule, lump-sum payments. Pension plans have been adopted by some major companies, and they are likely to become more prevalent in the future as the financial strength of Japanese companies improves, but at present they are not as common as they are in Western countries.

Income-tax on payrolls

SALARIES and bonuses are subject to withholding taxes when paid and to adjustment when returns are filed or to 'year-end adjustment' carried out by employers. The proper amount of withholding tax is obtained from withholding-tax tables and differs according to the nature of the salary concerned (salary from a main employer, another employer, or a bonus), the period of payment (day, month), and the number of dependents. The withholding tax is temporarily deducted at the source and must be paid to a local tax office on or before the 10th day of the month following the month of withholding. Final adjustment should be made by the company at the time of the last salary payment of the calendar year. If during the year an individual moves from one company to another, the latter company should make a year-end adjustment by obtaining salary information from the former company—a remarkable feature of the Japanese income-tax system that minimizes the possibilities of evasion.

Year-end adjustments usually result in refunds of income taxes withheld in prior months of the year since almost every year the government reduces individual income taxes by raising the level of certain exemptions and by lowering tax rates in view of the usual high-level economic growth of the country that brings about an increase in overall tax revenues.

Retirement benefits are subject to withholding taxes when paid, but not to later adjustments. In the 1967 tax reform, larger deductions and exemptions were allowed for retirement benefits so that most of them are now tax-free or taxed only slightly. For example, an employee retiring at the age of fifty-five after thirty years of service may ordinarily pay:

Income tax		*Retirement benefit*
None	on	¥3,000,000
¥59,000	on	¥5,000,000

Commutation expenses, meal expenses, and payments in goods and rent are not taxable within certain limits. For example, commutation expenses are not taxable up to ¥3,600 a month for use of public transportation. Any additional amounts are, however, taxable. At the same time, 70% of meal expenses is taxable unless the meals amount to only ¥700 or less per month, when they are not taxable. As for payment in goods, they are taxable at selling prices, but if the total amount is ¥700 or less per month, they are not taxable.

Rents involve a few complications. Those paid by employers for employees are taxable. In view of generally prevailing high rents and other housing difficulties, however, they can be treated as non-taxable if half of the 'rent equivalent' is paid by the employee to the employer. A monthly 'rent equivalent' is calculated as the total of the rent equivalent of both dwelling and land as follows:

$$\text{House rent equivalent} = \text{Registered value of the house per property-tax ledger} \times \frac{2}{1,000} + ¥12 \times \text{number of } tsubo \ (3.3^2 \text{ meters})$$

$$\text{Land rent equivalent} = \text{Registered value of the land per property-tax ledger} \times \frac{2.2}{1,000}$$

It should be carefully noted that if an employee's payment is less than half of the rent equivalent involved, his entire rent is taxable.

For directors of companies, however, this 'lenient' system of tax treatment with respect to rents was discontinued as of 1 August 1968. According to the new ruling, 'rent ordinarily payable' as applied to a director should be the larger of the following:

a one-half of the amount of rent actually paid by an employer

or

b $\begin{pmatrix} \text{Amount of tax} \\ \text{base for pro-} \\ \text{perty tax on} \\ \text{land for the} \\ \text{year} \end{pmatrix} \times 6\% + \begin{pmatrix} \text{Amount of tax base} \\ \text{for property tax on} \\ \text{house for the year} \\ \text{(in the case of non-} \\ \text{wooden structures: 10\%)} \end{pmatrix} \times 12\% \times \dfrac{1}{12}$

If the amount of rent actually collected from a director is lower than this calculation, the difference should be included in his gross salary. One-half of the amount of rent actually paid by an employer has become the minimum to be borne by a director, whereas only a nominal amount (10 to 20% of actual rent) is still acceptable in the case of an employee.

Travel expenses are not taxable in so far as they are supported by actual expense receipts or by a company's rules concerning travel expenses.

If a portion of a bonus is retained by a company as an employee's savings deposit, it should be accounted for as such. Individual withholding income taxes for payments in goods and individual deposits should be deducted at the source as in the case of cash payments. Therefore the employer should at least pay cash sufficient to cover the withholding income taxes incurred.

Accounting for the salaries of foreigners

THERE is no difference in accounting for salaries paid to foreigners except for income-tax treatment for 'non-residents' and 'non-permanent residents'. A withholding income tax only—a flat 20%—is imposed on a non-resident foreigner's income, and no further adjustment is required. A foreigner with a domicile in Japan or with residence in Japan for a period of one year (which makes him a 'resident taxpayer') is, however, subject to income tax on the total of his income derived from domestic sources inside Japan and from foreign sources outside Japan if paid in Japan or remitted to Japan if he has no intention of residing in Japan permanently and has maintained residence or domicile in Japan uninterruptedly for not more than five years (which makes him a 'non-permanent resident taxpayer'). If, however, he is a 'permanent resident taxpayer', his entire worldwide income is taxable.

A keen shortage of Western-style houses and apartments and a growing demand for them by foreigners have created unimaginably high rents in Japan. Foreigners ordinarily pay ¥150,000 to ¥200,000 ($400 to $600) or more per month for much smaller floor-space than that available in their home countries, and such rents are customarily paid by employers. In order for the entire rent to be non-taxable, however, an employee or director must bear a certain portion of it himself, as has already been indicated.

Legal benefits or social security taxes

JAPANESE social-security benefits range as follows, depending on salary income:

		Maximum
Health insurance	0.7% of basic salary	¥7,280
Welfare pension insurance		
Male	0.55% of basic salary	¥3,300
Female	0.39% of basic salary	¥2,340
Unemployment insurance	1.4% of gross monthly earnings	
Workmen's accident-compensation insurance in the case of an ordinary manufacturing business	0.3 to 0.5% of gross monthly earnings	

Source: Rate-tables of the respective Japanese laws.

Employers must bear half of the premiums for health insurance, welfare pension insurance, and unemployment insurance, and the entire amount of workmen's accident-compensation insurance. Premiums to be borne by employees are withheld from monthly salaries. All premiums are to be paid to the appropriate government agencies by the end of the month following the month of withholding.

Legal benefits together with voluntary benefits amount to about 14% of the total of monthly salaries and allowances in Japan. (Figure 2)

FIGURE 2

TREND OF FRINGE BENEFITS (1955–1966)

Survey period	Number of companies surveyed	Salaries and allowances (A)	Fringe benefits Total (B)	Legal	Voluntary	B/A
F.Y. 1966	715	¥55,431	¥7,698	¥3,382	¥4,316	13.9%
F.Y. 1965	739	49,273	6,674	2,897	3,777	13.5
F.Y. 1964	752	45,862	5,972	2,356	3,616	13.0
F.Y. 1963	680	43,531	5,346	2,188	3,158	12.3
Oct. 1961—Sept. 1962	707	37,038	4,750	1,908	2,842	14.8
Oct. 1960—Sept. 1961	575	35,041	4,554	1,842	2,712	13.0
Oct. 1959—Sept. 1960	495	33,174	4,431	1,772	2,659	13.4
Oct. 1958—Sept. 1959	500	29,444	4,231	1,692	2,539	14.4
Oct. 1957—Sept. 1958	485	28,674	4,169	1,705	2,464	14.5
Oct. 1956—Sept. 1957	434	26,926	3,922	1,600	2,322	14.6
Oct. 1955—Sept. 1956	327	23,967	3,505	1,463	2,042	14.6

Source: *Fukuri Kosei-hi Chōsa Kekka Hōkoku* ('Survey of Fringe Benefits'), Tokyo: Federation of Employers' Associations, December 1967, p. 11.

Voluntary fringe benefits

BESIDES legal benefits, Japanese companies themselves provide a variety of benefits, many of them very paternalistic. For example, company savings programs and loans for employees are very common. Most Japanese companies accept voluntary deposits—savings, time, instalment, and the like—from their employees at 8 to 10%

per year. The protection of such deposits was brought to the special attention of the public when, in 1964, the Sanyo Special Steel Company went bankrupt; such deposits can be withdrawn with the approval of the court even when a company is in the process of reorganization and all its other debts are shelved. At the same time, Japanese companies often make loans to their employees for specific purposes—for the construction or purchase of housing, for costs of marriage, or for investment in the company's stock, and so on.

The interest rates applicable to loans other than those for housing should be equal to or more than those of actually prevailing rates, but they may be as low as 6% per year (Civil Code rate) if so specified in an agreement. The interest rates for housing, however, have no minimum and may even be non-existent. Meanwhile, interest expenses paid to an employee to cover part or all of the interest he must pay to his bank for the purchase of a dwelling has not been subject to income tax since 1 June 1967. The purpose of these special treatments is, of course, the encouragement of home ownership and the alleviation of the Japanese housing shortage.

Other employees' benefits commonly available in Japan include group life insurance, the use of company-owned cafeterias, stores, clinics, and resort facilities, and special training both inside and outside of the company. The costs of all these benefits are deductible from company income and are not deemed to be related to individual income.

Entertainment expenses have traditionally been very loosely controlled in Japan and have hence been the target of much criticism as *shayōzoku* ('use of company funds for our purpose'). For example, a manager who receives a monthly salary of ¥100,000 might well spend even more than that amount for entertainment in a month. Even a lower ranking employee characteristically spends more than his salary for entertainment. This issue is primarily, of course, a matter of a company's internal discipline. Some years ago, however, the tax authorities took a first step to disallow 50% of such entertainment expense after deductions of ¥4,000,000 plus 0.25% of a company's capital stock and capital surplus. Then, in the 1967 tax reform, they took further steps to encourage the reduction of such expenses. Specifically, they ruled that in the computation of total entertainment expense (a) after the portion of current expense lower than the prior year's was deducted, half of the amount remaining would not be deductible and (b) 100% of the portion exceeding 105% of the prior year's expense would not be deductible.

A model calculation of total labor costs (Figure 3)

GIVEN the following assumptions, total labor costs should amount to about 180% of basic salary, or about 125% of the total of salaries, allowances, and bonuses together:

a	Basic salary	¥50,000 per month
b	Allowances, including overtime	10% of the above
c	Bonuses	A 2-month bonus paid twice a year, in June and December
d	Housing loans	¥1,000,000 at 4% p. a.
e	Commutation allowances	¥3,000 per month
f	Miscellaneous	2% of the total of salaries, allowances, and bonuses
g	Retirement benefits	1 month salary for each year's service (for persons with two or more years of service)

Legal benefits as shown in Figure 2 are lower than those in Figure 3 because lower basic salary and higher allowances are prevalent especially in old companies, and most insurance premiums are computed on the basis of basic salary exclusive of allowances. The voluntary benefits as shown in Figure 2 are also lower than those in Figure 3. One reason is that many employees who use company houses or dormitories or who own their own houses do not need

FIGURE 3

MODEL COMPUTATION OF ANNUAL SALARY
AND BENEFITS

Basic salary	¥50,000 × 12	¥600,000	100.0%
Allowances 10%		60,000	10.0
Bonuses 4 months		200,000	33.3
		¥860,000 100.0%	
Legal benefits:			
Health insurance	¥1,820 × 12	21,840	
Welfare pension insurance	¥1,650 × 12	19,800	
Unemployment insurance	¥340 × 12	4,080	
Workmen's accident	¥600,000 × 1.5%	3,000	
		¥48,720 5.6	8.0
Voluntary benefits (excluding free use of company facilities):			
Housing loan	¥1,000,000 × (9–4%)	¥50,000	
Commutation	¥3,000 × 12	36,000	
Others	¥860,000 × 3%	25,800	
		¥111,800 13.0	18.6
Retirement benefit:			
1 month		¥50,000 5.8	8.3
		124.4%	178.2%

housing loans and, in any case, junior employees are not entitled to
them. Another reason is that average commutation expense is not as
high as the one in Figure 3, especially in a company that has many
local offices and plants in the countryside, where bicycles are the
favorite means of commutation.

CHAPTER EIGHT

Private pension plans

BY MOTOSHI ISOMURA

The background of private pension plans—the qualified retirement pension plan—adjusted pension plans—non-qualified pension plans—management of pension funds

IN Japan there are two ways of providing for old age: by lump-sum retirement allowance systems (*taishoku-teate* or *taishoku-ichiji-kin*) and by pension plans, of which there are two kinds: public *(kōteki-nenkin-seido)*, which the government and other civil authorities have established for their employees, and private *(shiteki-kigyo-nenkin-seido)*, which corporations have voluntarily established for their employees.

Public pension plans are part of the Japanese social-security system and are of eight types (Figure 1), all of which require different premiums. The most relevant plan for discussion here is the Welfare Pension Plan.

With respect to tax treatment, private pension plans are either one of two types: qualified retirement pension plans or non-qualified pension plans.

The background of private pension plans

IT is generally understood in the world that so-called 'private pension plans' are a means of protecting workers retiring from

FIGURE I

TYPES OF PUBLIC PENSION PLANS (MARCH 1967)

	Public pension plans		Participants
1	Employees of the national government	*Kokka-kōmuin-kyōsai-kumiai*	1,130,000
2	Employees of local governments (e.g. perfectures, cities, towns)	*Chihō-kōmuin-kyōsai-kumiai*	3,000,000
3	Employees of public corporations (e.g. Japan National Railways or Japan Monopoly Corporation)	*Kōkyō-kigyōtai-shokuintō kyōsaikumiai*	770,000
4	Employees of Agricultural, Fishing or Forestry Cooperatives	*Nōrin-gyogyō-dantai-shokuin kyōsai-kumiai*	350,000
5	Seamen	*Sen-in-hoken*	260,000
6	Employees and teachers of private schools	*Shiritsu gakkō-shokuin-kyōsai-kumiai*	140,000
7	Professionals and self-employed (e.g. doctors, barbers, farmers, and fishermen)	*Kokumin-nenkin*	20,020,000
8	Most employees of private firms, (=Welfare Pension Insurance)	*Kōsei-nenkin-hoken*	19,160,000

Source: *Shakai-hoshō-nenkan* ('Social Security Yearbook'), Tokyo: Kenkō-hoken-kumiai-rengōkai, 1968, pp. 8–9.

employment because of old age and that they supplement social security. This definition holds good also in Japan, where during the past several years private pension plans have rapidly become popular. Their development and form, however, are greatly different from those of systems prevailing in Europe and the United States. Private pension plans in Japan have evolved around and remained inseparably related to the Japanese tradition of paying lump-sums as 'retirement allowances' *(taishoku-kin),* a system with no parallel in Europe and the United States.

The fundamental purpose of any pension plan is, of course, retirement *(taishoku).* In the United States reasons for retirement are

1 Old age (age limit)

2 Dismissal (retirement for reasons of management, including lay-off and complete severance)
3 Quitting (retirement for personal reasons)
4 Death (retirement through *force majeure* before the age limit)

In the United States a severance allowance of three to five months' pay is paid upon retirement for reasons of management, but none is paid for retirement for personal reasons. From the Japanese point of view, the typical American lump-sum allowance in case of dismissal is very small. In case of their retirement because of total disability American employees receive pensions from their government through social security or from their employers through private pension annuities. In Japan, however, the lump-sum retirement allowance is calculated both according to length of service and according to reasons for retirement.[1] The Japanese lump-sum system was conceived in the 1900s in order to enable corporations to induce employees to remain in service for a longer period of time than they would otherwise have done and to attract workers during the severe labor shortage caused by the rapid development of modern Japanese industry. The aim was to pay, as a means of controlling labor mobility, a retirement allowance designed to become larger as the period of service increased. Later, in the 1920s, this system also began to be applied at the request of labor itself, and today almost all enterprises that employ more than twenty or thirty persons have some form of retirement regulations derived from this system of allowance.

On the one hand, management regards the system as a token recognition of gratitude to retired employees who have faithfully discharged their duties for a long time and as remuneration for their contributions to the development of the corporation. Accordingly, in the assessment of retirement allowances, management believes that the merits or records of service of the employees concerned

[1] See Chapter Six.

should be taken into consideration. On the other hand, labor for its part regards it as only natural for management to guarantee economic security after retirement to employees who have dedicated the better part of their lives to the corporation. Accordingly, in the assessment of retirement allowances, labor believes that the living expenses of employees and their dependents after retirement should be taken into consideration. Whatever rationale is used, it is clear that the system is vitally necessary for most retired Japanese. One reason is that, because most of them have lived in company housing or have had to rent other housing, they want, upon retirement, to build their own homes with their allowances and thus provide shelter for themselves, their children, and/or their parents. Another reason is that they must often meet exacting expenses incurred for the education and marriage of their children.

The amounts involved in Japanese retirement allowances are substantial. Typically, after thirty years of service, employees can receive forty to fifty months' final pay when they retire for reasons of management and thirty-five to forty-five months' final pay when they retire for personal reasons. (Figure 2) Japanese firms usually state such figures in their wage regulations *(chingin kisoku)* or lump-sum retirement allowance rules *(taishokukin-kitei)* in the form of a 'Table of payment rates of retirement allowance' *(taishokukin-shikyūritsu-hyō)*.

The lump-sum retirement-allowance system has not become compulsory in Japan through labor legislation, but is demanded by usage or by labor management agreement. Its cost is totally borne by the employer. If bankruptcy occurs, it is possible that employees receive nothing. As for methods of accounting that the system requires, management is left free with respect to the way in which it accumulates the funds necessary for payment of the allowance. As salary levels keep rising year after year, even if the rate remained constant to the latest salary, the absolute amount of allowance nevertheless keeps increasing. (Figure 3) A tax-deductible account cannot be set aside, but a so-called reserve for employees' retirement

Chapter eight: Private pension plans

FIGURE 2

AVERAGE AMOUNTS OF LUMP-SUM RETIREMENT
ALLOWANCE, MALE UNIVERSITY GRADUATES
(APRIL 1967)[1]

Length of service (years)	Age at retirement[2]	Retirement for personal reasons		Retirement for management reasons	
		Amount	Rate[3]	Amount	Rate[3]
3	26	¥38,000	1.1	¥87,000	2.5
5	28	86,000	2.1	165,000	4.1
10	33	327,000	6.0	520,000	9.5
15	38	915,000	12.0	1,231,000	16.1
20	43	1,984,000	20.7	2,389,000	25.0
25	48	3,549,000	30.7	4,092,000	35.4
30	53	5,456,000	40.2	6,109,000	45.5
32	55	6,056,000	42.2	6,839,000	47.7

Source: "*Taishokukin-jijō-chōsa* ('Survey on the Lump-sum Retirement Allowance'),"
in *Chūō-Rōdō-Jihō* (April 1967) pp. 24–27.

Notes: 1 382 companies capitalized at over ¥5 billion and employing over 1,000 persons
were surveyed.
2 The age limit in Japan is 55 years in 60% of the cases, 56 years in 11% of the
cases, or shorter by about 10 years than the prevailing age limit in Europe
and the U.S.
3 Rate: i.e. times last monthly salary.

allowances *(taishoku-kyūyo-hikiatekin)*, which is equal to half of the
estimated amount, may be;[2] the system is, therefore, partially a
non-reserved or non-funding system. Meanwhile, it has become
urgent for management and labor to look for safer methods of secur-
ing the system.

Among Japan's social-security measures, its medical-insurance
plan *(iryō-hoken)* was inaugurated by the government in 1922 and
has since made remarkable strides. In fact, it has developed into one
of the most advanced systems in the world. But it cannot be denied
that Japan's pension plans, particularly private ones, have lagged

2 Corporation Tax Law Enforcement Order, Art. 108. In reserving a portion of the
retirement allowance to be paid in the future, a firm can dispose of it as a loss account
or as a loss reserve if it satisfies certain conditions provided for in the law.

far behind those of other countries. A quick look at past history will explain why.

Because it existed in Japan as a custom long before the introduction of any pension plans, the lump-sum retirement-allowance practice developed into a system unique to Japan. With the enactment in 1926 of the Retirement-Allowance Reserve and Retirement-Allowance Law *(Taishokukin-tsumitate oyobi Taishoku-teate-hō)*, it became compulsory for both labor and management to provide reserves for retirement allowances through premium payments. Hence the system became a substitute for a pension plan. Later, under the Workmen's Pension Insurance Law *(Rōdōsha-nenkin-hoken-hō)* of 1942, a public pension system was introduced. This law replaced the previous law and became much more widely applicable in scope. As a result, private industry seemed to feel no necessity for studying, devising, or instituting any independent pension plans. Then, in 1944, the Workmen's Pension Insurance Law was revised and renamed the Welfare Pension Insurance Law *(Kōsei-nenkinhoken-hō)*. This new law, which was meant to cope with a then troublesome spate of inflation, increased workers' benefits, but fell far short of providing adequate security. Moreover, because of a simultaneous lack of would-be pensioners, the expectations for a public pension plan increasingly diminished. As a result, a trend towards strengthening and increasing lump-sum retirement allowances became predominant as a self-defense measure in private industry.

Meanwhile, during the postwar period, because of an increase in the power of labor unions and disappointment over the public pension system, the tendency to seek old-age security through lump-sum retirement allowances grew stronger, and the actual demand for them as a means of acquiring housing after retirement took deep roots because of the serious housing shortage. Thus, the lag in Japan's development of private pension systems may be attributed to mixed influences: partly to the weakness of the public pension system and an increased demand for lump-sum retirement allowances, but partly also to the total absence of tax privileges that favored the establishment of private pension systems.

For a long time the lump-sum retirement allowance constituted an easy, non-accumulative system computed on the basis of final pay. That is to say, it was arrived at by multiplying an employee's pay at the time of his retirement by a rate proportional to his length of service. Consequently, any pay raise offsetting a basic wage resulted in an increase in retirement allowances. In addition, because labor unions continually demanded an increase in the amount of lump-sum retirement allowances, their total rose sharply, paralleling rises in the wage level. (Figure 3)

FIGURE 3

TREND OF THE AMOUNT OF LUMP-SUM RETIREMENT
ALLOWANCE AFTER 30 YEARS OF SERVICE AND IN
CASE OF RETIREMENT FOR MANAGEMENT REASONS.
(1956–1967)

Date of survey	Lump-sum retirement allowance (¥1,000)	Rate of last monthly salary	Index (Dec. '56=100.0)
December 1956	¥3,020	41.3	100.0%
January 1959	3,458	42.6	114.5
" 1961	3,969	44.7	131.4
" 1963	4,515	42.8	149.5
" 1965	5,399	45.2	178.8
April 1967	6,109	45.0	202.3

Source: *Rōmu-kenkyū* ('Study on Labor'), Tokyo: Rōmu-kenkyū-sha, March 1968, p. 25.

For their part, employers started considering the increment of these allowances independently, to be paid totally or partially in the form of annuities. Their reasoning ran as follows: 1) Although the amount of lump-sum allowance per employee had already reached ¥3 to 5 million, it was expected to continue to rise in the future. As a result, the increase in the number of employees who would retire before their age limits, together with the number who would retire at an advanced age, was sure to place an additional financial burden on corporations and lead to increases in unforeseeable payments.

The corporations therefore wanted to level off their financial burdens by paying retirement allowances in installments. 2) As long as the form of lump-sum payments was retained, retirement allowances were destined to rise because of the power relationship between labor and management, and it would be difficult to fix them at a reasonable level. With the introduction of a pension system, however, it might be possible. If, for instance, the living standard after retirement were assessed at 60 to 70% of that during employment and if the amount of social security to be received were then deducted, the balance might be provided as benefits through a private pension plan. 3) The procedure of a pension system, even though it really involved merely the pro-rated installments of a retirement allowance, could facilitate the employment of talented men. It would induce employees to serve for a long time by guaranteeing them economic security after retirement; it would make for smoothness of transition where retirement under the age limit occurred and thus for stabilization of labor control; and it would contribute ultimately to the improvement of productivity and labor-management relations.

Employees generally agreed to the transformation of lump-sum retirement allowances into pro-rated pensions, but for reasons that differed considerably from those of management. They felt that, since the lump-sum retirement allowance system was weak in providing for old age, a pension system would stabilize the standard of living after retirement even though the overall sum might have to be reduced! Furthermore, they felt that a large lump-sum for retirement was difficult to manage and subject to dangers of speculation, which a pension system would prevent.

Generally speaking, 'averaging out financial burdens' is the primary objective of transforming lump-sum retirement allowances into pensions, but that objective cannot be realized without the adoption of a prearranged reserve system by which payments may be set aside in a special fund from the time of initial employment. Until 1962, the Japanese taxation system provided no special privilege for this purpose. When management set aside reserves for lump-sum retirement allowances or for pensions (which, to reiterate, are a mere conversion of the lump-sum allowances into installments), it was allowed to set aside, as a loss account, only about one-half of its required total of payments, mostly internal reserves, in the form of a 'retirement-allowance reserve account' *(taishoku-kyūyo-hikiate-kin)*. Even when a pension plan was formulated on the basis of a prearranged reserve system, the premium paid by management was taxed at the source as wage income. In fact, Japanese tax law did not recognize pension plans in their proper sense. Finally, however, because of the strong demands of employer organizations and trust agencies, a tax reform carried out in 1962 allowed tax privileges for private pension plans that satisfied certain conditions stipulated in the Corporation Tax Law.

The qualified retirement pension plan

THE Qualified Retirement Pension Plan *(Tekikaku-taishoku-nen-kin-seido)* is not based on special legislation as such; it is an adjustment of part of the Corporation Tax Law *(Hōjin-zeihō)* and the Income Tax Law *(Shotokuzei-hō)*. From this point of view, it resembles the American qualified pension plan approved by the United States Code of Internal Revenue. The legal qualifications affecting the Qualified Retirement Pension Plan in Japan are given in the Enforcement Order of the Corporation Tax Law, Art. 159. It is limited to trust or insurance contracts connected with retirement pension plans and is approved by the Director General of the National Tax Administration Agency *(Kokuzeichō-chōkan)* provided that it fulfills the following qualifications:

1 Its objective must be to provide adequate retirement benefits. It should be so devised that the employer will pay an annuity *(nenkin)* at the time of an employee's retirement, although it is permissible to pay either a lump-sum or a small pension to an employee who retires before qualifying for the full pension.

Employers and business executives cannot become beneficiaries, and no discrimination against a specific employee is permitted.

2 Because the accumulated pension fund is a contribution of the employer and considered as a loss account, it should be completely independent from the enterprise. The agency in charge of its administration and operation as well as of the payment of pension benefits *per se* acts as a fiduciary; such agencies are restricted to trust banks and life insurance companies. The transfer of the premium to a loss account presupposes that the premium paid will be separated from the control of an enterprise. As a result, the premium paid and income accruing from it are not refunded to the employer, except, under certain conditions, for a surplus. The trust or insurance contract should be so arranged that when it is cancelled the pension fund on that date will belong to the employees of the enterprise concerned or to those who have the right to the benefits. The employer is prohibited from giving directions outside the scope of the contract to the trust bank concerning the operations of the fund and is further prohibited from receiving a loan on more profitable terms than usual, or similar benefits, from a trust bank or insurance company that holds the contract.

3 The amount of premiums and benefits should be computed in accordance with authorized actuarial procedures based upon standard practices. In the determination of normal cost, or the premium required of participants, whether payment is to be made in fixed amounts or through percentage deductions from pay must be decided in advance. Furthermore, the premium to be earmarked for refunding a liability incurred during past services is stipulated as an amount equal to less than 20% per year of the total amount of liability for past services.

4 The administrative requirement is that the initial number of subscribers to a pension plan should not be fewer than one hundred in the case of a trust-type of plan nor fewer than twenty in the case of an insurance-type of plan.

Chapter eight: Private pension plans

When a pension plan satisfies the foregoing qualifications, it will be accorded tax privileges applicable to the employer's contributions to the fund, the operation of the fund, and the distribution of benefits—privileges denied to unqualified pension plans. The employer's contributions to fund, whether earmarked for normal cost or for refunding a liability incurred during past services, are listed in the losses of the current business year and are exempt from tax. The so-called premium-paying pension system or employer-subscription system *(kyoshutsusei-nenkin)*, in which employees share part of the employer's contributions, is also approved. In this case, part of the premium paid by an employee can be legally deducted from his income, and when benefits are distributed to him, the premium he paid may be deducted. Income from the operation of the fund is exempt from tax, but a corporation tax of 1.0% per annum is levied on the property of the pension fund. This corporation tax should properly be levied as income tax from the point of view that the income involved has accrued to the employees whenever an employer makes contributions to the pension fund. Actually, the levying of the tax is postponed until the employee retires and receives a pension or a lump-sum as benefit. In recognition of the reason for the delay

FIGURE 4

QUALIFIED RETIREMENT PENSION SYSTEM: NUMBER
AND PARTICIPANTS (1963–1968)

Year	Trust type Funds	Participants (1,000)	Insurance type Funds	Participants (1,000)	Total Funds	Participants (1,000)
Mar. 1963	71	26	59	10	130	36
Mar. 1964	486	193	371	42	857	235
Mar. 1965	927	304	1,545	148	2,472	452
Mar. 1966	1,570	471	6,580	384	8,150	855
Mar. 1967	2,235	713	13,914	767	16,149	1,480
Mar. 1968	2,703	856	31,892	1,419	34,595	2,275

Source: *Tekikaku-taishoku-nenkin-shōnin-jōkyō* ('Report on the Approval of Qualified Retirement Pension Plan'), Tokyo: The National Tax Administration Agency, March 31 1968, p. 1.

FIGURE 5

QUALIFIED PENSION FUNDS AND PARTICIPANTS, BY TYPE

Participants per fund	Trust type Funds Number %		Trust type Participants Number % (1,000)		Insurance type Funds Number %		Insurance type Participants Number % (1,000)		Total Funds[1] Number %	
Fewer than 100	–	–	–	–	30,656	96	971	68	30,656	89
100–299	2,151	80	319	37	1,027	3	154	11	3,178	9
300–999	456	17	220	26	148	1	74	5	604	2
Over 1,000	96	3	319	37	61	–	220	16	157	–
Total	2,703	100	856	100	31,892	100	1,419	100	34,595	100

Source: *Ibid.,* p. 2.
Note: 1 Overlapping occurs because some funds (perhaps as many as 600) combine both types.

in tax payment, the tax itself is regarded as corresponding to overdue interest. Finally, an income tax is levied on the pension benefits themselves, and a retirement income tax is levied on the lump-sum retirement allowance.

During a period of five years, close to 35,000 qualified retirement pension funds have come into operation in Japan. (Figure 4) Because of the administrative requirement that the minimum number of subscribers should not be fewer than one hundred in the case of a trust type *(shintaku-gata)* and not fewer than twenty in the case of an insurance type *(hoken-gata),* the trust type is more popular among

FIGURE 6

QUALIFIED RETIREMENT PENSION PLANS BY AMOUNT
OF MONTHLY ANNUITY (1968)

Monthly annuity	Trust type Number	%	Insurance type Number	%	Total Number	%
Less than ¥5,000	93	3	884	3	977	3
¥5,001–10,000	613	23	7,858	24	8,471	24
¥10,001–15,000	667	25	4,563	14	5,230	15
¥15,001–20,000	520	19	6,595	21	7,115	21
¥20,001–25,000	341	13	3,093	10	3,434	10
Over ¥25,001	469	17	8,899	28	9,368	27
Total	2,703	100	13,892	100	34,595	100

Source: *Ibid.,* p. 3.

large enterprises and the insurance type among smaller enterprises. It is estimated that firms with more than one hundred employees number about 19,000, almost 20% of which (3,939) have adopted a qualified retirement pension plan. (Figure 5)

In the West, pension plans were considered from their inception as supplementing social-security systems. As for Japan, the Qualified Retirement Pension system remains deeply marked by its origin, for it is actually a system of the payment of annuities pro-rated from a portion of the traditional lump-sum retirement allowance or, at least, pro-rated from most of the increase of a given retirement allowance system. In 60% of the cases, the pension system is con-

FIGURE 7

QUALIFIED RETIREMENT PENSION FUNDS BY TYPE
AND AMOUNT OF MONTHLY CONTRIBUTION (1968)

	Trust type		Insurance type		Total	
	Number	%	Number	%	Number	%
Contribution						
By employer only	2,195	81	31,443	99	33,638	97
By employer and employee	508	19	449	1	957	3
Total	2,703	100	31,892	100	34,595	100
Type of contribution						
Flat amount	958	36	29,688	93	30,646	89
Proportional to pay	1,741	64	629	2	2,370	7
Other	4	–	1,575	5	1,579	4
Total	2,703	100	31,892	100	34,595	100
Amount of monthly contribution						
Less than ¥500	1,026	38	5,163	16	6,189	18
¥501–1,000	1,163	43	15,125	47	16,288	47
¥1,001–2,000	462	17	10,360	33	10,882	31
¥2,001–3,000	41	2	1,056	3	1,097	3
¥3,001–4,000	8	–	139	–	147	1
¥4,001–5,000	3	–	33	–	36	–
Over ¥5,000	0	–	16	–	16	–
Total	2,703	100	31,892	100	34,585	100

Source: *Ibid.* pp. 4–5.

tributed to exclusively by the employer because it is merely a modification of the retirement allowance system whose cost has always been totally borne by the employer. (Figure 6) Contributions to the fund generally take the form of a flat amount per employee, the reason being the need to 'sell' the plan to the entire work force on the simplest terms possible. Most contributions amount to between ¥501 and ¥2,000 per month. (Figure 7) Very few systems foresee that benefits will be paid during more than five to ten years. (Figure 8) All these facts confirm the view that the pension system in Japan is nothing but the payment in installments of a lump-sum retirement allowance.

FIGURE 8

QUALIFIED RETIREMENT PENSION PLANS BY LENGTH
OF BENEFITS (1968)

Length of benefits	Trust type		Insurance type		Total	
	Number	%	Number	%	Number	%
Up to 5 years	256	10	4,938	15	5,194	15
6–10 years	2,162	80	25,999	82	28,161	81
11–15 years	90	3	177	1	267	1
More than 16 years	2	–	8	–	10	–
Life-time pension	193	7	770	2	963	3
Total	2,703	100	31,892	100	34,595	100

Source: *Ibid.,* p. 4.

At any rate, the respective advantages and disadvantages of the trust-type or insurance-type of pension fund should be examined. As pointed out before, a minimum of one hundred participants is required for the trust type and a minimum of twenty for the insurance type. This requirement results from the fact that each trust plan is operated independently of its sponsoring enterprise and thus finds actuarial safety in the number of participants, whereas insurance plans provide for the combined operations of various additional funds such as life insurance, savings insurance, and the like and thus find actuarial safety in a complex of insurance funds. As far as the interest on such funds is concerned, it seems in 1967 to have averaged, after taxes and fees, 6.2 to 6.4% per annum for the trust type and 5.8 to 6.0% for the insurance type. The difference is due to legal restrictions imposed on life insurance companies in Japan; they are prohibited from distributing capital gains by investing in securities and increasing pension benefits. Such restrictions do not apply to trust companies that may distribute capital gains in the form of higher interest rates. As a result, the trust type of fund offers higher interest rates but does not guarantee the principal by reserving capital gains, whereas the insurance type bears lower interest, but provides an actuarial guarantee by reserving capital gains.

In the establishment of a qualified retirement pension plan, funding and planning have to be carefully considered. With respect to funding, the portion of the lump-sum retirement allowance to be paid in annuities should be decided with the agreement of the labor union. Initial objection should be anticipated, because the union will suspect an infringement upon what it considers the vested right of its members to their full allowances at time of retirement, but negotiations will overcome this objection. The technicalities of the transfer to annuities are complex and must be explained in detail. As for planning of the fund, the terms of the eligibility of participants and beneficiaries generally agreed upon are these:

> For *participants:* exclusion of all non-permanent staff, part-time employees, the two or three initial years of service, and younger employees below, for instance, the age of twenty-five.
>
> For *beneficiaries:* twenty years of participation in the plan and/ or the minimum age of fifty, usually both.

All other matters, such as amounts of contributions and benefits, past service liability, and so on, are settled by specific negotiation.

Adjusted pension plans

A new type of pension plan was recently developed in Japan, one related to Welfare Pension Insurance *(Kōsei nenkin hoken),* which plays an important role in Japanese business because all firms employing more than five persons must participate in it.[3] An arbitrary example may illustrate how its benefits are calculated. Under this plan, an employee with one dependent, having completed twenty years of service and twenty years of premium payments on average monthly earnings of, say, ¥25,000, would be entitled to a total monthly benefit of ¥10,400, as calculated by the following three formulas:

1 A flat benefit: 20 years × ¥250 per year = ¥5,000
2 An amount proportional to his pay: 20 years × ¥25,000 × 1% = ¥5,000
3 A dependent's allowance: 1 person × ¥400 = ¥400.

Such an amount remains a far cry from the ¥34,400 per month that an employee and his wife living in Tokyo reputedly need to cover their living expenses in May 1967![4]

At the time the Welfare Pension Insurance Law was revised in May 1965, the Adjusted Pension Plan *(Chōsei-nenkin-seido),* a semi-public plan, was enacted upon strong demand by employers. It entitles firms with more than one thousand employees, upon agreement of more than half the work force and with the approval of the Minister of Welfare, to establish a welfare pension fund *(kōsei-nenkin-kikin)* as a public corporation. This fund must be entrusted either to a trust company or to a life insurance company. The benefit issued is to replace the portion proportional to pay of the public Welfare Pension Insurance and must exceed it by at least 30%. After making a slight increase in his contribution, the employer now contributes directly to the firm's fund. The number of these

[3] Welfare Pension Insurance Law *(Kōsei Nenkin Hoken Hō),* Art. 6. The premium to be paid to the government amounts to 5.5% of the monthly salary for male and 3.9% for female employees, equally divided among employer and employee.

[4] *Rōsei Jiho Bessatsu 1968* ('Monthly Report on Labor Politics and Statistics, with Appendix'), Tokyo: Rōmu Gyosei Kenkyusho, 1968, p. 66.

Chapter eight: Private pension plans

funds and the number of their participants have increased steadily since inception in October 1966. (Figure 9)

FIGURE 9

DIFFUSION OF WELFARE PENSION FUNDS (1966–1968)

Date of survey	Funds	Participants (1,000)
Dec. 1966	13	28
Mar. 1967	142	490
June "	193	750
Sept. "	233	867
Dec. "	266	1,087
Mar. 1968	305	1,249
June "	364	1,682

Source: *Kōsei-nenkikin-ninka-jokyō* ('Monthly Report on Approvals of Welfare Pension Funds'), Tokyo: The Ministry of Welfare, various months.

Note: Trust type and insurance type are not recorded separately.

Non-qualified pension plans

A growing number of enterprises are reported as having adopted non-qualified pension plans that can be freely established and managed by employers. The funds for these plans are usually derived from a portion of net profits, which is established as an internal and voluntary reserve, besides the tax-allowed retirement-allowance reserve. All these funds amount to is thus the taxable portion of the retirement allowance reserve. There is no governmental objection to an employer's adopting qualified and non-qualified plans simultaneously; he will have, however, to pay close attention to his treatment of the allowable reserve. Comparing both plans, the following characteristics are apparent:

	Qualified	*Non-qualified*
Taxation of employer's contribution	None	Taxed
Taxation of employee's contribution	Taxed to a certain degree	—

[195]

Taxation of the profit of the fund's operation	None, but a corporation tax of 1% on fund	Ordinary corporation tax
Management of the fund	Must be external (trust or insurance); some restrictions by the National Tax Administration	Free

A special difficulty of non-qualified pension funds is the lack of professional and independent actuaries in Japan. The only meaningful recourse is therefore a trust or life insurance company.

Management of pension funds

IN Japan as elsewhere, the fundamental problem of pension funds is devising some method of protecting them against inflation. For several years the Japanese consumer price index has risen by a yearly average of 5%; if 1965 is taken as the base year, the index for 1968 stood at 113.3%.[5] Yet the Ministry of Finance, the governmental authority supervising qualified pension plan contracts, imposes the following restrictions upon them:

> investment in stock or trust-investment stocks is limited to a maximum of 30% of the fund;
> investment in real estate or real estate trusts is limited to a maximum of 20% of the fund.

Hence trust companies and life insurance companies handling pension funds have to invest more than 50% of those funds in instruments requiring the guarantee of principal (deposits, bonds, and the like). If, therefore, a 5% increase in prices is to be withstood, at least 15% in capital gains must be expected from the 30% allowable for stock investment, for investment of pension funds in real estate is still uncommon in Japan.

Protection of pension funds against inflation might be partly

[5] *Chingin-tsūshin* ('Report on Wages'), Tokyo: Chingin Tsūshin-sha, February 1968, p. 22.

Chapter eight: Private pension plans

strengthened by the proportional-to-pay system, by which premiums are reserved in proportion to total payrolls and increased as wages increase. Benefits are then calculated on the basis of a beneficiary's final pay.

The truth of the matter remains, however, that in today's Japan, a skillful combination of stock investment and proportional-to-pay system barely protects pension funds against inflation. Nonetheless, qualified retirement pension plans and adjusted pension plans keep spreading steadily, as shown by their total national reserves. (Figure 10)

FIGURE 10

DEVELOPMENT OF PENSION FUNDS (1963–1967)

		(¥ million)
Date of survey	Trust type	Insurance type
Mar. 1963	¥535	¥200
" 1964	2,674	741
" 1965	8,142	3,098
" 1966	16,359	8,035
" 1967	29,142	19,070
" 1968	57,484	42,753

Sources: Trust type: Monthly verbal report by the Trust and Banking Corporation (*Shintaku-kyōkai*).
Insurance type: *Hoken* ('Insurance'), Tokyo: Hoken Kenkyūsho, July 1967, p. 95.

Part IV

JAPANESE
INDUSTRIAL RELATIONS

CHAPTER NINE

The labor movement

BY PAUL TIMOTHY CHAN

Development of the labor movement—labor force and labor unions—wage issues and the labor struggle—the labor movement and politics

ODERN Japanese trade unionism is firmly founded on social, as well as legal, bases. Having received extraordinary impetus from the restoration of freedom at the end of the Pacific War and benefiting ever since from the rapid rise of industry as a whole, particularly during the last decade or so, the Japanese labor movement has grown at an unusual pace. Today, of an estimated labor force of about 30 million industrial workers in the nation, a total of about 35% is organized into trade unions. These unions are in turn federated into four national trade-union centers constituting major socio-political and economic forces that have a determining influence upon the character of the entire labor movement.

The General Council of Trade Unions of Japan *(Sōhyō)*, with a membership of 4,200,000, is the largest and hence the dominant national trade-union center in the country and represents left-wing political radicalism. The Japan Confederation of Labor *(Dōmei)*, with a membership of 1,800,000, ranks second and is noted for political moderation. The Federation of Industrial Unions *(Chūritsu Rōren)*, with a membership of 1,037,000, and the National Federation of Industrial Organizations (NIO), with a membership of 69,800, have usually associated themselves practically, if not ideologically, with Sōhyō.

Several factors are requisite to any understanding of the character of Japanese labor organizations and the Japanese labor movement in general. Politically, persistent ideological assertions made by labor leaders, especially those of Sōhyō, have actually hampered the case of the workers, while organizationally, the unions still suffer from the effects of the enterprise-union system that grew out of traditional Japanese paternalistic feudalism. Although there are some universally recognizable features in Japanese labor organization, a close examination shows that traditionalism has conditioned it in several unique ways.

Development of the labor movement

THE organized labor movement of Japan can be traced in its modern sense to the late 19th century, when, some hundred years ago, it coincided with the restoration of imperial rule. Rickshaw men, printers, blacksmiths, miners, and (interestingly enough) the geisha girls of Tokyo were among the first Japanese to attempt organization, but these attempts were only sporadic and short-lived. A more sustained effort was carried out in the prewar period, when the struggle, basically for legal recognition, was designed to break the policy of repression that persisted with ever increasing intensity until the end of the war. The formation in 1912 of *Yūaikai*, the forerunner of Dōmei, which culminated in 1920 in the organization of the Japanese Federation of Labor *(Sōdōmei)*, was the first real breakthrough for organized labor in prewar Japan. Yet even Sōdōmei, moderate as it was, was forced to dissolve in 1940. And for the duration of the Pacific War, Japan was without any labor organization with even a semblance of independence, for all workers were organized and controlled by the government. Thus not until the end of the war in 1945 did the Japanese labor movement make its first appearance in any viable sense.

Chapter nine: The labor movement

The sudden end of the war was in every respect so revolutionary for the people of Japan that it affected all components of their lives. The actions undertaken in rapid succession by the Occupation forces during the first several months after their arrival were electrifying in their effect. The SCAP Directive of October 1945 ordering the repeal of all legal instruments suppressing civil rights and freedom of religion, speech, political activity, and association; the purge of the militarists and their collaborators from public office; the Emperor's denial of the divinity that had theretofore been the major symbol of Japanese political extremism—these were only a few of the major steps taken to liberate the people and introduce democracy as proclaimed in the Potsdam Declaration of 1945.

Within weeks some three thousand political prisoners inside Japan, most of them Communist leaders, were released, and their compatriots streamed back to Japan from exile abroad. In November of 1945 the Japan Socialist Party (JSP) was formed. In December the Communists emerged from underground and openly regrouped themselves at the 4th National Convention of the Japan Communist Party (JCP). In January of 1946 Sōdōmei reopened its office; in August the left-wing Socialists and Communists joined to form the National Congress of Industrial Unions *(Sambetsu)*; and by March 1947 the Communists organized the National Liaison Council of Labor Unions *(Zenrenkyo)*. The JCP forthrightly called the Occupation forces 'the liberation army', a remarkable compliment for a Communist institution to give a non-Communist one. In any case, all these developments reflected the strong encouragement that the Occupation gave to Japanese labor. Within two years under its protection, the Japanese labor movement grew to over 28,000 unions with a total membership in excess of six million workers, representing well over 45% of the total labor force of the nation.

One of the determining influences shaping the Japanese labor movement has always been the ideological force of Communism. Because they have long recognized, in theory as well as in practice, that labor unions occupy an extremely important strategic position in modern industrial society, the Communists have always made intense efforts to capture controlling positions in the labor movement. As may be seen, both the actions of the Occupation and the prevailing mood of the people who were faced with hopeless inflation and imminent mass starvation favored the Communists. Conflict among the national Japanese trade-union centers where the Communists were organized and agitating for sole political hegemony in labor and politics was an inevitable outcome. Since a more detailed account of these consequences will be discussed in the sections following, suffice it to say here that the conflict brought about recurring cycles of splits and reorganizations that contorted the labor movement as paralyzing convulsions would contort a giant. Finally toppling by force of its own failures of infiltration, exploitation, and agitation, the Japan Communist Party brought about the collapse of both Zenrenkyo and Sambetsu, which disbanded in 1950.

Sōhyō was formed in the same year by those labor leaders of the Japan Socialist Party who were opposed to the domination and exploitation of Japanese labor organizations by the JCP. Thus, although Sōhyō began its life as a labor organization opposed to monolithic Communist control, it soon changed from 'chicken to duck', in the famous phrase of Minoru Takano, then secretary-general, who used the expression to characterize its shift from a moderate left-wing stance to a more militant left-wing radicalism closely identifiable with the JCP at home and Communist China and the USSR abroad.

Emerging from the ruins of Sambetsu and Zenrenkyo, Sōhyō, with three million members, became the only strong national trade-union center in Japan. But moderate leaders in the organization were forced to withdraw from membership as soon as they saw that it had become the mainstay of left-wing political operations. During 1951 and 1952, as a matter of fact, Sōhyō was rent with internal division between left-wing Socialists and Communists on the one hand and moderate Socialists on the other. They were hopelessly divided on the issue of the Japanese Peace Treaty, which was then being negotiated by the governments of Japan and the United States and her allies. Finally, in 1953, four large affiliated unions represented by the unions of seamen and textile workers openly condemned the political actions of Sōhyō that were ideologically motivated at the expense of the welfare of its members; and, in 1944, with those four unions as the nucleus, the moderates formed the Japanese Trade Union Council *(Zenrō)*.

From a theoretical point of view, labor unions serve as channels and administrative agencies for the protests of workers. Under normal conditions, therefore, the unions are charged with the task of exercising what may be termed a proprietary interest in expressing such protests through collective bargaining, grievance procedures, and strikes. They are expected to reflect the changing nature of the workers' needs and desires. Accordingly, the scope of union activities is broad, and it tends to broaden continually as the manifold nature of the workers' needs and aspirations also broadens. The critical test of those labor organizations formed in protest to the leftwing domination of their counterparts lay in this area, where the success of Zenrō was considerable; hence the attractiveness of the organization to the rank and file of workers both in Sōhyō and in fields still to be organized. Zenrō's successful graduation into Dōmei, achieved through a merger with Sōdōmei in November 1964, was no occasion for surprise for those who had followed the labor movement in Japan.

Today, in any case, Sōhyō and Dōmei stand as the two major rival organizations in Japanese labor. Dōmei has shown its viability in a consistent policy characterized by conscious avoidance of ideological implications and a steady rise in membership, whereas Sōhyō has pursued an erratic line of action vacillating between left-wing political radicalism and traditional unionism that has emphasized economic interests exclusively. The only occasional check against Sōhyō's characteristic and habitual return to left-wing radicalism has been the desertion of its members, which has at times threatened the very foundations of the organization. Yet the leaders of Sōhyō have persisted in pursuing in their struggles political objectives merely sugar-coated with wage and benefit demands.

The cost of the ideologically motivated leadership of, first, Sambetsu and, later, Sōhyō has been high, and damaging to Japanese labor. Under the shadow of political radicalism, the Japanese labor movement has been unable to grow out of an archaic structure and wage system. The effect on the morale of workers both inside and outside the unions has been far-reaching, indeed.

The labor force and labor unions

THE rapid expansion of Japanese industry during the last decade has resulted in a phenomenal growth of urban centers and a concomitantly phenomenal growth in the industrial labor force. According to a Ministry of Labor survey published in 1967, that force, which was about 6 million at the end of the Pacific War, was 29 million in 1967. During the same period the population shift from rural to urban centers was heavy and intense. Under such circumstances, some change in the character of the labor force was inevitable, but not sufficiently strong to remold it fundamentally, so that certain historical peculiarities continue to condition that character.

Because of the socio-economic background of the nation, industry in Japan was originally forced to rely heavily on the rural population for its supply of labor, for there was no urban population large enough to serve it as a pool of manpower. Since, by its very nature, the labor drawn from a rural population was seasonal and migratory, it shared no common feature with its counterparts in Western Europe where there seems always to have been an adequate reservoir of urban workers available. The historical motives of Japanese labor cannot therefore be regarded as very much like those that obtained in the West. Originally drawn from among surplus farmhands, Japanese labor has traditionally been far less concerned with such basic issues as a viable wage system, better working conditions, and the development of effective bargaining and grievance procedures than it has come to be in the last decade or so. The primary reason Japanese farm-hands originally sought urban employment was to earn enough for remittance to their families in depressed rural areas. Hence their earnings were only supplementary in value. Chained as they were to their strong family obligations, they were quite content to accept whatever wages their employers gave them; needless to say, such an attitude is not conducive to the development of a healthy labor movement in modern terms.

The Japanese familial structure itself also affected the character of the labor force. The traditional system of primogeniture, designed to preserve the family line through inheritance reserved to the eldest son, forced second and third sons in rural areas to seek their opportunities elsewhere, in urban areas. This situation had two distinct effects upon molding the character of the labor force. First, required by necessity to seek an immediate and simple source of income and discouraged by a sense of insecurity from exploiting new tracts for cultivation in regions which were already short of arable land and which promised only marginal rewards at best, those second and third sons sought to establish socio-economic security by entrusting themselves to a variety of basically societal groups built upon paternalistic concepts. Second, chiefly depending upon the support and protection of the leaders of such groups, they deprived themselves of that very independence that is essential for the development of a modern labor movement. Meanwhile, of course, the groups served several useful purposes. The leader, or *oyabun* ('master' or 'father-surrogate'), acted as provider, protector, and negotiator for his followers, or *kobun,* who unquestioningly accepted his terms of employment in exchange for security. In effect a labor boss, the *oyabun* was a useful broker for employers, and the familial bonds that tied his group together tended to curtail widespread absenteeism and desertions. Although today such terms as *oyabun* and *kobun* are rarely used in labor circles, the underlying mental attitudes peculiar to the relationship are still powerful, particularly in the medium and small industries that constitute the major portion of the Japanese industrial complex. This fact, in turn, negates the very purpose of unionism.

Since, as a matter of fact, females constituted the majority of industrial workers in Japan for a long time, their situation is little different. Japanese industry began to grow with heavy emphasis upon the development of textiles, and it was chiefly young girls drawn from chronically depressed rural regions who 'manned' the machines. Leaving their families as soon as they finished elementary school in order to spend the interlude between adolescence and marriage in earning, saving, and remitting to their families whatever they could, they were not very much concerned with a better wage system or with better conditions, despite the harsh ones under which they were working. Theirs, again, was only a temporary migration to urban areas.

During the early years of the Occupation, several important labor laws were passed to correct some of the sorrier strictures of the Japanese labor movement, for example, the Trade Union Law (1945), the Labor Relations Adjustment Law (1946), and the Labor Standards Law (1947). Yet, even now, the forces of feudalistic traditionalism continue to influence the attitudes of Japanese workers in one way or another inimical to the healthy growth of the labor movement. The recent sudden upsurge of Japanese industry has generated a powerful impetus towards change in the traditional mentality of the labor force, but it has not yet effectively brought about the kind of change that is needed.

The term 'enterprise' is used attributively to define the dominant structural characteristic for which Japanese labor unions are known. Unlike their Western counterparts, which are organized on an industry-wide basis with central organs supervising locals of the same industry but of different capitalizations and managements distributed over a wide geographical area, Japanese unions are organized strictly within units of individual enterprise. In a nutshell, then, a Japanese enterprise union is one organized exclusively among the members of one firm or one plant. Over 90% of Japanese unions organized at the end of the war belong to this category, whereas 10%, or fewer, are industry-wide. The All Japan Seamen's Union, as a matter of fact, is about the only Japanese union that can qualify as an industrial union in a Western, classic, and technical sense, and it is an exception. The extremity of the Japanese situation may be seen in the independent identities the unions maintain even when they represent the workers in the plants and establishments of the same industrial management situated in different geographical areas, for example in the miners' unions of the Mitsui Company, which owns and operates several collieries in the nation. More specifically, although the union in Sunagawa, Hokkaido, and the one in Miike, Kyushu, are both connected with collieries owned and operated by Mitsui, each of them is organically independent. Thus, even in a situation where an enterprise is built upon a number of plants and establishments of its own, the union in each separate unit insists upon organic independence and eschews any structural links with the others, except through loose liaison or federation.

The development of the enterprise-union system in Japan can be attributed to several factors. First, from a structural point of view, Japanese industry is a complex of small firms and plants that are independent, usually acting as sub-contractors of larger enterprises. Feudalistic traditionalism with its omnipresent paternalistic influence has been another important factor. Employed only in small plants and firms, the employees in such enterprises have typically placed more importance on their paternalistic ties with their employers than on other matters. The consideration of the economic solvency and prosperity of the enterprise concerned has been more vital to them than the consideration of union activities and the bettering of their lot.

Under the Occupation, labor unions were given strong encouragement and naturally, therefore, grew rapidly. The measures taken by

SCAP to free the people had an effect that was like the opening up of floodgates. Freed from the suppressions of wartime existence and released from their prison cells, political and labor leaders found it no longer necessary to stand outside a plant-gate to distribute leaflets soliciting the workers' support for union activities. The liberty that came so suddenly made individual approaches no longer necessary or useful; the organizers could take whole firms as the units of their organizational efforts—as, indeed, they did. They simply moved into a company compound, assembled the hungry and bewildered workers around them, and declared the formation of a union then and there. Given such inaugural assemblies, strengthened as they were by the general national outcry for food and justice, the organizers understandably paid more attention to the formation of unions on enterprise bases than on industrial bases. Nor was the World Federation of Trade Unions (WFTU), whose headquarters are in Moscow, idle during this chaotic postwar period. Obviously, for tactical reasons, it ordered left-wing labor leaders to organize according to individual enterprises in order to facilitate the creation of such worker-management committees as would give Communist-controlled employees power to dictate policies of operation for eventual take-over.

Although one must grant some merits to the enterprise-union system, fundamentally it was not, and is not, ideal from the point of view of labor's genuine interests. This fact was particularly true in Japan up until about 1950 when the members of enterprise unions included all categories of employees, even the managerial.

Of the many weaknesses basic to the system, the one that heads the list is perhaps its organizational structure, which leaves itself wide open to exploitation with respect to specific political objectives. When the JCP controlled the operations of enterprise unions during the first several postwar years, they boldly attempted to resort to direct action for the take-over of enterprises in the name of revolution. In a union organized on the basis of one enterprise only, where the members comprised all employees including the managerial, the implanting of a handful of activists as leaders was all that was necessary for turning the union into a militant revolutionary committee for control. The failure of the JCP's tactics is ↙ not attributable to any inherent merits in the system, but rather to the party's miscalculation in timing and to the impact created by cold-war tensions.

Second, the Japanese enterprise union is in effect an association of employees with little or no concept of the principles that ought to govern labor-management relations. As a result, rather than reflecting the principle of trade unionism by which labor and management face each other horizontally, on a plane of equality, it presents a structure of verticality, a channel of human relations that link the entrepreneur with his employees only through manifold chains of administrative personnel down through the union officials to the union members and other employees. Since, in such a structure, bargaining, negotiation, and settlement are made strictly within the confines of the enterprise involved, labor's disadvantage is evident. Unions with such a structure are likely to degenerate into mere company unions.

Third, because the influence of traditionalism is strong in the enterprise-union system, there is a strong natural inclination for the union officials to adopt dual standards in approaching problems inside and outside their respective unions. This duality gives rise to the rather baffling phenomenon of some labor officials making, on the one hand, radical political statements advocating a militant revolutionary struggle to overthrow 'imperialism' and 'monopoly capitalism', while at the same time, on the other hand, doing their utmost to maintain the best conceivable human relations with management.

Fourth, since enterprise-union officials are also employees, they are exposed to constant danger of dismissal, which, needless to say, could force them out of their union positions as well as their jobs. The seriousness of the psychological effect inherent in such a contingency requires no illustration.

Wage issues and the labor struggle

THE problem of wages is the central issue between labor and management in any industrial society, and Japan is no exception. Yet the Japanese wage structure is so confusing that in many cases it is difficult even for union officials to explain. The conglomeration of numerous terms expressing it testifies to one aspect of its difficulty. For example, a few of the most commonly used terms are *nenkō joretsu chingin* ('wage by seniority'), *shokukaikyū* ('pay according to job classification'), *shokumukyū* ('pay according to job position'), *nōritsukyū* ('pay according to work results'), and *ōdan chingin* ('lateral industrial wage scale'). Most such terms were devised, particularly since 1948, to meet problems created by the changing structural shape of Japanese industry and attendant necessities of adjusting labor-management relations. The confusing features of the wage structure are further compounded by the absence of any commonly accepted wage standard. Athough a minimum wage law was passed in early 1959, it has failed to serve as an effective guideline. Essentially, Japanese wages are determined on a subsistence basis designated in Japan as the 'base-pay', which is tied in with a cost-of-living allowance system, the scale of which is determined in theory by the prevailing cost-of-living index. A survey of its background and development will be helpful.

During the war, as a means of controlling and maintaining wages, the government introduced a system based on a cost-of-living allowance to be paid in cash, goods, and services to supplement wages that fell far short of the prevailing real value of money. To illustrate, the average retail index in 1930 was ¥100 and the wage scale was also ¥100. But when the retail index rose to ¥229 in 1944 and to ¥752 in 1945, the wage scale lagged far behind, at ¥183 in 1944 and ¥300 in 1945. Accordingly, the figure shows a drop in real wages of well over 60% by 1945. This difference the government attempted to make up by issuing a cost-of-living allowance rather than permitting a rise in the wage scale. When the retail index rose to ¥2,906 by 1946 and began to get out of control, soaring up to a critical point for postwar Japan, still the wage scale continued to trail far behind. Indeed, inflation rampaged throughout the Japanese economy until, in 1949, Joseph Dodge, Minister of the United States Embassy, formulated the Nine-Point Economic Stabilization Program known as the Dodge Plan and it was applied.

Basically, the Dodge Plan was designed to check inflation by means of a reinforced austerity program coupled with fiscal reformation. In the meantime, however, labor was faced with the desperate need to work out a wage formula that would at least assure the workers subsistence. With labor struggles marked by frequent violence and often accompanied by a Chinese Communist fashion of 'people's trials' of entrepreneurs, the nation was sinking rapidly in a turbulent sea of labor unrest. A wage system based on a uniform percentile increase over the existing wage scale was no longer efficient, for it fell far short of the cost of living. It was in the midst of this severe political and economic turmoil, in December 1956, that the Electrical Workers Union won a new wage system based on a formula of its own. The event was extremely significant not only because it was labor's own initiative, but also because it involved the first concrete postwar wage theory leading to future solutions of the nations' labor problems.

Specifically, the wage formula devised by the Electrical Workers Union, the *Densen-gata* Wage Plan, combined two schemes: 1) a fixed scale of subsistence wages and 2) a sliding scale of incentive wages determined by work results *(nōritsukyū)*. The subsistence wage scale was further broken down into differing classifications for single and married workers, according to which size of family was taken into account. The success of the formula was especially important because it set the pace for the subsequent actions of both government and labor with respect to the wage problem. In July 1947 a Socialist government established the average occupational wage scale at ¥1,800, thereby fixing base-pay for the first time in

[213]

postwar Japan. Then, in February 1948, an *ad hoc* committee on wages and allowances recommended a plan that was both more concrete and more realistic; this plan set ¥2,920 for a worker twenty-nine years of age with a family of 2.5 persons as the base wage for employees of public enterprises. To be sure, protests and objections followed—the protest strike of the Postal Workers Union was particularly intense. But finally labor as a whole, both in public and private enterprise, accepted the scale as the lesser of evils. When the National Railway Workers Union accepted it, the ¥2,920 base-wage system rapidly spread among labor unions as well as among entrepreneurs.

The base-wage system became popular in the labor movement because of the convenience it offered in the organization of different enterprises with varying scales of base wages. Japanese labor's continued acceptance of base-wage increases as a standard tactical goal in its struggles is therefore readily understandable. To the entrepreneurs also the system was convenient because it relieved them of complicated procedures of having to work out complex wage increases. Logically, then, base-wage increases have become the issue most central in practically all Japanese labor disputes.

Yet the base-wage system had definite disadvantages for labor. First, struggles for increases in base wages in effect resulted in the shelving of the minimum-wage issue and thus forced labor more or less to abandon its demand for a wage scale that would guarantee minimum subsistence. Struggles for increases uniformly applied to all enterprises regardless of size or kind unavoidably resulted in growing divergencies among the wage levels of large and small enterprises. This development had the effect, in turn, of creating discontent and discord among the unions, especially involving the national trade-union centers to which they respectively belonged, and seriously threatened unity within individual unions, at great cost to solidarity, strength, and morale. For instance, in an enterprise union organized on a basis that included linemen, foremen, white-collar workers, upper-class workers, petty intellectuals, and many of those in managerial positions, a natural outcome was arguments among them concerning larger portions of wage settlements. Widening differences in wage levels among the union members themselves created an ideal opportunity for management to restore job-classification systems and cost the unions the loss of numerous able officials and petty intellectuals who were important agents of leadership. Summarily considered, the Dodge Plan, increasing pressure from the Association of Japanese Employers *(Nikkeiren),* and, in 1947, an action known as 'the Red Purge' that rooted Communists and militant left-wing leaders out of the labor movement had altogether such telling effects that the movement was depressed throughout Japan, and the unions floundered.

In 1952, as a counter-measure to these effects, Sōhyō worked out a plan popularly known as 'the Market-Basket' wage plan, the aim of which was twofold: 1) to mitigate the damage of the base-wage increase system, also known as the BE-A or 'base-up' system, and 2) to expand the labor struggle to include the housewives of strike-bound union members. More directly exposed to the cost-of-living issue than their husbands, the housewives had an especially exploitable sensitivity for labor and political purposes. Yet even this effort failed to eradicate the problems involved in the inflexible principles of the base-up system.

Then, in 1954, Nikkeiren initiated a movement for adoption of a plan of long-term wage agreement accompanied by regular increments. Although many unions subscribed to the plan, Sōhyō opposed it on the grounds that it tends to freeze wages at subsistence level. According to the latest report of the Ministry of Labor, published in June 1967, the average monthly wage scale in a plant employing five hundred or more workers is ¥48,000, that in a plant with one hundred to five hundred workers ¥42,441, and that in a plant with one hundred to thirty workers ¥39,525. However, the scale drops sharply as the size of the enterprise grows smaller, and small enterprises constitute the major part of Japanese industry. For

[215]

this reason, the low wage scales will continue to foment labor unrest in the nation.

The militant nature of the terminology that Japanese unions use to describe their activities is peculiar to the Japanese labor movement. One term constantly used is 'struggle', which in the labor context has many different meanings. Stated simply, it chiefly denotes collective bargaining and other grievance procedures that may or may not involve strikes. A struggle itself goes on in two major areas: one is economic, involving traditional wage, benefit, and job-security issues, safety regulations, working hours, automation, and the like; the other is purely political—ideologically motivated and politically projected. More often than not, labor struggles in Japan mix the two and thus make analysis of central issues difficult.

The most commonly used term is 'BE-A struggle', in which BE-A' stands for 'base-up,' or base-wage increases. Inasmuch as the wage structure in Japan is built on the concept of the base-wage system discussed earlier, any activities designed to bargain with the management for wage increases is called a 'BE-A struggle'. It is thus the basic form of struggle in the Japanese labor movement.

In 1952, for tactical as well as ideo-political purposes, Sōhyō under Minoru Takano formulated a new type of struggle called *Gurumi.* Japan was then undergoing a severe strain of political and economic ferment resulting from the cold-war tensions localized in the hot Korean War. Having turned from 'chicken to duck' and become a militant vanguard in the struggle against 'imperialism' and 'monopoly capitalism', Sōhyō adopted the *gurumi* struggle as a tactical means of attaining its political objectives. As a matter of fact, the *gurumi*-concept had its origin in the principle of the 'People's Struggle' that emanated from Peking. Specifically meaning 'to include' or 'inclusive of', *gurumi* can best be translated as 'constituent-wide'. Thus calling for constituent-wide participation, the plan involved two aspects. One was expansion beyond the scope of individual enterprise unions, a goal that required ways and means of overcoming the serious limitations of the enterprise-union system. The other was an economic program sufficiently attractive to engage that portion of the public not directly connected with union activities.

As implementation, the planners conceived of a three-stage development. The first was the organization of the families, principally the wives, of strike-bound union members, as a means of eliciting whose support as a dependable auxiliary Sōhyō worked out the Market-Basket plan mentioned earlier. Naturally attractive to housewives, it was based on a flexible principle that called for an equilibrium between market prices and the housewives' need to fill their grocery baskets. Then, with organized families as operational bases, the second stage was to be the organization of community-wide areas, and the third the organization of regional areas. Full success in the *gurumi* venture would have effectively eliminated the weaknesses inherent in the enterprise-union system. Although the mine workers' unions made impressive headway with it, their success was local and limited. All in all, Sōhyō's attempt thus to broaden labor's struggle beyond the realms of individual enterprise unions failed.

Organizationally, the Japanese labor movement as based on the concept of the enterprise union has developed in two broad directions. Horizontally the unions have grouped themselves into regional or prefectural federations while vertically they have grouped themselves into national industrial associations that are in turn joined together to form national trade-union centers such as Sōhyō or Dōmei. Since, whether regional or national, such alliances are leagues of independent unions, the structure itself has serious endemic weaknesses, particularly pronounced in finance. The only two sources of necessary operational funds a national trade-union center so organized has are dues payments and general fund-raising campaigns, chiefly the latter. But the responses of the enterprise unions have been so poor that, by and large, Sōhyō has been compelled to program its struggles without the backing of adequate funds.

The *gurumi* struggle was staged under such circumstances. Lacking adequate funds and still burdened by the strong influence of feudalistic traditionalism, the participating unions and their women auxiliary organizations found themselves unable to carry the burden to its ultimate end. In many cases, separate struggles were supported by loans arranged on an interunion basis, but such financing resulted only in disputes that brought about splits and desertions of individual unions from regional and national organizations.

There are several other kinds of Japanese labor struggle that have different names. *Shuntō* ('the Spring Struggle') is one of the most common, but there are also those called *sukejūru rōsō* ('the Schedule Struggle') and *sangyō-betsu rōsō* ('the Industry-wide Struggle'). The major focus for all unions in the world is, of course, the struggle for wage increases, which follows either biennial or annual cycles, depending upon the fiscal system of a given firm or nation. In modern Japan, particularly since 1953 when Nikkeiren began to agitate with increasing pressure for adoption of its suggested system of long-term wage agreements, the negotiations involving wage increases have been conducted shortly before the end of each fiscal year in coincidence with the Spring season. Moreover, public enterprise unions like the National Railway Workers Union have found it tactically advantageous to press for increases through collective bargaining during the budgetary sessions of the Diet, which are held each spring just before the end of the governmental fiscal year. Accordingly, the *shuntō* plan, adopted by Sōhyō in 1954, derives its name from the custom of conducting struggles for wage increases during the Spring season.

Circumstances surrounding the origin of *Shuntō* suggest deeper motivations than a mere tactical shift in Sōhyō's pattern of struggle. Mainly the work of Kaoru Ota, who succeeded Minoru Takano as chief of Sōhyō, the plan was recommended at a time when the *gurumi* system with all its ideo-political implications, and perhaps because of them, was reaching an impasse. At any rate, there is

[218]

strong evidence that the authors of the *shuntō* plan made a conscious effort to avoid ideo-political implication by placing primary emphasis on wage increases. In effect, the plan was an open repudiation of the leadership of Minoru Takano and his policy of left-wing political radicalism oriented towards the Communist bloc, especially Communist China, and reflected a serious internal dispute between factions led by pro-Chinese Takano on the one hand and Soviet-oriented Ota on the other. But even more profound in meaning was the concomitant revelation of the disinterest of the general membership of the unions under Sōhyō with respect to ideo-political matters, for it forced the leadership to revert to traditional emphasis on the economic aspects of unionism. The basic dilemma of Sōhyō must be sought in this area. Time and again its leadership has departed from traditional economic concerns for militant ideo-political radicalism, and time and again the general attitude of its members has forced a reversion to those basic economic concerns, as the cases of both Minoru Takano and Kaoru Ota illustrate. In short, the dilemma basic to Sōhyō, the largest national trade-union center in Japan, is the paradox of two basically incompatible elements—an ideo-politically motivated leadership and a general membership that lacks the class-consciousness requisite to any interest in ideo-political problems.

To be sure, from labor's point of view, the *shuntō* plan has had significant merits. As a procedure of collective bargaining, it has been by far the most effective method yet devised in Japan of strengthening labor's position *vis à vis* management. Whether locally or regionally federated for a struggle, Japanese labor has characteristically long been unable to mount a common offensive with collective pressure because of the independent fragmentation of the enterprise-union system. The *shuntō* plan was labor's answer to this situation, as it was especially formulated for the purpose of plugging the structural loophole in the system. Through this plan the Sōhyō leadership hoped to utilize the existing vertical organization that combines the unions of the same trade or industry into national industrial federations that in turn form a national trade-union center. The plan envisaged the creation of a joint struggle conference with those national industrial federations *(tansan)* as the components. If successfully realized, the plan would shift the burden of the pressure building operation from individual enterprise unions to the national body—specifically, to a joint-struggle conference, whose participants would each year by a sort of selective-service system choose an especially heavyweight *tansan* to lead the struggle for an optimum rate of wage increases. Thus won, that optimum rate could then be used by other unions in their disputes. In other words, the basic dual purpose of the *shuntō* plan was, first, the organization of separate unions into one affiliated, key struggle and, second, the establishment of an optimum 'base-up' to facilitate and support individual unions in their bargaining.

According to this plan a joint-struggle conference with five major *tansan* was organized in the Fall of 1954 and augmented by three more major *tansan* in early 1955. The unions began to support the plan, and the Spring labor offensive became widely accepted. In the joint-struggle conference of that first year the eight major *tansan* represented the enterprise unions respectively affiliated with them. By early 1956 the National Council of Public Enterprise Workers Unions joined the conference. Since this development, almost all the major *tansan* in Japan participate in the joint-struggle conference, and it has become a formidable power capable of mounting serious offensives. Public enterprise unions that once scheduled their labor campaigns in the fall have now moved their schedules up to the Spring in order to coordinate their efforts with the private enterprise unions. Largely, although not completely, the *shuntō* plan has succeeded in organizing in Japan an impressive common labor front for meeting the impact of annual confrontations with management, and it is no longer necessary for individual enterprise unions to negotiate from an inferior position.

To exert maximum pressure against management with optimum results, the planners of *Shuntō* adopted several distinctive tactics.

For one thing they based their wage concept on the principle of 'a little more' that Samuel Gompers, the pioneer American labor leader, advocated, although Sōhyō prefers to call it a 'uniform rise plus *alpha* ("a little more")'. For another thing, they made use of what they called 'the schedule struggle', which simply means prearranged timing for several waves of action: work slow-downs, workshop rallies, demonstrations, and other such pressure-building operations. Their term 'top-batter' simply signifies the pacemaker selectively chosen by the joint-struggle conference, as discussed before, from the ranks of those in the conference who can bargain from the best conceivable position of strength. In this way, members who must work at a slower pace are not forced out of the struggle. And, as indicated before, the rate of increase the 'top-batter' wins becomes the basis for the wage movement of the entire labor market.

Efficacious as it has been, the *shuntō* plan has its weaknesses, some endemic and others extraneous. One problem has arisen, for example, from the fact that Japanese labor law forbids public enterprise unions the right to bargain collectively and to strike. Accordingly, when the 'top-batter' of the year was once selected from the ranks of the Council of the Public Enterprise Workers Unions, its participation in *Shuntō* resulted in heavy casualties in the form of dismissals and other penalties, as well as in financial and organizational costs to the unions involved, which have long shown a tendency to be strongly ideo-politically oriented and a struggle pattern very militant—to their detriment, in the long run. Then, as *shuntō* began to change character and grew even more ideo-political, and the members of the joint-struggle conference became over-involved in political activities not really essential to effective unionism, the inevitable consequence was demoralization of the rank and file union membership, intra-union unrest, and a weakening of inter-union solidarity. Sōhyō's membership began to decline.

From about 1954, Sōhyō began to show increasing concern over a growing movement in Japan for industrial automation and rationalization which the leaders maintained indicated a deliberate design to reduce manpower. On that premise, Sōhyō staked out an absolute opposition to these measures of modernization. It is true that there have been cases involving several major Japanese industries in which rationalization has caused mass relocation of workers or actual dismissals where a considerable number of plants and mines have been closed down. But, by and large, automation and rationalization have not resulted in industrial contraction and mass unemployment in Japan. Quite the contrary: reinforced by carefully planned capital investments, Japanese industry has progressively strengthened its viability through automation and rationalization. The general consequence has been healthy and constructive in that the mass of medium and small enterprises, which are essentially sub-contractors to larger industries, have found themselves in improved economic conditions. The upshot has been a rapid rise in the employment rate, so that there now exists an acute shortage of manpower. While this phenomenon would appear to negate the logic of doing so, the leaders of Sōhyō find themselves in the embarrassing position of having to continue their policy of opposition to automation and rationalization.

The labor movement and politics

No labor movement can be completely apolitical. As an important socio-economic organization occupying an extremely important place in a nation's economy, it cannot but be expected to play a commensurately significant role in the nation's politics. In this respect, Japan is no exception. All four Japanese trade-union centers have been, and are, active in politics. The Democratic Socialist Party (DSP) has been consistently supported by Dōmei, and the Japan Socialist Party (JSP) has been consistently supported by Sōhyō, as well as by the grass-roots members of the labor movement. Having been rather normal, the political activities of the national trade-union centers therefore present little need for detailed analysis. Yet the special character of Sōhyō's relations with the JSP deserves close examination, for the ideo-political character of this party may well illuminate some of the reasons underlying the political behavior of Sōhyō.

The JSP is, of course, a class party. When it was first formed in November 1945, its membership was made up of both rightwing and left-wing socialists, thus embodying from the outset an essential incompatibility that continued to trouble the party polemically until its final split in 1959. As a matter of fact, the party has undergone two schisms since its original organization. The first occurred in October 1951 on the issue of the San Francisco Peace Treaty and the United States-Japan Mutual Security Agreement, both of which the left-wing members rejected, but which the right-wing members accepted as a *modus vivendi*. Although in 1955 political pressures reunited the two opposing factions, the merger was short-lived, for again in 1960 over the issue of the revision of the United States-Japan Security Agreement the two factions collided violently and then broke in a final schism. Led by Hiroo Nishio, who was expelled from the JSP, the right wing moved to form the DSP in January 1960, while the JSP, under the leadership of Inejiro Asanuma, increasingly inclined towards Communist China, an inclination that culminated in the issuing of a famous joint communiqué from Peking that called the United States the common enemy of the peoples of Japan and China.

At any rate, since its own formation in 1950, Sōhyō has maintained intimate relations with the JSP, especially in the struggle for common political goals. Sōhyō leaders have held seats in the party's Central Executive Committee and have frequently sat in party councils where important policies were discussed and decided. Differences between the two organizations were only to be expected, of course, but those that occurred were more tactical than strategic. Most significant is the fact that the two organizations have long stood ideologically together with only fluctuating variations of attitude.

At its annual convention in 1951, taking an irretraceable step, Sōhyō rejected the San Francisco Peace Treaty and condemned the

Mutual Security Agreement. At the same time, it adopted a resolution containing four basic principles concerning war and peace that have served as its basic guiding political line ever since. The resolution called for 1) a universal peace treaty, 2) a policy of neutrality, 3) opposition to foreign military bases in Japan, and 4) opposition to rearmament. Although on the surface the resolution suggested nothing ulterior, it should be remembered that the world was under severe strain at the time because of tension between the United States and the Soviet Union. The Korean War was raging with all its ramifications, and the Red Star dominated China. Since Sōhyō's demand for universal peace was to include the Soviet Union and Communist China, its opposition to foreign military bases and rearmament was clearly directed only against American defense establishments in the Far East. Then, openly branding the United States an imperialist, Sōhyō simply nullified its policy of neutrality.

Against this background, there are two theories concerning the nature of the labor struggles that Sōhyō sponsors. One school of thought contends that the political components of the struggles are no more than trimming for concealment of their real nature, which is basically and merely labor's campaign for wage increases. Another school argues, however, that the wage-increase demand merely sugar-coats the ideo-political objectives that are the genuine goals of such struggles. The case requires careful examination. Meanwhile, it must be said that the left-wing political radicalism that one segment of labor has followed despite the heavy price it has had to pay for it in loss of membership gives weight to the second view.

The Japanese labor movement has made great strides, thanks— and rightfully—to the labor leaders of the nation. Their efforts to overcome the serious limitations that the enterprise-union system has imposed on the Japanese labor movement should receive proper recognition. Yet there are still several problems that require solution. One is the strong influence of traditional Japanese paternalism that continues to play a role in the attitudes of the Japanese labor force. In a nation as highly industrialized as Japan, this phenomenon will change, as it has changed and must change, but the change has so far been too slow. Another problem is the fact that labor has made very tardy progress in organizing the immense labor force engaged in the small and medium enterprises that are virtually unique in Japan; certainly this force has been extremely important in the development of Japanese industry to a position of third rank in the world. Another problem is that the large scale reorganization Japanese industry has been undergoing demands that labor, too, come forward with new concepts and plans to meet changing situations. Indeed, labor's responsibility here is profound. Since it occupies such an important place in the socio-economics of the nation, it should have an equivalent place in the politics of the nation. But undue energy directed towards ideo-political issues at the expense of traditional unionism does not serve the proper interests of Japanese labor, and the fact that the morale of a large segment of the union members has been thus affected during recent years must be viewed with serious concern.

These are only a few observations touching upon the problems inherent in the Japanese labor movement. The improvement of working conditions and the steady progress of the movement as a whole while the labor force itself expands in this highly industrialized society will depend largely on the success or failure of Japanese labor leaders in solving such basic problems.

Enterprise unionism and wage increases

BY MAKOTO SAKURABAYASHI

Enterprise unionism—enterprise unionism and management— enterprise unionism and interfirm wage differentials— enterprise unionism and the wage level

THE largest labor union movement in non-Communist Asia is to be found in postwar Japan. Immediately after the war, the rapid development of trade unionism was the result, on the one hand, of the American Occupation policy of encouraging voluntary unionism as an integral part of the demilitarization program and, on the other hand, of galloping inflation that was wiping out all cash income. After 1948, however, when inflation was brought under control by the Dodge Plan, the atmosphere turned less favorable for the unions: the 'Red Purge' laid off a great number of Communist labor leaders, and recently enacted labor legislation was revised in order to limit organized labor's excesses. Between 1945 and 1949, the rate of labor organization increased in Japan from 0 to 56% of the salaried labor force, bringing the number of unionized workers to 6.7 million, more than fifteen times the prewar maximum. Thereafter, it started to decline steadily, reaching 36% in 1968, though the absolute number of unionists now reaches more than 10 million.

Since their beginnings immediately after World War II, Japanese labor organizations have been beset by an ominous characteristic, their very structure, which is enterprise unionism. 'Enterprise unionism' does not necessarily mean, of course, management domination, but such a danger nevertheless exists, as evidenced by the collective bargaining and wage increases taking place at every level of employment in today's Japan. The present discussion will, however, be concerned only with unions in the private sector, and with the regular or permanent employees they organize.

Enterprise unionism

THE enterprise union is the key structure of Japanese trade unionism and its actual bargaining unit. It clearly distinguishes itself from any Western type of union structure. The enterprise-wide or plant-wide union structure called enterprise union *(kigyōbetsu kumiai)* is the organizational structure of 90% of all local unions in Japan and covers more than 80% of Japanese union members.[1] Such a union organizes primarily, if not exclusively, the regular employees of a firm, the members of the enterprise 'family', for whom employment from the time of school graduation to the age limit of 55 or more is a definite prospect. The essential characteristic of an enterprise union is, therefore, that its very existence depends entirely upon the survival and growth of the firm to which it is related; its primary wage function is not so much to maximize the wage income of its members as to guarantee the security of lifelong income while protecting lifelong employment. As a result, the bargaining power of an enterprise union is severely handicapped. As a general union within a firm, it embraces all the regular employees whatever their occupation and age. It is thus confronted with the

[1] *Showa 37-nen rōdō-kumiai kihon-chōsa hōkoku-sho* ('Basic Survey Report on Labor Unions 1962'), Tokyo: The Ministry of Labor, 1963, p. 14. No such data are available after 1962.

ever-present danger of conflict of interests among different ingroups. Strikes are limited to, at most, a few days so as not to jeopardize a company's position in its competitive markets and to avoid the formation of a 'second union' *(daini kumiai)*, a rival union within the same firm, which might oppose a strike.

Enterprise unionism prevents occupation-wide bargaining. It cannot set uniform time rates or piece rates for all firms so as 'to take labor out of competition'. Unions in the same industry have not attempted to equalize unit labor costs. If only one enterprise is struck or concedes its union's demand for higher wages, it may lose customers to competitors. The union's gain will cause a disadvantage affecting both unionized and non-unionized competitors. Because its bargaining is limited to a company-wide or plant-wide basis, the union cannot realistically hope to standardize wage increases throughout a whole industry or a whole occupation; nevertheless, external factors such as the overall Japanese labor shortage, the increase in consumers' prices, the increase in the value productivity of labor, and, most importantly, the so-called Spring Wage Offensive, to some extent conterbalance that handicap.

Finally, even in giant corporations, where an enterprise union may count several thousands of members, the advantages of large-scale organization are missing. It is a fact that operating finances are insufficient and that strike funds are often non-existent.[2] Professional union leaders and specialists are hard to come by, and union officers are neither assisted by a competent staff nor economically or psychologically independent of their employers. Like other employees, they remain bound by their lifelong employment and fear to be displaced or discriminated against by an employer after their return to work. This fact also explains why outside pro-

---

[2] According to the *Asahi Shimbun*, August 6, 1966, the National Railway Locomotive Engineers' Union *(Dōryokusha)* with 60,000 union members decided to collect ¥2,500 per member for the Wage Offensive of 1966, but the total amount collected was only half of the ¥300 million required to cover part of the living costs of those discharged by the Japanese National Railway Corporation as punishment for work stoppage.

fessional leadership and assistance are frowned upon by the union officers themselves.

The upshot is that the procedures by which wages are bargained for are highly decentralized, involving tens of thousands of individual enterprise unions and their firms, for no industrial federation participates in negotiations involving important companies and therefore no pattern emerges for others to follow. What is meant by collective bargaining *(dantai kōshō)* in Japan is substantially different from what is meant in the West. It is not a process by which unions deal with employers in order to arrive at and administer agreements governing terms of employment. In Japan, such is the purpose of the employment regulations *(shūgyō kisoku)*, though there may be some distinct agreement on wages and seasonal allowances. What is called the collective agreement *(dantai kyōyaku)* amounts essentially to a ratification of a union's legal rights and a declaration of an intention to establish friendly union-management relations. It has practically no provision establishing the ways of interpreting an agreement or of solving the problems that will arise under it.

Enterprise unionism and management

KEEPING in mind that the majority of large Japanese firms are unionized, whereas small firms are not (Figure 1), most employers give in to a union's demands for higher wages, despite its very limited power to bargain and strike. In recent years, the ability of large as well as small Japanese firms to pay has increased rapidly because of the increased value productivity of labor. (Figure 2) Yet, for its part, Japanese management is not fully motivated by profit maximization. It is more concerned about the 'harmony' *(wa)* within a firm, requiring 'fair' treatment of the individual worker and his lifelong commitment with the firm, as well as 'fairness' in the relative treatment of all employees. In the Japanese context, therefore, management is not concerned with substituting

[230]

Chapter ten: Enterprise unionism and wage increases

FIGURE I

ESTIMATED RATE OF UNIONIZATION, BY SIZE OF FIRM
(1966)

Size of firm	All industries	Manufacturing industry
Total	27.7%	37.3%
500 and more	64.0	78.7
100–499	31.6	35.8
30– 99	9.6	11.4
Less than 30	3.8	2.1

Source: *Rōdō Hakusho 1966* ('Labor White Paper'), Tokyo: The Ministry of Labor, 1967, p. 205

FIGURE 2

ANNUAL RATE OF INCREASE OF GROSS ADDED VALUE PRODUCTIVITY OF LABOR AND LABOR COST, PER EMPLOYEE, PER MONTH, IN MANUFACTURING
(1961 and 1965)

Size of firm by number of employees	Gross added value productivity of labor per employee, per month				(thousand) Labor cost per employee, per month			
	1961 (A)	1965 (B)	B–A	$\left(\dfrac{B-A}{A}\right)$	1961	1965	B–A	$\left(\dfrac{B-A}{A}\right)$
50– 99	¥45.0	¥67.8	¥22.8	(50.7%)	¥25.2	¥41.2	¥16.0	(63.5%)
100–199	48.7	74.8	26.1	(53.6%)	25.6	43.6	18.0	(74.2%)
200–299	55.7	77.3	21.6	(38.8%)	28.3	43.9	15.6	(55.1%)
300–499	61.7	88.0	26.3	(42.6%)	30.2	47.1	16.9	(56.0%)
500–999	74.0	100.7	26.7	(36.1%)	34.1	51.9	17.8	(52.2%)
1,000 & more	108.5	149.4	40.9	(37.7%)	43.7	64.1	20.4	(46.7%)

Sources: *Kibobetsu Kigyō Keiei Bunseki—1961 nendo* ('Analysis of Enterprise Management by Size of Firm'), Tokyo: The Bank of Japan, 1962, pp. 18–19; *Kibobetsu Kigyō Keiei Bunseki—1965 nendo* ('Analysis of Enterprise Management by Size of Firm'), Tokyo: The Bank of Japan, 1966, pp. 18–19.

lower-paid temporary employees for higher-paid regular employees unless the firm's survival and growth are threatened. In view of the rapid growth of the economy and intensified international competition, employers fear the loss of industrial harmony within their

[231]

firms that could result from work stoppages. This loss would be
not only financial, but also 'psychological'. For example, not the
least consideration is the fear of damaging their credit position with
the banks, particularly in view of the well-known fact that the debt-
equity ratio of large firms is extremely low.

FIGURE 3

PERCENTAGE OF SHORTAGE OF NEW MIDDLE-
AND HIGH-SCHOOL GRADUATES, BY SIZE OF FIRM
(1965)

Size of firm	Percentage
Average	21.7%
500 and more	10.3
200–499	17.9
100–199	25.9
15– 99	33.6

Source: *Rōdō Hakusho, 1966* ('Labor White Paper'), Tokyo: The Ministry of Labor,
1967, p. 240.

In Japan, both large and small employers are closely watching
one another and both are under strong pressure to raise wages.
They confront one another in a labor market where the demand for
professional specialists and young employees far exceeds the
supply, forcing them to pay precipitate attention to starting wages.
Between 1961 and 1965, the rate of wage increase in the badly unionized smaller firms was higher than that in the highly unionized
larger firms because the badly unionized smaller firms had a higher
rate of increase in labor productivity and, at the same time, keener
labor shortages. The gross added value productivity and labor cost
per employee increased by 151% and 164% respectively in small
firms, but only by 138% and 147% in large firms. (Figure 2) But
in 1965, the percentage of shortage of middle-school and high-school
graduates in small firms with 15–99 employees was three times
that in large firms with 500 and more employees. (Figure 3) This
remarkable difference is due mainly to lower wage levels in small
firms, as well as to other inferior factors, such as working hours, condi-

tions, opportunity for vocational training, and employment stability.

Enterprise unionism and interfirm wage differentials

BECAUSE of their lack of control over the labor market, enterprise unions cannot set standard wage rates throughout a whole occupation or industry so that every employee with the same job receives a similar minimum rate. Also, they have little effect upon reducing interfirm wage differentials in the same industry or occupation, but, as a matter of fact, perpetuate the wage gaps normally resulting from interfirm differentials in labor productivity. In 1965, the monthly gross value of added labor productivity in small manufacturing firms (¥67,000) was less than half that in large firms with 1,000 and more employees (¥149,000), and the average monthly labor cost per employee (¥41,000) was two-thirds that of large firms (¥64,000). (Figure 2)

Consequently, any attempt at equalizing interfirm wage differentials by labor mobility in Japan seems doomed to be slowed down by differentials in technological levels and management organization. The fact is that immobility perpetuates the conformity of employees with both their enterprises and their enterprise unions. In large firms employees hired upon graduation from school are trained in order to fit into particular technical setups and managerial organizations and thus meet the skill requirements of imported or ever advancing technology. By contrast, in small firms employees are taught necessary skills by informal on-the-job training given by senior workers: the ideal is to enable everybody to handle any job or piece of machinery available in the shop upon any kind of request or order.[3]

---

[3] In 1965, 30% of the firms surveyed had some sort of apprenticeship system for high-school graduates. The ratio varied widely according to size of firm: firms with 1,000 and more employees, 38%; firms with 500–999 employees, 25% firms with 100–499 employees, 18%. (R.J. Ballon, M. Sakurabayashi, and I. Tsunekawa, *Wage Survey of Male Blue-Collar Workers,* Tokyo: Sophia University Socio-Economic Institute, Industrial Relations Section, Bulletin No. 14, 1967, p. 11.).

Japanese hiring practices are themselves discriminatory. Usually only fresh graduates are hired as candidates for regular employment, whereas workers with former experience are hired only as temporary or lower-paid regular workers. In 1965 the ratio of new graduates to the total number of newly hired regular employees in Japan was 58.9% in firms with five hundred and more regular employees, but only 22.5% in small firms with thirty to ninety-nine regular workers.[4] Large-plant employees, hired upon school graduation, remain tied to their companies until the mandatory retirement age and show no interest in supplementary labor-market information unless discharged as a result of company reorganization or extraordinary disciplinary action. Big firms are few and powerful; small firms are numerous and weak. At any rate, the brunt of the population pressure and its concomitant of employment instability has been largely borne by these small enterprises. It is little wonder therefore that enterprise unions in small firms are much more handicapped not only by low organization rate and employer's resistance (due mainly to pressures of strong wage costs in non-unionized competing firms), but also by a lack of trained union leaders and of effective support from national labor organizations. The smaller the union, the more unstable an organization it is.

Given the absence of industry-wide bargaining in Japan, interfirm differentials in bargaining ability are considerable. Bargaining ability is usually greater in large firms and large unions than in small firms and small unions. Since large firms have a policy of hiring the cream of new graduates, both they and their related unions benefit from better inherent qualities and the better education of their employees. They have better corporate staffs, and their unions can elect more skilled union leaders from among the better-trained employees of the firm. As a result, both sides in large firms

---

[4] See *Rōdō Hakusho, 1966* ('Labor White Paper'), Tokyo: The Ministry of Labor, 1967, p. 90.

are more capable of passing proper judgment on overall market situations and more skilled at negotiation. Thus, the ability to score advantages at the bargaining table, which rests a great deal on the knowledge and experience of each bargainer and on mutual trust, is far greater in larger firms and their larger unions.

It must also be stated that the effect of enterprise unions upon their firms, as compared to conditions in a non-union situation, is not so much that of the so-called 'economy of high wages' or the 'shock effect of high wages' as it is of improvements in personnel administration, such as more careful policies of recruitment and transfer, more thoughtful systematization of personnel administration itself and a concomitant increase in professionalization of the personnel department, and more explicit attention being given by top management to personnel policies in general.

Enterprise unionism and the nation-wide wage level

I T has already been pointed out that, in order to allow their related enterprises to survive and grow in exchange, as it were, for the security of lifelong employment, Japanese unions, precisely because they are enterprise unions, are forced to hold the frequency and duration of their strikes to a minimum.[5] Consequently, wage increases in Japan are a matter of much less concern at the enterprise level than at the national level. Japanese organized labor aims at raising the national wage level, and for that purpose has devised a tactic repeated annually, every Spring, called the "Spring Wage Offensive" (*Shunki Chin-age Kyōdō Bōsō*, abbreviated to *Shuntō*). It strengthens and complements the weak bargaining power of enterprise unions and their greatly limited power of striking. *Sōhyō* ('General Council of Trade Unions of Japan'), the largest national labor center in Japan, is the moving spirit of this action,

[5] See *Shōwa 40-nen Rōdō-sōgi Tōkei Chōsa Hōkoku-sho* ('Statistical Survey Report on Labor Disputes 1965'), Tokyo: The Ministry of Labor, 1966, p. 37.

which in 1965 streamlined 66% of all strikes for wage increases.[6] *Shuntō* provides its affiliated leaders with the means of informing the nation at large, including both management and the rank and file of organized labor, that wages should be increased *(base-up)*, thus voicing a general need resulting from the annual increase in the Japanese cost of living. It also helps promote a psychological climate that practically forces all unions to join in the so-called 'scheduled struggle' *(sukejūru tōsō)*. This is a labor-dispute tactic which was outlined for the first time in November 1955 in an 'Action Schedule' *(kōdō hōshin)* promulgated by the new Sōhyō leadership and which became the accepted pattern of *shuntō* from 1961 on, when rising prices and a labor shortage started to manifest themselves as results of the nation's rapid economic growth. It consists essentially of two phases: in the first phase, unions participating in the coming *shuntō* announce well in advance a schedule of strikes simultaneously with their demands for the wage increase agreed upon as the objective of the nation-wide offensive; in the second phase, some short-duration strikes are staged, whatever the employer's concessions may be.

Notwithstanding the desire of the *shuntō* leaders to develop thereby a wider labor solidarity expressed by industry-wide unionism, the offensive in fact perpetuates enterprise unionism. On the one hand, by offering the maximum concession proposed by *Nikkeiren* (Japan Federation of Employers' Associations) or by the industrywide employers federation, *plus* some additions of its own, management fosters the enterprise-consciousness of the employees and thus reduces labor problems. On the other hand, by insisting upon the unified wage demand heralded by the *shuntō* leaders or their industrywide federation, *minus* some amount conceded by the enterprise union or agreed upon after some 'sweetheart' negotiations with management, the union fosters conformity with the enterprise as well as its union. At the final settlement, employer and

---

6 See *Rōdō Hakusho 1966, op. cit.*, p. 307.

employees' representatives strike a delicate face-saving balance of wage increase by combining two distinct increases:

1 the annual wage progression *(teiki shōkyū)* based on
   a the enterprise salary tables embodying the *nenkō* system (education and length of service),
   b employer's appraisal of each regular employee;
2 a certain percentage increase called *base-up* agreed upon through collective bargaining.[7]

In 1966, for example, the Japan-wide increase averaged 12%, comprising 7% *base-up* and 5% annual wage progression.[8]

Japanese social behavior contributes greatly to this situation. It amounts to balancing the dichotomy between, on the one hand, external behavior *(furumai)*, whereby one 'follows the leader' or 'keeps pace' *(tsukiai)* for the purpose of saving face, and, on the other hand, one's real intentions *(honne)*. In practice, this means that the excessive wage demand propounded by the *shuntō* leaders is rarely criticized by the participating unions; and the too low initial wage proposal advanced by Nikkeiren is neither criticized nor followed by its member companies, which will, after all, settle for a wage offer above what Nikkeiren considers 'feasible'. Neither side will feel defeated, but will claim victory, when, say, only half of labor's initial demand is granted.

As a matter of fact, enterprise-union officers and members are more concerned about their own lifelong employment security and promotion than about wage maximization. To wit, the *base-up* copes with the increase in consumer prices (about 7% in 1966), but does not, for example, take proper advantage of the general increase in starting wages *(shonin kyū)* that in 1966 increased by 13 and 14% respectively for male and female middle-school graduates and by

---

[7] See *Wage Survey of Male Blue-Collar Workers, op. cit.,* p. 7.

[8] Noboru Furukawa, *1967 Nendo Ban Jinkenhi o Chūshintoshita Chingin Kentō Shiryō,* ('Labor-Cost Oriented Wage Data,' 1967 Edition), Tokyo: Nihon Hōrei Yōshiki Publishing Co., 1967, pp. 134, 143, 223.

16 and 17% for high-school graduates.[9] Furthermore, despite the pressure on the wage level generated by the annual 'offensives', the fact remains that, between 1961 and 1965, the increase in the monthly labor cost per employee in manufacturing firms with 1,000 and more employees was ¥20,400, whereas gross value of added labor productivity per employee increased twice as much, or by ¥40,900. (Figure 2)

The built-in pattern of a typical unionized enterprise's wage increase is determined by the union's allowing a high productivity of labor, which secures employment by the enterprise, and obtaining only a moderate share of the enterprise's better performance. It is little wonder therefore that industrial federations, particularly in the chemical, oil, steel, auto, electrical, and other technologically advanced industries, are frequently threatened by withdrawal on the part of their affiliated enterprise unions. In these large enterprises, unions gradually strengthen union autonomy by organizing the workers in subcontracting firms, to the detriment of a strengthening of the industrial federations.

Let it be said that the Spring Wage Offensive has also political and ideological implications. In the absence of industrial unionism, the bargaining power of the enterprise unions is so weak that it needs political and legislative support. Moreover, industrial federations and their leaders have to justify their existence. Ideological rivalry is rife among them and is heightened by the rivalry among the political parties (Japan Socialist Party, Japan Democratic-Socialist Party, and Japan Communist Party) they belong to. Prevented by an enterprise and its union from participating in the collective bargaining process, the labor leaders of industrial federations and of the national centers turn to nation-wide objectives that necessarily become political and ideological. In this connection, it seems that some international labor organizations, especially the

---

[9] *Rōdō Mondai no Shōri* ('Guide to Labor Problems'), Tokyo: The Ministry of Labor, 1967, p. 80.

Chapter ten: Enterprise unionism and wage increases

International Metal Federation, Japanese Conference (IMF-JC), are destined to an important role in the annual *shuntō*; they might focus the attention of labor leaders not tied down by an enterprise union on the need to consider properly the industry-wide economics of collective bargaining. Such a development is greatly helped by the growing pressure and awareness of international competition in Japan's industrial world.

There is a tendency to assume that Japanese labor unions are changing their outlook on enterprise unionism. The data presented here do not, however, encourage such a view. The Japanese economic situation, like any other, is changing, but the human relations in Japanese industry as found in labor unions and management alike seem to be its most conservative components. Japanese enterprise unionism is not about to change readily, unless the intensified influences of economic maturity, international business competition, and international labor organizations grow into vital forces challenging the built-in pattern of enterprise unionism. The primary function of Japanese unionism will continue for the time being to be the safeguarding of lifelong income security however much appearances may change. It is as yet by no means clear that the evolution of Japanese unionism, as it occurs, is moving toward the Western model; it may rather move toward a mixture of, on the one hand, enterprise unionism modified by multi-employer bargaining, at least for groups of large firms of similar size, and, on the other hand, expanded enterprise union autonomy by which the unions of large enterprises would control the unions in related subcontracting firms.

CHAPTER ELEVEN

Labor disputes
and
their settlement

BY TADASHI HANAMI

Settlement of industrial disputes—nation-wide dimensions of labor disputes

I N Western countries union organizations are not characteristically limited to one enterprise, but cover an industry or a craft and therefore are not especially close to the workshop. Some lower union officers may be close to actual work situations, but such negotiations as they engage in do not include formal bargaining. Representatives of employees at the workshop level are not necessarily union officers and, indeed, like some shop stewards in Great Britain, may not even be formally recognized by the unions. Any strike they might call is considered a 'wild-cat' or 'unauthorized' strike. In Germany, representatives of employees at the workshop level are clearly separated from union organization and are prohibited from organizing or carrying out any strike action. In such countries collective bargaining and its resulting collective agreements are made on an industrial or craft basis, regionally or nationally. Disputes concerning the application or interpretation of these agreements are solved by consultation between representa-

Q   [241]

tives of management and representatives of employees. If no agreement is reached, the matter is handled through established procedures that include private arbitration or court procedures. Unlike Germany or France, the United States has no system of labor consultation, but it has developed a highly sophisticated system of channels of grievance and arbitration, so that grievances rarely become issues in American industrial disputes.

By contrast, in Japan, where unions organize and represent the employees of a specific enterprise or plant exclusively (*kigyō-betsu kumiai:* 'enterprise union'), their function is not only to conclude collective agreements *(rōdō kyōyaku),* but also, even more so, to administer them or, better, to 'express' the daily routine of the industrial relationship itself. In Japanese industrial relations, therefore, a dispute can be industrial in the sense that it is a conflict between union and employer, but it can also be individual. Formal grievance procedures are uncommon. By the very nature of enterprise unionism, Japanese union officers are usually in daily contact with rank-and-file employees and hear their grievances directly. Since many of those officers are the union representatives that sit at bargaining tables and, if need be, call strikes, they readily confront management representatives with individual grievances and make them an issue for bargaining, which might possibly degenerate into a dispute and a strike.

As such agreements do anywhere else in the world, Japanese collective labor agreements need interpretation in their daily relevance. It must be emphasized, however, that Japanese agreements are couched in abstract and general terms open to widely divergent interpretations. The reason for this ambiguity goes back to the Japanese sociological context of any contractual relationship. It is deeply felt that the contract need not be specific and exact; its terms are not too important. Rather than depending on the written word, the parties rely on their relationship itself, the circumstances that brought them together, the background against which their relationship has evolved, the human *rapport* established between them.

Chapter eleven: Labor disputes and their settlement

It is this harmony *(wa)* that counts; the contract is a mere formality! It is expected that problems and difficulties will arise, but it is not the written word that will solve them, however specific it may be; the solution, if it is to be found at all, is to be found in the presupposed harmonious relationship.

At the enterprise level, the relationship between employees and management is not different; it implies 'harmony' as a precondition of the daily routine. The gist of the so-called collective agreement is, therefore, a mere declaration of principles: the friendly relationship between labor and management, the recognition of the union's rights, and other general provisions already found in governmental labor legislation. The problems arising out of the interpretation and implementation of these general principles must be solved by mutual understanding within the familial atmosphere of the enterprise. When this fails, the parties are faced with a 'dispute'.

Settlement of industrial disputes

As applicable to disputes arising in industrial relations, private arbitration and grievance procedures are remarkably underdeveloped in Japan, for reasons that are rather complex. The most important one is the characteristic way disputes are settled in Japanese society in general and the special nature of Japanese industrial relations.

Briefly speaking, the Japanese way of settling disputes is amicable, consisting primarily of a 'soothing' of the existing dissatisfaction. Japanese social relations are still more or less hierarchical and 'harmonious', especially among small social groups; in principle a dispute is not expected to arise here, since it disturbs the harmonious relationship. If it does arise, however, it should be solved by mutual understanding; it will not be solved in a 'rational' way, by negotiations appealing to an objective standard, but in an 'irrational' way by appealing to the emotions of the disputants. If, however,

[243]

the dispute is not solved by the disputants themselves, it will usually be solved by some go-between. Again, his role does not consist in solving the dispute by any universal standard; his task is persuasion by appealing to the emotions of the disputants. The go-between is usually a man of prestige and authority in the given society. The disputants will come to concessions not because they admit the reasonableness of the solution, but because they do not want to damage the go-between's authority and prestige. He should not lose face, for such an event would destroy the harmony of the society in which all are living. The favorite saying concerning dispute settlement in such a traditional society is: 'Let the dispute flow to the water', which means that all discrepancy should be forgotten and harmony should be re-established.

When disputes arise outside the 'harmonious' social group, for instance between different social groups, the traditional way of settlement does not work. If these groups belong, however, to a superior or wider society and thus are subject to the latter's harmonious order, the dispute can be solved in the traditional way. Otherwise, amicable behavior from both parties is not to be expected. In these cases the dispute usually takes on a bitter and protracted form, sometimes accompanied by exacerbated feelings and violence. It will be solved only when the parties recognize the disadvantage of continuing the disagreement and seek a third party with enough prestige and authority to submit to.

Industrial disputes share in this sociological context. Specifically, Japanese unions have two sides to their character: they participate in the harmony of an enterprise society, or 'family', as employees' organizations and, at the same time, come under the influence of a force outside of the enterprise, class-consciousness, which would have them look at an employer as an innate opponent and forego the common ground on which to negotiate with him.

Basically, then, in the daily routine of Japanese enterprise, disputes are not expected to arise, and individual grievances should be solved by mutual understanding. Even grievances taken up by unions are usually solved by mutual agreement between an enterprise-conscious union and management. Still, some disputes grow beyond the limits of 'harmony'; they then risk becoming long-standing and bitter conflicts accompanied by fierce utterances and violence. Their settlement can only be expected from a government institution with enough prestige and authority to persuade the parties that now stand joined in battle outside their own sphere of possible mutual understanding. This is the function of the Japanese Labor Relations commissions. Even here, however, settlement is reached in a Japanese fashion. The disputants, as elsewhere in Japanese society, prefer conciliation to mediation or arbitration, for it is closer to the traditional approach of mutual understanding.[1] Settlement by a Labor Relations commission as a third party is not reached by the application of some universal standard, but by an appeal to the sentiments of the disputants. No clear-cut decision on which of the parties is right or wrong need be pronounced. Even if a case is submitted for mediation or arbitration, a commission will try to persuade both parties. Though legally different, the three methods of dispute settlement are, therefore, substantially similar[2].

Nation-wide dimensions of labor disputes

JAPANESE labor and management have been criticized for depending too much on the Labor Relations commissions for the settlement of their disputes. Cases are brought to the commissions before all possibilities of negotiation have been exhausted. On the surface,

---

[1] The three methods are described in the Labor Relations Adjustment Law (1946), Arts. 17ff. In 1966 the commissions handled 1,621 disputes, of which 1,542 were submitted for conciliation. See *Rodoiinkai Nenpo No. 21* ('Yearbook of the Central Labor Relations Commission'), Tokyo: Churoi Jimukyoku, 1967, p. 102.

[2] The procedures of the commissions are described in 'Wage Adjustment Machinery in Japan', *Japan Labor Bulletin*, Vol. IV, No. 6, Tokyo: Japan Institute of Labor, 1965. See also Tadashi Hanami, 'Twenty Years of the Labor Relations Commission System', *Japan Labor Bulletin*, Vol. V, No. 1.

the criticism is correct. Nevertheless, it overlooks some deep-seated peculiarities of Japanese industrial relations.

Enterprise unions enjoy only a very blunted bargaining power in Japan, since they are directly hedged in by the business conditions of the particular enterprises they organize. Furthermore, as mentioned earlier, the parties cannot solve their disputes by negotiation once a certain critical stage is reached, since they are not used to discussing matters in a 'rational' way by calling on objective principles. The negotiators, officers of the union and management representatives, are not confident of being able to persuade their constituencies, union members or stockholders, of the wisdom of the arguments that bring about settlement. A commission's proposal, then, becomes the excuse for reaching a compromise that otherwise might appear unreasonable to those not directly involved in the negotiations.

Accordingly, it is quite natural in Japan that at the enterprise level considerations emerge that transcend the enterprise. At this point, the nature of industrial relations at the national level enters the stage. In Japan, only about half of the unionized workers enjoy free bargaining rights and freedom to strike. In 1966, of a total of 10,404,000 union members, 17.5% were civil-service employees who have no right to bargain or to strike; and 11.4% were employees of public corporations and national enterprises, who have only a nominal right to negotiate, for they are not allowed to strike and their disputes are handled by the Public Corporations and National Enterprises Labor Relations Commission (P.L.R.C.). The rest of organized labor, about 71% (7,393,000) in 1966, was employed in the private sector, but about 15% of them were working in public utilities where acts of dispute are subject to a special adjustment procedure of the Central Labor Relations Commission.[3] Thus, not much more than half of Japanese organized labor enjoys *de jure* complete freedom to bargain.

[3] *Rodo Kumiai Kihon Chosa* ('Basic Survey of Trade Unions'), Tokyo: The Ministry of Labor, 1966, pp. 80–81.

Chapter eleven: Labor disputes and their settlement

The labor movement has tried to compensate for its inherent weaknesses in bargaining at the enterprise level by using dispute tactics such as the scheduled strike *(sukejūru tōsō)*, pattern-setting bargaining *(sōba zukuri)*, political struggle *(senji tōsō)*, and so on. All of these tactics are part and parcel of the Annual Spring Wage Offensive *(Shuntō)* that was started in 1955, when several major industrial union federations, under the leadership of *Sōhyō*, decided on a coordinated joint wage-increase demand and coined a new Japanese word, *base-up*, meaning a general rise of the wage level. Repeated every year, the *shuntō*, after enlisting also *Chūritsurōren* (The Federation of Independent Unions), soon set a pattern for about 80% of organized labor.

In the Fall of the year preceding *shuntō* Sōhyō solicits unions to join a united demand for wage increases and forms a Joint Committee for the Spring Offensive *(Shuntō Iinkai)*. The main job of this committee is to determine a schedule of dispute tactics culminating in the Spring, at about the time when the new fiscal year starts on the first of April. It selects so-called 'top-batters' or 'pattern-setters'. These are 'strong' unions, well organized and with a fighting spirit, in industries where business conditions are good. The unions are the vanguards of the offensive. Experience has taught that such a choice must remain flexible: economic and political developments may modify the effectiveness of these unions, and in a given industry some unions are more open than others to guidance from national headquarters. In any event, once a favorable wage increase has been obtained in a particular large enterprise, a 'pattern' is set.

In most cases, such increases have been influenced by the activities of the Central Labor Relations Commission or the Public Corporations and National Enterprises Labor Relations Commission. In the last thirteen years, important pattern-setters have been *Shitetsu Rōren* (General Federation of Private Railway Workers' Unions) and *Kōrōkyō* (Public Corporations and National Enterprises Workers' Council). The Spring Offensive is predicated on the expectation that these government agencies will take a stand favora-

[247]

ble to an increase of the wage level, since work stoppages in these industries may seriously affect the daily life of the nation. Such was the development of the *shuntō* in 1957, 1958, 1961, 1963, and 1965. In 1966, however, a seeming change took place: when the Central Labor Relations Commission failed to settle a dispute between *Shitetsu Rōren* and private railway employers, the parties themselves, after a series of strikes, reached agreement. Then, in 1967 and 1968, the market price of the *shuntō* wage increase emerged from management's favorable offer in the steel industry.

By such experience it has been learned that under prosperous business conditions unions obtain a substantial increase in the wage level when they manifest their will to struggle by announcing a strike schedule and staging some short demonstration strikes. In depression years, of course, unions have to rely on the intervention of government agencies. In both cases, however, except for the pattern-setters, unions are 'free-riders' and share an increase that cannot be wholly attributed to their own pains.

Part V

FOREIGN MANAGEMENT
AND
JAPANESE EMPLOYMENT

CHAPTER TWELVE

Personnel management
in
foreign corporations

BY RYOKICHI HIRONO[1]

*The personnel department—jobs and performance—functional
versus personal—individualism*

I T is natural and proper to assume that when a foreign firm that
has developed in an alien economic, political, and social environment starts a business undertaking in Japan either by itself or
with a Japanese partner, it will behave in some measure differently
from a typical Japanese firm owned and operated completely by
Japanese nationals. In essence, the distinct features of the management philosophy, policy, and practices underlying these foreign,
predominantly American, corporations, wholly or jointly owned,

---

[1] The author participated in two research projects on which this chapter is based.
The first was sponsored by the Japan Economic Research Institute, and published
in 1965 under the title: *Gaishikei Kigyō Jittai Chōsa Hōkokusho* ('Report on Foreign Investment in Japan'.) The second, financed by the Asia Foundation, has just been
conducted by *Gendai Chingin Mondai Kenkyukai* ('Research Group on Contemporary Wage Problems'.) Other publications called upon are a comprehensive study
conducted by the Ministry of International Trade and Industry in 1958–59, a general
study by the Japan Economic Research Institute in 1964–65, and, finally, a comparative
study conducted by *Nikkeiren* in 1967.

may be characterized as the influences of democratic individualism and economic rationalism, whose extent differs among different establishments presumably depending upon such factors as type and pattern of ownership of a firm, its competitive position in its field, its period of operation, the area of management functions in question, the organizational goals and behavioral patterns of its parent firm(s), and the personal beliefs and attitudes of its top management.

At one extreme position, these influences assert themselves very strongly throughout an organization, and the organizational goals and behavioral pattern of an American subsidiary are accordingly very much like those of its counterpart in the United States. The management philosophy and techniques of such a firm are ideally based on a full recognition of a belief that 1) individual rights and freedom, including the right of developing capabilities and unlimited appropriations, are fundamental human rights, that 2) individuals should be afforded the maximum possible opportunity to exercise these rights and freedom, and that 3) the economic well-being of a society, a community, and a corporation is maximized only through the maximum exercise of their inalienable human rights. They are also ideally based on an explicit understanding and belief that the pursuit of maximum utilities and profits is the ultimate objective of the economic activities of individuals and corporations and that it is therefore both natural and rational that everything else, including other aspects of human rights, should be subjected as an effective and appropriate means, or as an auxiliary, to the fulfillment of this ultimate objective of human endeavor.

At the other extreme, however, there could be a foreign subsidiary which purports to minimize the influences of such Western liberal-democratic market principles and stick to the traditional values and principles of Japanese business behavior, which only now are gradually changing. The management philosophy and techniques of such a firm would be ideally based on a full belief that 1) the interest of a group, a corporation, and a community of which individuals are members is superior to individual rights and freedom, that 2) the rights and freedom of individuals must therefore be subordinated to the higher level of group interest, and that 3) the economic well-being of individuals is maximized only through the maximum realization of the interest of their group, corporation, community and/or society at large. They are also, however, vaguely based on a belief that the principle of economic rationalism is a necessary evil and must be restrained in its exercise by principles of a higher order, such as those of mutual obligation and social harmony.

In fact, nearly all the American subsidiaries operating in Japan come somewhere in between these two extreme positions, blending the philosophy and techniques of American management with the Japanese in such a way as their top management discerns to be most appropriate to relevant conditions both internal and external to the firms. The blending of two such intrinsically opposed patterns causes in different firms differences of view not only among top managers, but also among employees who have differing scales of values. To the extent, of course, that employers have freedom of choice in the matter, the distribution of employees with differing scales of values can be made any way the managers wish, e.g., either on a norm of compromise or slanted towards the American or the Japanese pattern, but this distribution is itself subject to environmental constraints, including the view of organized labor, with which the employers must, in many cases, come to agreement in order to run their businesses at all. The acceptability of American values among the members of such companies naturally varies with variations in the acceptability and consistency of such values among the larger society surrounding them.

Aware of the fact that the major difference between a foreign corporation abroad and its subsidiary in Japan is the human factor of production and its related institutions, foreign firms in Japan have tended in general to emphasize the corporate goals of ensuring their employees a materially decent and ever rising standard of living; challenge, satisfaction, and security in their jobs; and safe and pleasant working conditions—all at least equal to, or even better

[253]

than, those provided by leading Japanese firms in the same industry and locality. To realize these all-important goals, many of them have formulated a basic policy of personnel management, whether written or unwritten, that goes something like this:

1 Optimum use of manpower must be a major policy of organization. Therefore a proper mixture of skills and capabilities must be maintained in accordance with technology, production processes, and projected growth rate. Both the optimum use of manpower and the attraction of other employees of superior quality require payment of a maximum feasible remuneration, a clear congruity between remuneration and job performance, and an orderly promotion from within of employees of the highest demonstrated quality, not to mention the encouragement of communication, whether vertical or horizontal, as essential to morale.

2 The development of individual employees must also be a major policy of organization, especially the development of their intellectual capacities and technical skills and the fulfillment of their diverse personal needs. Hence the most minute care must be taken with respect to changing levels of individual challenge and satisfaction, as well as of changes in production processes, organizational structure, and work groups. Explicit encouragement should be given to the self-appraisal of individual employees, and its results should be used as a guide to transfers or work assignments within the organization. All sorts of educational and training opportunities should also be provided for employees who might want to take advantage of them in order to qualify themselves for positions of increasing responsibility or for any other reason. The company should also pay remuneration commensurate with the increasing levels of family and community responsibilities that employees must face as years accumulate.

In striving for these goals of personnel management, foreign companies reveal themselves to be cognizant of the overriding importance of respect for the traditional customs and institutions of the community in which they are operating, as long as the goals can be accommodated without conflict with an efficient fulfillment of the primary corporate objectives of steady growth and maximum long-run profits. Such cognizance among foreign companies is evidenced by the fact that many of them provide welfare programs for their employees—for example, flower-arrangement and tea-ceremony lessons for women. But how have foreign corporations actually translated their personnel goals into concrete work rules and regulations and day-to-day practices?

Personnel management is assumed to cover such wide areas of activity as recruitment, placement, and separation; training, transfer, and promotion; wage, salary, and working-hours administration; health and welfare programs; and even union relations where no separate divisions charged with industrial relations exist.

The personnel department

THE first major difference evident in the personnel practices of foreign and Japanese companies is found in the roles played by personnel departments. In most Japanese firms the various activities that fall under personnel are ordinarily grouped in a personnel department and supervised by a personnel manager or department head. In some of the largest companies there is even a director of personnel who oversees the personnel manager and his department. In foreign companies in Japan, however, more often than not organizational structure and job description for personnel departments are quite different from those in Japanese companies. Though clearly related to the size of company operation, the personnel department in a foreign firm is invariably much smaller than in a Japanese firm, and the personnel manager has less authority and responsibility than the personnel manager in a Japanese firm. Actually, it has been found that in some foreign firms the personnel manager is merely a person charged with the staff responsibility for personnel activities, from recruitment to retirement, without any line responsibility whatsoever, whereas in other foreign firms he is in practice more than a staff manager, for his advice carries weight equal to, if not greater than, the line manager's in personnel decisions. In many foreign firms the actual pattern of relationship between personnel and line managers often depends upon their relative personalities and their respective relations with top management. It is important, however, to note that under all circumstances the personnel manager acts only in a staff relation to the line managers—for example, a sales or production manager—and that it is the line manager who is solely responsible for personnel decisions, whereas in Japanese firms staff and line managers have co-responsibility. In some foreign companies line managers dare neither ignore nor override the personnel recommendations of a personnel manager, particularly in larger firms where organizational complexity has imposed on line managers a rigid compliance with the rules and standards set by the personnel manager. In some firms the personnel manager as a staff manager may be authorized only to set company-wide personnel standards, often minimum only, such as those that involve recruitment, promotion, and wage and salary administration. In such firms line managers are left perfectly free to make their own discretionary decisions concerning personnel matters within their own departments as long as those decisions do not conflict with company-wide rules and standards.

The foreign practice of placing heavier responsibility for personnel decisions on line managers than on personnel managers stems from the fact 1) that because the firms are usually not so big and complicated as their parent firms, either Japanese or American, the line managers can both supervise their subordinates easily and communicate easily among themselves regarding standards, 2) that the top managers of foreign firms, particularly those who are themselves foreign, believe that line managers know better than personnel managers about the responsibilities and technical requirements of jobs in their departments, and 3) that personnel ought to be assigned to jobs rather than jobs to personnel.

In Japanese firms employees tend to be moved around under the supervision of the personnel department in and across workshops, and line managers and departments tend to be on the receiving rather than on the initiating end, particularly in larger firms and with respect to salaried, non-production employees. This traditional practice seems to be based on the concept that employees are not hired for specific jobs but are initiated into a firm as lifetime members of the corporate 'family' and it is therefore to the firm itself that they develop permanent attachments rather than to specific jobs. It is as though the Japanese personnel department were a locomotive pulling employees like railway cars in any direction and at any speed dictated by the corporate schedule and the central automatic traffic control (ATC) system, while their jobs in the line departments were merely stations they pass while moving to the terminal station of their promotion. Presumably, of course, the direction and size of the terminal station where each car ends depend upon its continuing value and importance both between and at the stations it passes, for station-masters are in constant communication with the locomotive engineers following the company's train schedules and central ATC system.

This essential difference between foreign and traditional Japanese companies appears in every area of personnel practices. With respect to recruitment, for instance, in most foreign firms once a plan is approved by top management, line-department managers become solely responsible for the selection, placement, and pay rates of successful applicants. They are also expected to take the initiative in planning, executing, and controlling various requisite kinds of technical training, both on and off the job, and in supervising transfer and promotion programs for their subordinates. Of course, foreign personnel departments acting in a staff capacity place job advertisements, process applications, assist line managers in interviewing, and execute final employment contracts in the name of the

R   [257]

company's representative director. Often it is also their responsibility to oversee induction training, helping the line managers in every way in providing whatever technical education of new employees is necessary, and in making the best use of manpower. For successful operation, this kind of staff relationship of personnel departments with line departments in foreign corporations presupposes the existence of clearly delineated organizational goals, the distribution of functional authority and responsibilities among different organizational levels and departments, and technically detailed job descriptions and definitions of management responsibilities in all departments. Although they are gradually emerging, it is just such presupposed conditions that are lacking in most traditional Japanese companies, which are highly structured organizationally and personnally, but on an authoritarian and paternal, rather than a functional basis.

Jobs and performance

IN fact, the second major difference between foreign and traditional Japanese companies arises in this very area. Even where such clearly defined conditions of organization may exist in Japanese companies, the 'presupposed' aspect of them may not exist; hence the employees concerned neither consciously understand nor actively apply them. As pointed out before, new employees in a traditional Japanese corporation are initiated into it as members of a family rather than as workers hired for particular jobs. Apart from certain technical work, professions, and traditional crafts, the concept of exclusive occupations or jobs is almost nil in the minds of most Japanese employees as well as in the organizational structures of Japanese corporations. At the time of hiring, most Japanese neither anticipate nor concern themselves with the kinds of jobs they may be assigned to despite the fact that a hierarchy of jobs inevitably exists in any company. The fact that payment and promotion depend primarily upon such personal attributes as education, age, and length of service rather than upon the nature of particular jobs and job performance is not only clear evidence of the insignificance of the concept of occupations or jobs in the Japanese mind, but it also further obscures it. One consequence is the oft-cited situation in which Japanese employees, asked what they do for a living, identify themselves with the companies for which they work rather than with their occupations. In Japan's status-oriented society, company affiliation is much more important than job identification, particularly among those within the same echelons of corporate hierarchy.

The priority that workers in some foreign companies in Japan give to job identification over company affiliation is shared and strengthened by the companies themselves in all fields of personnel practice. Unlike traditional Japanese firms, such companies recruit new workers by advertising job openings, for they are more interested in the technical capabilities and individual aspirations of their potential employees with respect to the jobs at stake than in their overall personal and familial backgrounds. Thus, ordinarily, foreign firms do not, as traditional Japanese companies do, conduct extensive non-technical and academic employment tests that seem only indirectly or remotely related to the immediate requirements of extant vacancies. The difference in the degree of attachment to job or company that workers feel in foreign or Japanese companies is also evidenced and reinforced by the kinds of development programs the companies provide for their workers. In foreign firms training programs as distinguished from educational programs are emphasized, are by definition technical, and are often given only on the job for the purpose of improving the technical capability of employees. By contrast, in Japanese firms training and educational programs are stressed equally and are often highly organized for the purpose of stamping employees with a corporate image. This difference between job priority in foreign firms and company priority in Japanese firms also underlies the higher incidence of labor mobility, both inter-employer and intra-occupational, in foreign companies.

As for remuneration systems, these also differ in foreign as compared with Japanese firms. In foreign firms payment is made for jobs—in other words, according to job rates. In Japanese firms, however, payment is personal. When in overall requirements—general knowledge, technical skill, experience, responsibility, and physical strength, as well as in working conditions—jobs are comparable, payment tends to be equal in foreign companies, but varied in Japanese companies. Whereas in foreign companies it makes no difference who performs a job since he is paid at the same rate as anyone else who does the same job, in Japanese companies *who* performs a job is the determining factor in remuneration. In other words, in Japanese companies workers performing identical jobs are paid at different rates, for their personal circumstances such as schooling, age, and length of service differ. Thus, while the concept of occupations or jobs is clearly established and widely recognized in many foreign firms, it is not clearly established and widely recognized in traditional Japanese firms.

Functional versus personal

THE emphasis that foreign companies place upon the functional rather than the personal aspects of organizational activity gives rise to a third feature that differentiates their personnel practices from those of Japanese companies. In foreign companies, through and across all departments of organization, there is a greater degree of, and a greater respect for, specialization, as evidenced in the higher ratio of specialists to company staff in foreign than in Japanese firms. As a matter of fact, foreign companies grant better opportunities for specialized training, both inside and outside the organization, and reward specialization with higher potentials of position and higher incentives of pay. Japanese companies, on the other hand, traditionally emphasize the development of what might be called for want of a better word 'generalists' who are supposed to be widely experienced and take a broader and longer-term look at situations facing them than specialists can do.

Chapter twelve: Management in foreign corporations

In a foreign company a man may start and end his employment as a salesman, but along the way he accumulates all sorts of experiences with a variety of products. In a traditional Japanese company, however, a man may start his employment as a salesman and end as a production or planning manager, or in any of a number of other jobs not even related to sales. In a multiproduct foreign company the pattern of intracompany mobility, including promotion, involves intra-occupational movements through different product divisions, whereas in a traditional Japanese company the pattern tends to be rotational, reflecting a movement from one functional department to another on a regular and continuing basis. For potential managers who must view their functional activities from an overall corporate standpoint, rotation has advantages over specialization, but it works against the interest of many other employees who may end their careers mainly as first-line managers and/or specialists because the rotational pattern has restricted their chances of intercompany promotion. This is one of the major technical reasons that Japanese employees tend to be less mobile among different employers than their foreign counterparts. It may even be said that the traditional Japanese company's lesser emphasis on specialization has acted, even if only by chance, to bind employees to employers in such a way that remuneration and promotion have had to be formalized upon the hierarchy of education, age, and length of service rather than that of specific jobs and job performance.

Combined emphases upon jobs and specialization have led most foreign companies to rely heavily on the open labor market for their recruitment of workers in addition to the traditional Japanese method of recruiting them fresh from schools. Unlike many Japanese companies, foreign firms seem to be more concerned with procuring workers with the skills and experiences necessary for their functional activities than with initiating them into permanent membership in their organizations. Given this point of view, as long as the workers satisfy requisite technical, sales, servicing, and administrative requirements, the source of their recruitment matters little. In fact, some foreign firms have constantly preferred open-market recruitment to the traditional Japanese method of closed-market recruitment because of the greater likelihood that the open-market system provides richer and readier skills, experience, and capabilities than the closed-market system can provide. It goes without saying that traditional Japanese companies have no such view. Until only recently they have usually restricted their recruitment of new employees, particularly key ones, to applicants fresh from school regardless of educational level. Only during the last several years and only under the pressure of increasing labor shortages have they also resorted to open-market recruitment to supplement employees recruited by the traditional method. In addition to the fact that labor is cheaper when paid according to the Japanese system of remuneration, it is mainly because Japanese companies are more interested in molding their employees to their own corporate images than they are in procuring the skills and experience new employees might have at hand that the traditional method of recruiting workers fresh from schools has not only survived but also been chiefly relied on in Japan. The importance traditional companies attach to the molding process is so great that they deliberately hire young workers fresh from schools without any technical skills or previous work experience whatsoever, simply because such recruits are most amenable to the process. Indeed, they form the core of both the production and non-production work force of the companies. As a corollary, most Japanese companies classify those workers they hire in the open labor market as 'non-regular', thus distinguishing them from 'regular' employees hired fresh from schools. Often these 'non-regular' employees are regarded as merely 'temporary' and therefore subject to all sorts of financial and other special handicaps as compared with other employees. In other words, considered unfit for the molding process, they form an 'outgroup' distinct from the 'ingroup' regardless of their kinds and levels of specialization. Recently, however, some upward movement from outgroup to ingroup has been discernible, but only since the beginning of the 60s as traditional attitudes and personnel procedures have begun to break down in Japanese companies, mainly under the pressures of continued high growth, technological change, and a prevailing shortage of labor, particularly among the young people leaving school.

In foreign companies, especially those wholly-owned foreign companies where most employees happen to have been recruited in the open market, there seems to be no distinction or discrimination between those employees recruited by the one system and those recruited by the other. In most joint-venture companies, however, there are two distinct groups of employees: those hired directly by the joint-venture companies themselves and those on secondary assignment from their Japanese parent companies, in which case they may feel superior and may, in fact, receive higher remuneration than that of the other employees. Because, however, such discrimination can be, and often is, a cause of disunity and trouble among employees, most joint-venture companies make special efforts to integrate the employees garnered from the Japanese parent company with the other employees by changing their status to that of direct hiring and/or strictly applying the same financial and other compensation to all employees at every level of the job hierarchy. Thus, in both wholly-owned foreign and joint-venture companies operating in Japan there appears to be little emphasis on either the molding process or the concomitant discrimination in status that are widely prevalent in traditional Japanese companies; on the contrary, there is widespread disapproval of such personnel practices.

It is not only because they are primarily interested in qualifications for specific jobs and in specialization that foreign companies have relied heavily on the open-market method of recruiting new employees in Japan. Because many of them were only recently established, sometimes without any formal ties with well-known Japanese companies or other, even slighter connections, they have had to compete for labor in an ever tighter market with large and medium Japanese companies of long standing that offered greater long-range economic security and social prestige to the typical Japanese applicants for whom these two values seem more important than high remuneration with great risk or job challenge and satisfaction. In other words, given both economic and social factors, there has been no choice for many foreign companies in Japan but to rely on the unorthodox method of recruitment, drawing on that segment of Japanese workers who would dare a greater risk in order to enjoy higher earnings and who would value job challenge and satisfaction much more than such traditional values as long-range security and social standing. In this sense it may be valid to state that, in terms of values, the employees of foreign companies form a group psychologically distinct from those working in traditional Japanese companies. At this stage, however, this observation is mere conjecture requiring a separate investigation, which may yet throw a very interesting light on the attitudes towards work that may dominate Japanese workers five to ten years from now.

Individualism

CLOSELY associated with concepts of functionalism, job-centricity, and specialization, a philosophy of individualism and self-identification constitutes a fourth characteristic of the personnel practices of foreign companies operating in Japan. As indicated in a 'Statement on Corporate Objectives and Principles' of one of the foreign companies that have successfully operated here for some time, the 'provision of opportunities to develop their skills through training, to qualify for positions of increasing responsibility and to gain personal satisfaction through making the most use of their abilities' is a standard for employees that is similarly stressed by many foreign companies as a primary corporate objective, along with such objectives as continuing growth, production of the highest quality of goods at the lowest prices, and provision for remuneration and working conditions comparable with or superior to those prevailing in the same industry or locality.

Foreign companies commonly recognize through their personnel policies that there are differences in objectives among differing individual employees, as well as between individual employees and the organization employing them, and that these different objectives should not only be allowed to operate but should also be assisted towards fulfillment in order to ensure the continuing stability and growth of an organization. In such companies individual objectives are not suppressed on behalf of corporate objectives, for they are considered an integral part of corporate objectives. It is doubtful, however, whether in traditional Japanese companies the satisfaction of personal needs among employees and the development of their personal abilities, have, in themselves, any significant place, for in Japanese companies authoritarianism so often dominates employer-employee relations that the satisfaction of personal needs is subordinated in every way to the primary objectives of continuing corporate growth and the maximization of profits. Although Japanese industrial paternalism may look like concern for the welfare of individual employees, it operates only in exchange for complete devotion on the part of the employees and thus discourages any meaningful kind of individualism or the attainment of any reasonable level of personal fulfillment. In traditional Japanese companies such paternalism has only one purpose: to strengthen the group spirit and the devotion of employees to corporate objectives, which have nothing to do with individualism and self-identification.

In foreign companies in Japan personnel policy is centered in an individualistic orientation. Indeed, foreign companies often show preference for recruits who have distinctive personality traits and superior capabilities rather than, say, outstanding academic records. Unlike traditional Japanese companies, they seem to be uninterested in well-rounded but personally unambitious applicants who tend to be conformists with little understanding of unity in diversity and the value of constructive criticism. In interviews with job applicants, also, foreign companies show high regard for individualism and personal fulfillment; for example, assuming that their applicants all seek high pay, they encourage them to state the remuneration they desire. If confronted with questions about their desired remuneration, most Japanese applicants coming to a traditional Japanese company would be baffled, sometimes quoting figures lower than they considered they deserved, but often leaving them unspecified at all in the hope that they would get whatever rates their referential peers were being paid. Studies show that more individualistic and self-selling responses occur among job applicants in foreign companies than among those in traditional Japanese companies.

Although brainstorming is a day-to-day method of conference in foreign companies that has been increasingly adopted by Japanese companies, the legacy of authoritarian conformism and the lack of a ready acceptance of individualism have hindered the successful implementation or desired outcome of this technique of personnel management in Japan. Meanwhile, placing a greater emphasis on merit ratings with respect to remuneration and promotion than traditional Japanese companies, foreign companies also hold their individual employees more strictly responsible for their decisions and the consequences of those decisions as a logical concomitant of the greater autonomy they attach to job performance. At the same time, the foreign companies seem also to offer a larger number of organized facilities for internal, especially vertical, communication, by which individual employees can effectively participate in and influence policy formulation, revision, and implementation at section, departmental, and even company levels.

It would be misleading to contend that individualism alone, despite its obvious psychological force, can motivate employees of an organization to personal fulfillment. Particularly in traditional Japanese companies, many Japanese employees work so hard for their employers that they sacrifice their family lives in not insignificant ways. Although it is true that many of them do so because of their personal ambitions to rise in the hierarchy of corporate management, many others, especially older employees, find their richest sense of personal fulfillment in devotion and self-sacrifice to their employers.

Thus the concept of 'groupism' and self-denial does not necessarily conflict with that of personal fulfillment. Yet the social environment in which this combination is tolerated, or even encouraged, certainly differs from the social environment in which the combination of individualism and personal fulfillment is embodied and idealized. Could it be said that the one combination represents the values of a 'traditional' society, while the other represents the values of a 'modern' society?

In any case, it is essential finally to note that functionalism, job-centricity, specialization, and individualistic self-fulfillment neither exhaust all the characteristics observed in the personnel practices of foreign companies nor exist to the same degree and in the same density in all foreign companies. Moreover, they may have been more harshly contrasted here with characteristics of personnel practices in traditional Japanese companies than the reality warrants, and at the risk of misrepresentation either through simplification or complication. Certainly, it can generally be said that the foreign characteristics that make differences most obvious are more strongly and clearly observable in wholly-owned foreign subsidiaries than in joint ventures, in smaller foreign companies than in larger ones, and in non-unionized foreign companies than in unionized ones. Nevertheless, it can honestly be maintained that the characteristics here presented fairly represent the fundamental features of the personnel practices of foreign companies now successfully operating in Japan.

The major personnel problems that foreign companies face in Japan stem chiefly from the modifications they must make in their policies and practices in order to adjust them to the socio-economic, organizational, and cultural aspects of the Japanese environment. The functionalistic features of the management of foreign companies tend to conflict with the traditional features of Japanese enterprise that are still sentimentally preferred by many Japanese employees. At the risk of repetition it must be pointed out again that, traditionally, the Japanese regard an enterprise as a kind of familial organization in which a close personal relationship binds members together, even though degrees of obligation vary among different enterprises. It is for this reason that Japanese employees in a joint-venture company, for example, particularly those recruited from a Japanese parent firm, often complain that employee relationships are too impersonal and that the strong sense of prevailing rationalism is suffocating. Specifically, they complain about such things as an excessive rigidity in working hours, over-emphasis on fulfillment of production, sales, and other goals, and so on.

While job-centricity has come to be increasingly appreciated as a working concept in many Japanese corporations, it has also created some delicate problems among employees. Those upholding the traditional Japanese philosophy of personnel management question the validity of a whole range of personnel practices oriented upon it, holding it responsible for the 'dehumanization' of management in foreign corporations. Even those employees favorable to it are uneasy about, if not actually frustrated by, the degree to which it 'interferes' with their long-range security and progression of earnings. And when, in Japan, these two sacrosanct areas are considered to be infringed upon, there is likely to be some outbursts denouncing management as encroaching with alien concepts upon vested rights. As for employers, some of them maintain that job-centered management decreases loyalty among workers, particularly of the younger generations. Meanwhile, for some members of senior and middle management of a foreign, especially a joint-venture company, job-centered management based on functionalism has caused great frustration by limiting the exercise of their authority over subordinates. Whereas in traditional Japanese companies such managers are able to command varying degrees of total personal obedience from their subordinates, whether inside or outside a firm, in foreign companies they must confine their authority to specific jobs and the performance of them inside the firm in strict accordance with the job descriptions concerned. Beyond the requirements of a hierarchy of jobs, their subordinates have as many rights and discretions as they in their day-to-day conduct inside the company and total freedom outside the company. Despite its underlying rationale, such equality is very hard for traditionally authoritarian Japanese managers to take.

A strong foreign emphasis on specialization has influenced traditional Japanese management to adopt a number of restructuring measures in personnel so that professional employees, actually specialists, may be assigned to functionally proper roles. Needless to say, the number of such specialists has greatly increased in Japan as research and development activities, at both corporate and national levels, have increased. By and large, because such specialists are more interested in their professional status and advancement than in ordinary promotion along the lines of the corporate hierarchy, more and more Japanese companies have had to create specialist positions with corresponding levels of authority, responsibility, and remuneration. Because, however, of the traditional Japanese view that managers are superior to specialists in any corporate hierarchy, management has been somewhat reluctant to create positions as high in status for its professional employees as for its managers in line and staff organizations. Naturally enough, such reluctance seems to have been highest in traditional Japanese companies and greater in joint-venture than in wholly-owned foreign subsidiaries. At any rate, having overcome an initial psychological difficulty arising from the creation of a special hierarchy for these professional employees, the foreign companies that have done so have begun to draw high-calibre people from other Japanese corporations where such an innovation has not yet been introduced. Obviously, this labor drain has caused a grave concern among the Japanese firms that have suffered from it, but at the same time it has forced them to take defensive measures of organizational restructuring with respect to their professional personnel.

Having given rise to a strongly self-conscious group of professional employees, including numerous salesmen, the high degree of specialization in foreign companies has brought about a pluralistic type of organization quite different from the monolithic type traditionally dominant in most Japanese companies. The consequence is that the management of companies with such an organization must concern itself not only with union relations involving production employees but also with group relations involving non-unionized professional employees. Indeed, in some cases, professional employees have united with production employees to provide strategic assistance to union activity, thus boosting strength that has often tended to be only nominal, especially among non-production employees, despite their high rate of unionization. Since, when they are militantly organized, professional employees because of their strategic positions can be a real threat to management, their demands have been increasingly accommodated. Yet there is no denying the fact that a pluralistic type of organization in foreign companies has invariably contributed to further complications of conflict and its mitigation within such organizations. Meanwhile, the fact that many senior and middle Japanese executives of joint-venture companies have had little experience in supervising and coordinating the functional activities of their professional employees as distinct from ordinary clerical and administrative employees has exacerbated the problem.

It is the individualistic orientation of their personnel practices that more than any other feature has baffled many Japanese employees in foreign companies, particularly those hired from their Japanese parent companies. Individualism, with all it represents, is at the root of all the other features of foreign personnel policy, such as functionalism, job-centricity, and specialization—all of which are intricately interrelated. Although individualism as an analytical concept is understandable and even acceptable, the Japanese have never embraced it as a popular, living philosophy; in prewar Japan, in fact, it was summarily suppressed. Thus individualistic orientation in the recruitment, work assignments, wage and salary administration, promotion, educational and training activity, and other areas of personnel practices in foreign companies has caused serious problems of adjustment among Japanese employees, generating irritation, frustation, and friction. Naturally, those employees recruited in the open labor market, who have come by their own choice to foreign companies, are the least sensitive to such problems.

Finally, as might be expected, the extent to which individualistic orientation in personnel practices has given rise to problems of self-adjustment among Japanese employees appears to be smallest at small wholly-owned foreign subsidiaries, where the employees manifest the greatest psychological acceptance, and the largest at large joint-venture companies, where the employees manifest the greatest preference for the traditional personnel practices of long-established Japanese companies. Accordingly, as might also be expected, the personnel practices of most foreign companies in Japan appear to follow the traditional pattern as the path of least resistance. Because of the socio-economic, technological, and institutional changes that have been taking place in postwar Japan, however, this pattern is itself subject to pressures of change. At the same time, it should be noted that the outward appearance of personnel practices in foreign companies can be deceptive, for more often than not the spirit in which those practices have been carried out has continuously changed from that in which they were originally introduced into traditional Japanese companies. The speed with which the gap can be closed between guiding spirit and actual practices, particularly in joint-venture companies, must depend not only on the conscious efforts of managers, but also on the acceptance of Japanese society. After all, if it is to be successful, every practice of personnel management in any foreign company in Japan must be tailored to the needs that obtain both inside and outside of the organization.

Statistical Appendix

COMPILED BY ROBERT J. BALLON

I: EMPLOYMENT

II: WAGES

S

Statistical appendix

Statistical appendix

I EMPLOYMENT

LIVING STANDARDS IN JAPAN ARE STEADILY IMPROVING: the GNP per capita was $564 in 1962, $863 in 1965, and keeps increasing year after year. The main reason it does so is that industrialization and the employment it offers have continued unabated. With growing national affluence, the schooling of the young is extended and the labor-force participation rate is diminished for the nation as a whole (Tables 1 and 2), but most of all in agriculture. (Table 3) Japan still has a fairly large number of unpaid family workers (Table 4) distributed in small shops and stores, but more characteristically Japanese is the distinction between regular (or permanent) and temporary employees, (Tables 5 and 6) as well as the concept of "length of service" with the same employer. (Table 7) Labor turnover is by far the largest among younger employees and tapers off as length of service, and consequently age, extend. (Tables 8 and 9)

TABLE 1

LABOR FORCE AND LABOR FORCE PARTICIPATION

			(thousand)
Population and labor force	1960	1963	1966
Total population	93,250	95,940	98,920
15-years old and more (A)	65,670	69,380	74,320
Male (B)	31,730	33,580	36,020
Female (C)	33,910	35,810	38,310
Labor force (D)	45,150	46,520	48,910
Male (E)	26,870	27,910	29,420
Female (F)	18,280	18,620	19,490
Employed	44,720	46,130	48,470
Unemployed	430	400	440
Labor force participation			(%)
D/A	69.2%	67.1%	65.8%
E/B	84.8	83.1	81.7
E/O	54.5	52.0	60.2
E/D	59.6	60.0	60.2
F/D	40.5	40.0	39.8

Sources: *Year Book of Labour Statistics,* Tokyo: The Ministry of Labor, various years, and *Fujin Rōdō no Jitsujō 1966* ('Facts on Female Workers'), Tokyo: The Ministry of Labor, 1967, p. 3.

TABLE 2

LABOR FORCE AND LABOR FORCE PARTICIPATION
BY AGE BRACKET
(1966)

Age	Labor force (1,000)		Labor force participation	
	Female	Male	Female	Male
Total	19,490	29,420	50.9%	81.7%
15–19	2,140	2,220	38.0	37.9
20–24	3,100	3,830	70.1	85.7
25–29	2,060	4,010	48.7	96.9
30–39	4,340	7,640	54.7	97.3
40–54	5,300	7,040	61.5	96.3
55–64	1,790	3,110	45.9	86.9
65–	780	1,580	21.7	56.2

Source: *Fujin Rōdō no Jitsujō, 1966* ('Facts on Female Workers'), Tokyo: The Ministry of Labor, 1967, p. 4.

[278]

TABLE 3

EMPLOYMENT BY INDUSTRIAL SECTORS

(thousand)

Industrial sector	1960	1963	1966
Primary industry 1	15,540	12,960	11,730
Secondary industry 2	12,010	14,250	15,490
(Construction)	(2,350)	(2,730)	(3,290)
(Manufacturing)	(9,120)	(11,120)	(11,870)
Tertiary industry 3	14,790	18,890	21,230

Source: *Year Book of Labour Statistics,* Tokyo: The Ministry of Labor, various years.
Notes: 1 Agriculture, forestry, fisheries and aquaculture
        2 Mining, construction, manufacturing
        3 All others

TABLE 4

EMPLOYMENT STATUS

(thousand)

	1960	1963	1966
All industries	44,720	46,130	48,470
Agriculture and forestry			
Total	14,920	12,400	11,140
Self-employed	5,470	4,670	4,340
Family workers	8,870	7,340	6,420
Employees	590	390	390
Non-agriculture and forestry			
Total	29,790	33,690	37,300
Self-employed	5,370	5,140	5,440
Family workers	3,060	3,160	3,230
Employees	21,320	25,380	28,620

Source: *Year Book of Labour Statistics,* Tokyo: The Ministry of Labor, various years.

TABLE 5

DISTRIBUTION BY TYPE OF EMPLOYMENT AND SEX

Year	Female				Male			
	Total	Regular	Temporary	Daily	Total	Regular	Temporary	Daily
		1	2	3		1	2	3
1960	100.0	92.0	3.4	4.6	100.0	88.2	6.1	5.7
1963	100.0	86.4	8.4	5.3	100.0	91.9	4.0	4.2
1966	100.0	85.6	8.9	5.5	100.0	92.3	3.8	3.9

Sources: *Fujin Rōdō no Jitsujō 1966* ('Facts on Female Workers'), Tokyo: The Ministry of Labor, 1967, p. 17, and based on *Year Book of Labour Statistics, 1960,* Tokyo: The Ministry of Labor, 1961, p. 16.

Notes: 1 Employees who have a contract of employment without a specified period of employment or with a period of more than a year.

2 Employed for a specific period of more than a month but less than a year.

3 Employed daily or for a specific period of less than a month.

TABLE 6

REGULAR AND TEMPORARY EMPLOYEES IN SELECTED
INDUSTRIES BY SEX

(thousand)

Industry and sex	1960		1963		1966	
	Regular	Temporary	Regular	Temporary	Regular	Temporary
Manufacturing						
Total	7,160	290	8,720	540	9,290	580
Male	4,990	150	6,090	240	6,540	230
Female	2,170	150	2,630	300	2,760	350
Wholesale, retail						
Total	3,770	120	4,850	210	5,720	280
Male	2,350	50	2,940	70	3,380	100
Female	1,420	70	1,910	130	2,340	180
Services						
Total	3,530	120	3,770	180	4,470	230
Male	1,900	40	2,010	50	2,430	70
Female	1,640	80	1,760	120	2,050	170

Source: *Year Book of Labour Statistics,* Tokyo: The Ministry of Labor, various years.

TABLE 7

AVERAGE AGE AND LENGTH OF SERVICE IN ALL INDUSTRIES,
BY SIZE OF ESTABLISHMENT AND SEX

Size and sex	Age			Length of service (years)		
	1960	1963	1966	1960	1963	1966
Total						
All employees	30.9	31.3	31.9	6.7	6.8	6.8
Male	32.8	33.0	33.5	7.8	7.9	8.0
Female	26.3	27.2	28.5	4.0	4.0	4.0
1,000 and more						
All employees	32.4	32.0	32.3	9.8	9.6	9.7
Male	34.6	34.1	34.3	11.2	11.1	11.4
Female	25.5	25.8	26.5	5.3	5.2	5.1
500 to 999						
All employees		29.4	29.8		5.9	6.1
Male	*100–999*	31.8	31.8		6.9	7.1
Female	All employees	24.3	25.1		4.0	3.7
100 to 499	29.5			5.1		
	Male					
All employees	31.8	30.1	30.6	5.9	5.0	5.2
Male	Female	32.0	32.3		5.7	6.0
Female	24.8	26.1	27.0	3.5	3.5	3.4
30 to 99						
All employees	*10–99*	31.0	32.1		4.3	4.7
Male	All employees	32.2	33.3		4.9	5.4
	30.1	28.6	29.9	4.3	3.1	3.3
Female	Male					
10 to 29	31.1			4.8		
	Female					
All employees	28.0	31.8	33.2	3.3	4.6	4.8
Male		32.4	33.7		5.0	5.4
Female		30.5	32.3		3.6	3.7

Source: *Year Book of Labour Statistics,* Tokyo: The Ministry of Labor, various years.

TABLE 8

PERCENTAGE DISTRIBUTION OF NEWLY HIRED AND
SEPARATED EMPLOYEES, BY AGE AND SEX (1966)

Age	Hiring With previous experience		Hiring No experience		Severance	
	Female	Male	Female	Male	Female	Male
Total	100.0	100.0	100.0	100.0	100.0	100.0
Less than 20	20.0	34.3	25.3	17.1	20.2	19.1
20–24	22.6	25.1	32.8	26.1	38.7	25.4
25–29	15.0	12.9	13.5	19.5	16.0	16.6
30–34	13.4	8.2	6.7	12.4	7.1	11.4
35–39	10.9	4.8	6.8	8.2	6.0	6.9
40–49	13.2	6.4	10.2	9.1	7.9	8.4
50–59	4.0	4.9	3.9	5.9	3.3	8.8
60 and more	0.9	3.4	0.7	1.6	0.7	3.3

Source: *Fujin Rōdō no Jitsujō 1966* ('Facts on Female Workers'), Tokyo: The Ministry of
Labor, 1967, p. 27.

TABLE 9

NUMBER AND PERCENTAGE DISTRIBUTION OF SEPARATED
EMPLOYEES BY DURATION OF SERVICE, ALL
INDUSTRIES, BY SEX (1966)

Length of service	Total	Male	(thousand) Female
Total	3,351.1 (100.0%)	1,739.7 (100.0%)	1,611.4 (100.0%)
Less than 6 months	750.0 (22.4)	406.7 (23.4)	343.3 (21.3)
6–12 months	550.5 (16.4)	295.7 (17.0)	254.9 (15.8)
1–2 years	598.6 (17.9)	301.5 (17.3)	297.1 (18.4)
2–5 years	849.5 (25.4)	397.6 (22.9)	451.9 (28.0)
5–10 years	388.1 (11.6)	177.3 (10.2)	210.8 (13.1)
10 and more years	211.9 (6.3)	159.8 (9.2)	52.1 (3.2)

Source: *Year Book of Labour Statistics 1966,* Tokyo: The Ministry of Labor, 1967, p. 43.

II WAGES

A WAGE LEVELS AND DIFFERENTIALS

AT THE OFFICIAL RATE OF EXCHANGE (¥360=US$1.00), THE 1966 *average monthly salary in Japan was about US$120. (Table 10) With 1965 as the base year, wages have almost doubled since the beginning of the 1960s, (Table 11) but averages vary according to industry and size of establishment. (Tables 12 and 13)*

The sex differential in wages is substantial, (Table 14) but should be understood in the light of the lifetime dimension so characteristic of employment in Japan. In postwar years, the wage gap between white-collar and blue-collar employees has been steadily narrowing. (Table 15) However, the wage differential between large and small enterprises, though improving, remains a sore point. (Table 16)

TABLE 10

WAGE INDICES AND AVERAGE MONTHLY CASH EARNINGS
OF REGULAR EMPLOYEES, IN ALL INDUSTRIES
(ESTABLISHMENTS WITH 30 OR MORE EMPLOYEES)
(1957–1966)

| Year | All industries | |
	Indices (1965=100)	Monthly cash earnings
1957	52.3	–
1958	53.9	–
1959	57.2	–
1960	61.1	–
1961	68.0	–
1962	75.0	¥29,458
1963	83.0	32,727
1964	91.3	35,774
1965	100.0	39,360
1966	110.8	43,925

Source: *Year Book of Labour Statistics 1966*, Tokyo: The Ministry of Labor, 1967, pp. 52 and 62.

TABLE 11

PERCENTAGE WAGE INCREASE IN SELECTED INDUSTRIES

	1960	1963	(1965=100) 1966
Manufacturing	61.8	83.2	111.6
Food	56.7	81.9	108.4
Textile	57.7	81.2	109.8
Pulp, paper	64.5	83.5	111.8
Printing	57.4	82.3	110.2
Chemical	65.9	82.3	111.2
Oil	62.0	83.2	112.3
Iron, steel	68.4	82.7	112.7
Machinery	62.6	85.7	115.1
Precision machinery	61.9	86.0	113.6
Wholesale, retail	61.5	86.3	110.5
Finance, insurance	63.9	84.9	109.7

Source: *Rōdō Hakusho 1967* ('Labor White Paper'), Tokyo; The Ministry of Labor, 1967, p. 243.

TABLE 12

MONTHLY CASH EARNINGS IN SELECTED INDUSTRIES (SIZE OF ESTABLISHMENT: 30 AND MORE EMPLOYEES)

Industry and earnings	1960	1963	1966
Manufacturing			
Total	¥22,630	¥30,204	¥40,510
Contract	18,319	23,987	32,064
Special	4,311	6,217	8,446
Wholesale, retail			
Total	23,139	30,592	40,544
Contract	18,191	23,577	31,327
Special	4,948	7,015	9,217
Finance, insurance			
Total	32,191	43,222	56,204
Contract	23,642	30,872	39,103
Special	8,549	12,350	17,101

Source: *Rōdō Hakusho 1967* ('Labor White Paper'), Tokyo: The Ministry of Labor, 1967, p. 242.

TABLE 13

AVERAGE MONTHLY CASH EARNINGS BY SIZE OF ESTABLISHMENT, IN MANUFACTURING

Size and earnings	1960	1963	1966
500 and more employees			
Total	¥28,690	¥35,745	¥47,513
Contract 1	22,409	27,432	36,464
Special 2	6,281	8,313	11,049
100–499 employees			
Total	20,293	28,299	38,419
Contract	16,501	22,472	30,283
Special	3,792	5,827	8,136
30–99 employees			
Total	16,897	24,587	33,174
Contract	14,742	20,940	28,050
Special	2,155	3,647	5,124
5–29 employees			
Total	13,270	20,764	29,259
Contract	12,136	17,405	25,881
Special	1,134	2,359	3,378

Source: *Rōdō Hakusho 1967* ('Labor White Paper'), Tokyo: The Ministry of Labor, 1967, pp. 246–7.

Notes: 1 Earnings computed by a formula previously determined by the labor contract, collective agreement, or wage regulations of the establishment.

2 Amount actually paid to the employee during the period for extraordinary or emergent reasons, and without any previous agreement, contract, or rule. Retroactive payment of wages for past months as a result of a new agreement is also included. Though their terms and amounts are established by collective agreement, payments such as summer and year-end bonuses, which are paid for each period longer than 3 months, and allowances such as marriage allowances, which are paid for unforeseen events, are included.

TABLE 14

AVERAGE MONTHLY SALARY, BY SEX (SIZE OF ESTABLISHMENT: 30 OR MORE EMPLOYEES)

Year	Total cash earnings		Increase over previous year	
	Female	Male	Female	Male
1961	13,923	31,868	12.2%	9.8%
1962	16,000	35,012	14.9	9.9
1963	18,039	38,780	12.7	10.8
1964	19,877	42,551	10.2	9.7
1965	22,275	46,571	12.1	9.4
1966	24,867	51,856	11.6	11.3

Sources: *Fujin Rōdō no Jitsujō 1966* ('Facts on Female Workers'), Tokyo: The Ministry of Labor, 1967, p. 32, and based on *year Book of Labour Statistics*, Tokyo: The Ministry of Labor, various years.

TABLE 15

MONTHLY CONTRACT CASH-EARNINGS DIFFERENTIALS
BETWEEN WHITE-COLLAR AND BLUE-COLLAR EMPLOYEES,
BY SEX, IN MANUFACTURING

Status and sex	1960	1963	1966
White-collar employees			
Male (A)	¥30,301	¥38,015	¥48,218
Female (B)	11,941	16,383	21,753
Blue-collar employees			
Male (C)	20,476	26,197	35,263
Female (D)	8,557	12,250	16,755
B/A	39.4%	43.1%	45.1%
D/C	41.8	46.8	47.5
C/A	67.6	68.9	73.1
D/B	71.7	74.8	77.0

Source: *Rōdō Hakusho 1967* ('Labor White Paper'), Tokyo: The Ministry of Labor, 1967,
p. 249.

TABLE 16

WAGE DIFFERENTIALS IN MANUFACTURING, BY SIZE OF
ESTABLISHMENT AND SEX (1966)

	Total cash earnings	Increase over previous year	Differential by size
Female			
Total	¥22,083	11.6%	
500 & more employees	25,270	12.6	100.0
100–499 "	21,671	11.4	85.8
30–99 "	19,370	10.7	76.7
5–29 "	17,685	9.4	70.7
Male			
Total	¥49,686	12.1%	
500 & more employees	55,804	12.4	100.0
100–400 "	47,774	12.7	85.6
30–99 "	41,861	10.6	75.0
5–29 "	36,707	10.0	65.8

Source: *Fujin Rōdō no Jitsujō 1966* ('Facts on Female Workers'), Tokyo: The Ministry of
Labor, 1667, p. 36.

B WAGE INCREASES

THE STRUCTURE OF JAPANESE WAGES REFLECTS VALUES *scarcely familiar to the non-Japanese employee. Granted that Japanese employment is by and large a lifelong proposition, Japanese wage "history" begins with a starting salary determined by degree of schooling and sex, (Table 17) as well as by size of establishment. (Table 18) From the date of employment on, the Japanese basic salary increases almost automatically every year (in recent years, however, besides this increase, there is also the so-called "base-up", an increase of the general wage level obtained by the unions for reason of increased cost of living) (Table 19). It is, therefore, to be expected that the years of service (Table 20) and size of establishment (Table 21) are decisive factors in the determination of wage increases. Years of service, in Japan, can be equated with age differentials (Tables 22 and 23) and are, in turn, influenced by sex. (Table 24)*

TABLE 17

STARTING SALARIES BY SEX AND DEGREE OF SCHOOLING
IN MANUFACTURING

Sex and school		1960	1963	1966
Male:	University	¥13,300	¥20,040	–
	High school	8,220	13,250	¥17,810
	Middle school	6,020	9,910	14,120
Female:	University	12,740	18,500	–
	High school	7,370	12,060	16,330
	Middle school	5,680	9,780	14,090

Source: *Rōdō Hakusho 1967* ('Labor White Paper'), Tokyo; The Ministry of Labor, 1967, p. 270.

[287]

TABLE 18

STARTING SALARIES, BY DEGREE OF SCHOOLING
AND SIZE OF ESTABLISHMENT

Size and year		Male graduates			Female graduates	
	University	High school	Middle school	University	High school	Middle school
Total						
1960	¥13,330	¥ 8,220	¥ 6,020	¥12,740	¥ 7,370	¥ 5,680
1963	20,040	13,250	9,910	18,500	12,060	9,780
1966	26,150	17,810	14,120	24,460	16,330	14,090
500 and more employees						
1960	14,660	9,250	6,470	12,860	8,340	6,450
1963	20,980	13,650	9,260	18,670	12,560	10,120
1966	26,540	18,290	13,820	24,830	16,680	14,260
100–499 employees						
1960	13,200	8,330	6,140	12,890	7,620	5,890
1963	19,300	12,910	9,860	18,180	11,860	9,710
1966	25,530	17,690	14,100	24,510	16,550	14,040
15–99 employees						
1960	12,970	7,380	5,930	12,450	7,050	5,530
1963	19,210	13,200	9,980	18,960	11,780	9,470
1966	25,400*	17,590	14,260	23,530*	16,180	13,680

Sources: *Rōdō Hakusho 1967* ('Labor White Paper'), Tokyo: The Ministry of Labor, 1967, pp. 270, 271, and *Showa 41 Nendo Daigaku Sotsugyōsha Shūshoku Jōkyo Chōsakekka Gaiyō* ('Summary of the Results of the Survey on the Employment of University Graduates, 1966'), Tokyo: The Ministry of Education, 1967, p. 15.

Note: * The smallest size of establishment for the starting salaries of university graduates is "less than 100" instead of "15–99".

TABLE 19

NUMBER OF ESTABLISHMENTS BY SIZE AND NUMBER OF
REGULAR WAGE INCREASES PER YEAR, IN
MANUFACTURING AND WHOLESALE, RETAIL
(1966)

Size and increases	Manufacturing	Wholesale, retail
Number of establishments	47,112	16,375
Increase once per year	32,930	12,058
twice p/y	13,645	4,238
other	537	79
5,000 and more employees	591	219
Increase once p/y	546	219
twice p/y	44	–
other	1	–
1,000–4,999 employees	1,231	568
Increase once p/y	1,144	541
twice p/y	81	18
other	6	9
500–999 employees	1,380	594
Increase once p/y	972	566
twice p/y	400	28
other	8	–
100–499 employees	12,550	3,934
Increase once p/y	9,898	3,172
twice p/y	2,620	762
other	32	–
30–99 employees	31,360	11,060
Increase once p/y	20,370	7,560
twice p/y	10,500	3,430
other	490	70

Source: *Year Book of Labour Statistics 1966*, Tokyo: The Ministry of Labor, 1967, p. 186.

T

[289]

TABLE 20

AVERAGE MONTHLY CONTRACT CASH EARNINGS, BY SEX AND YEARS OF SERVICE (APRIL 1966)

Years of service	All employees	Male	Female
0	¥22,100	¥27,100	¥16,100
1	23,900	28,800	17,500
2	25,600	30,500	18,500
3–4	28,400	32,900	20,100
5–9	35,000	38,900	23,000
10–14	44,500	47,400	27,600
15–19	51,300	53,600	32,100
20–29	56,800	58,100	39,300
30 and more	69,300	70,600	41,700

Source: *Year Book of Labour Statistics 1966,* Tokyo: The Ministry of Labor, 1967, pp. 132–3.

TABLE 21

DURATION OF SERVICE, MONTHLY CONTRACT CASH EARNINGS AND ANNUAL SPECIAL CASH EARNINGS, OF BLUE-COLLAR WORKERS, BY SIZE OF ESTABLISHMENT AND SEX, IN MANUFACTURING (APRIL 1966)

Size and earnings	All employees	Male Years of service	Earnings	Female Years of service	Earnings
1,000 and more employees					
Monthly contract	¥ 36,500	10.4	¥ 42,700	4.6	¥19,600
Annual special	119,500		143,300		55,000
500–999 employees					
Monthly contract	31,200	7.6	37,300	3.9	18,900
Annual special	89,300		110,500		46,300
100–499 employees					
Monthly contract	29,200	6.4	35,700	3.6	17,700
Annual special	67,400		85,900		34,700
30–99 employees					
Monthly contract	28,400	5.7	35,100	3.6	17,300
Annual special	46,300		59,700		24,200
10–29 employees					
Monthly contract	27,500	5.7	33,900	3.9	16,800
Annual special	35,300		44,500		19,800

Source: *Year Book of Labour Statistics 1966,* Tokyo: The Ministry of Labor, 1967, pp. 146–9.

TABLE 22

WAGE DIFFERENTIAL RATIO BY AGE AND SIZE OF
ESTABLISHMENT, IN MANUFACTURING

(age 20–24=100)

Age	1,000 and more employees		30–99 employees	
	1961	1966	1961	1966
17 and less	50.4	56.3	56.9	56.0
18–19	78.2	76.2	76.8	73.9
20–24	100.0	100.0	100.0	100.0
25–29	136.7	124.5	126.6	120.6
30–34	182.0	151.6	141.1	132.3
35–39	210.1	179.8	153.5	133.7
40–49	237.0	199.3	153.2	136.1
50–59	240.5	211.6	139.7	125.8

Source: *Rōdō Hakusho 1967* ('Labor White Paper') Tokyo: The Ministry of Labor, 1967
pp. 264–5.

TABLE 23

WAGE PROGRESSION BY YEARS OF SERVICE AND SELECTED
AGE BRACKETS, IN MANUFACTURING

(thousand)

Age bracket

Years of service	20–24		30–34		40–49	
	1961	1966	1961	1966	1961	1966
1	¥13.3	¥23.8	¥17.6	¥28.7	¥19.2	¥25.5
2	13.4	23.4	18.7	30.7	17.7	26.4
3–4	14.2	24.6	21.3	33.5	20.2	28.8
5–9	14.3	26.1	26.0	40.3	24.5	35.4
10–14	–	–	29.7	44.2	33.2	45.9
15–19	–	–	30.5	43.9	40.4	54.9
20–29	–	–	34.4	45.0	48.9	63.9
30 and more	–	–	–	–	48.4	69.4

Source: *Rōdō Hakusho 1967* ('Labor White Paper'), Tokyo: The Ministry of Labor, 1967,
pp. 266–7.

[291]

TABLE 24

WAGE DIFFERENTIAL FOR FEMALE EMPLOYEES BY AGE
(REGULAR SALARY)

Age	1961	1964	1965	(Male=100) 1966
–18	95.8	95.1	96.5	92.5
18–19	76.6	79.9	83.1	83.5
20–24	67.7	68.8	71.5	71.3
25–29	60.2	58.7	61.0	60.4
30–34	52.7	52.1	53.5	52.2
35–39	42.4	45.3	47.9	48.1
40–49	37.0	39.8	41.5	42.5
50–59	39.2	41.5	43.2	45.0
60–	44.6	50.2	52.6	52.7

Source: *Fujin Rōdō no Jitsujō 1966* ('Facts on Female Workers'), Tokyo: The Ministry of
Labor, 1967, p. 46.

C WAGE COMPONENTS

IN JAPAN, MOST WAGES ARE PAID BY THE MONTH; ABOUT *80% is given as a basic salary and the rest in the form of allowances. (Table 25) Such a wage composition is fairly uniform whatever the size of establishment. (Table 26) However, when the yearly income is considered, a large part is covered by seasonal allowances (Table 27) ; and at the end of the employment period, a substantial retirement allowance is paid out (Table 28), which varies according to degree of schooling and, of course, size of establishment. (Table 29) Such a retirement allowance may or may not be combined with a pension system. (Table 30) It is, therefore, little wonder that Japanese industry gives close attention to the age limits of retirement, the time when lifelong employment and its salary system come to an end. (Table 31)*

TABLE 25

RATIOS OF COMPONENTS OF THE MONTHLY CONTRACT
CASH-EARNINGS IN SELECTED INDUSTRIES
(SIZE OF ESTABLISHMENT: 30 OR MORE EMPLOYEES)
(SEPTEMBER 1966)

Components	All industries	Manufacturing	Wholesale, retail	Finance, insurance
Grand total monthly earnings	(¥35,140) 100%	(¥33,656) 100%	(¥34,070) 100%	(¥41,572) 100%
Total contract cash earnings	88.5 (100%)	86.9	95.5	95.5
Basic wage	(82.8)	(85.1)	(84.3)	(81.9)
Incentive wage	(5.9)	(4.4)	(1.9)	(4.0)
Duty allowance	(3.5)	(2.9)	(4.5)	(5.2)
Cost-of-living allowance	(6.0)	(5.6)	(7.2)	(8.5)
Attendance allowance	(1.4)	(1.7)	(1.2)	(0.1)
Other allowance	(0.4)	(0.3)	(0.9)	(0.3)
Overtime	10.7	12.1	4.3	4.3
Others	0.8	1.0	0.2	0.2

Source: *Year Book of Labour Statistics 1966,* Tokyo: The Ministry of Labor, 1967, pp. 172–
173.

[293]

TABLE 26-1

COMPOSITION RATIO OF VARIOUS COMPONENTS OF THE MONTHLY CONTRACT CASH-EARNINGS IN ALL INDUSTRIES AND MANUFACTURING, BY SIZE OF ESTABLISHMENT (SEPTEMBER 1966)

Size of establishment Components		All industries				
	Total	5,000 employees and more	1,000 to 4,999	500 to 999	100 to 499	30 to 99
Total monthly contract cash-earnings	100.0%	100.0%	100.0%	100.0%	100.0%	100.0%
	(¥35,140)	(¥42,241)	(¥38,467)	(¥35,046)	(¥35,737)	(¥31,182)
Cash earnings	88.5%	84.9%	87.3%	87.8%	89.6%	90.8%
	(¥31,099)	(¥35,860)	(¥33,582)	(¥30,776)	(¥30,220)	(¥28,328)
Basic salary*	(82.8)	(81.8)	(85.3)	(82.3)	(82.7)	(82.3)
Incentive wage*	(5.9)	(8.1)	(3.4)	(5.8)	(5.7)	(5.9)
Duty allowance*	(3.5)	(2.8)	(3.2)	(3.6)	(4.0)	(3.7)
Cost-of-living allowance*	(6.0)	(6.7)	(7.2)	(6.8)	(5.3)	(5.2)
Attendance allowance*	(1.4)	(0.4)	(0.6)	(1.2)	(1.9)	(2.3)
Others *	(0.4)	(0.2)	(0.3)	(0.3)	(0.4)	(0.6)
Overtime allowance	10.7	13.7	11.9	11.4	9.7	8.6
Miscellaneous allowances	0.8	1.4	0.8	0.8	0.7	0.6

TABLE 26–2

Size of establishment Components	Total	Manufacturing				
		5,000 employees and more	1,000 to 4,999	500 to 999	100 to 499	30 to 99
Total monthly contract cash-earnings	100.0%	100.0%	100.0%	100.0%	100.0%	100.0%
	(¥33,656)	(¥40,700)	(¥37,404)	(¥33,408)	(¥31,152)	(¥29,827)
Cash earnings	86.9%	83.2%	85.9%	87.0%	87.9%	89.6%
	(¥29,238)	(¥33,857)	(¥32,122)	(¥29,028)	(¥27,386)	(¥26,741)
Basic salary*	(85.1)	(82.8)	(87.2)	(85.1)	(85.9)	(84.9)
Incentive wage*	(4.4)	(8.5)	(2.6)	(3.7)	(3.0)	(4.1)
Duty allowance*	(2.9)	(2.2)	(2.6)	(3.1)	(3.2)	(3.0)
Cost-of-living allowance*	(5.6)	(6.1)	(0.8)	(0.3)	(5.2)	(4.8)
Attendance allowance*	(1.7)	(0.3)	(0.7)	(1.5)	(2.3)	(2.8)
Others*	(0.3)	(0.1)	(0.1)	(0.3)	(0.4)	(0.4)
Overtime allowance	12.1	15.2	13.3	12.1	11.2	9.7
Miscellaneous allowances	1.0	1.6	0.8	0.9	0.9	0.7

Source: *Year Book of Labour Statistics 1966*, Tokyo: The Ministry of Labor, 1967, p. 171.
Note: * These percentages represent the ratio to the "cash earnings" above.

TABLE 27

SEASONAL ALLOWANCES, BY SIZE OF ESTABLISHMENT,
IN MANUFACURING

Size and seasonal allowance	1960	1963	1966
500 and more employees			
Total	3.36*	3.64	3.62
Mid-summer	1.49	1.60	1.58
Year-end	1.72	1.81	1.73
100—499 employees			
Total	2.76	3.11	3.20
Mid-summer	1.12	1.28	1.35
Year-end	1.44	1.56	1.59
30—99 employees			
Total	1.75	2.09	2.22
Mid-summer	0.66	0.83	0.91
Year-end	0.97	1.10	1.16

Source: *Rōdō Hakusho 1967* ('Labor White Paper'), Tokyo: The Ministry of Labor,
1967, p. 251.
Note: * Numbers are "times monthly salary".

TABLE 28

AVERAGE RETIREMENT ALLOWANCES, ALL INDUSTRIES, BY SIZE OF ESTABLISHMENT (1966)

(thousand)

School graduation and retirement		30–99 employees	100–499	500–999	1,000–4,999	5,000 and more
University graduate Voluntary retirement:						
Years of	10	¥ 267	¥ 256	¥ 275	¥ 289	¥ 263
service:	20	902	986	1,192	1,434	1,590
	30	1,886	2,185	2,781	3,547	4,494
Age limit		2,429	2,841	3,577	4,520	5,637
High-school graduate Voluntary retirement:						
Years of	10	204	194	207	213	180
service:	20	698	763	908	1,035	1,045
	30	1,493	1,687	2,132	2,616	3,083
Age limit		2,062	2,421	3,150	3,948	4,353
Middle-school graduate Voluntary retirement:						
Years of	10	146	147	153	174	139
service:	20	492	584	693	805	763
	30	1,035	1,299	1,633	1,946	2,143
Age limit		1,515	1,959	2,610	3,109	3,269

Source: *Chingin Rōdō Jikan Seido Sōgō Chōsa 1966* ('General Survey on Wages and Working Hours'), Tokyo: The Ministry of Labor, 1967, pp. 212–221.

TABLE 29

AVERAGE RETIREMENT ALLOWANCES, BY TYPE OF EMPLOYEE
AND SIZE OF ESTABLISHMENT, IN MANUFACTURING
(SEPTEMBER 1966)

School graduation and size	Voluntary retirement Years of service			(in thousands) Retirement at age limit
	10	20	30	
College graduates				
5,000 and more employees	¥253	¥1,529	¥4,423	¥5,547
1,000–4,999 employees	286	1,403	3,500	4,485
500– 999 employees	265	1,150	2,741	3,516
100– 499 employees	240	914	2,060	2,694
30– 99 employees	225	778	1,607	2,138
High-school graduates (white-collar)				
5,000 and more employees	210	1,000	3,025	4,447
1,000–4,999 employees	208	994	2,524	3,875
500– 999 employees	193	856	2,059	3,067
100– 499 employees	180	710	1,581	2,280
30– 99 employees	175	605	1,264	1,762
Middle-school graduates (blue-collar)				
5,000 and more employees	169	748	2,145	3,313
1,000–4,999 employees	167	772	1,904	3,087
500– 999 employees	146	677	1,622	2,630
100– 499 employees	144	571	1,282	1,961
30– 99 employees	143	490	1,022	1,518

Source: *Year Book of Labour Statistics 1966,* Tokyo: The Ministry of Labor, 1967, p. 189.

TABLE 30

RETIREMENT ALLOWANCE SYSTEM, ALL INDUSTRIES, BY
SIZE OF ESTABLISHMENT, AND SELECTED INDUSTRIES (1966)

Industry	Total	Retirement allowance system				No system
		Total	Retirement allowance	Pension	Both	
All industries	100.0	82.7				17.2
		(100.0)	(86.4)	(0.1)	(13.3)	
5,000 & more employees	100.0	96.8				3.1
		(100.0)	(45.8)	(–)	(54.1)	
1,000–4,999 ”	100.0	97.8				2.1
		(100.0)	(59.0)	(–)	(40.9)	
500– 999 ”	100.0	95.2				4.6
		(100.0)	(77.3)	(–)	(22.6)	
100– 499 ”	100.0	93.7				6.2
		(100.0)	(85.5)	(0.0)	(14.3)	
30– 99 ”	100.0	75.5				24.4
		(100.0)	(92.8)	(0.1)	(6.9)	
Manufacturing	100.0	80.1				19.8
		(100.0)	(88.2)	(0.0)	(11.7)	
Wholesale	100.0	90.7				9.2
		(100.0)	(83.8)	(0.4)	(15.7)	

Source: Based on *Chingin Rōdō Jikan Seido Sōgō Chōsa 1966* ('General Survey on Wages & Working Hours'), Tokyo: The Ministry of Labor, 1967, pp. 201, 202.

TABLE 31

RATE OF APPLICATION OF AGE LIMIT AND AGE DISTRIBUTION,
BY SIZE OF ESTABLISHMENT, MANUFACTURING (1966)

Size	Rate of application	Total	Age							
			–50	50–54	55	56	57	58	59	60–
White-collar, male Employees										
5000 and more	96.9	100.0	–	–	76.2	12.8	7.6	0.8	–	2.2
1000–4,999	98.8	100.0	–	–	76.1	7.4	6.0	2.9	0.1	7.2
500– 999	96.6	100.0	–	–	76.6	4.6	6.8	1.8	–	9.9
100– 499	84.3	100.0	0.2	1.0	69.7	3.8	4.9	2.6	0.4	17.1
Blue-collar, male Employees										
5000 and more	96.9	100.0	–	0.2	75.7	13.1	7.5	0.7	–	2.5
1000–4,999	98.8	100.0	–	0.1	76.4	8.1	6.1	2.7	0.1	6.1
500– 999	96.6	100.0	–	0.3	78.2	4.8	5.8	1.6	–	9.0
100– 499	84.3	100.0	–	1.5	71.2	3.9	4.5	2.4	0.4	15.8

Source: *Chingin Rōdō Jikan Seido Sōgō Chōsa 1966* ('General Survey on Wages and Working Hours'), Tokyo: The Ministry of Labor, 1967, pp. 188, 190.

[299]

III LABOR ORGANIZATION

THE RATE OF ORGANIZATION OF JAPANESE LABOR COM-
*pares favorably with that of other industrialized nations. This rate,
largely achieved twenty years ago, has remained fairly stable, notwithstanding the nation's tremendous economic growth and the doubling
of its labor force. (Table 32) The coverage of union members by the
various labor laws reveals that one-third of organized labor is found in
the public sector. (Table 33) The most heavily organized industry is
manufacturing, followed by transportation and communication (Table
34) and, roughly speaking, only large establishments are organized.
(Tables 35 and 36) One out of three union members is a female employee. (Table 37) Labor unions in Japan are mostly enterprise-wide
(Table 38) and their membership fee is about ¥520 per month. (Table
39) One-third of the unions are independent; all others are affiliated
with a national center. (Tables 40 and 41). The breakdown of this
affiliation by industry indicates where the strength of the main national
centers lies. (Table 42)*

TABLE 32

NUMBER OF UNIONS, MEMBERSHIP, AND RATE OF ORGANIZATION

	Number of unions	Membership	Rate of organization
1947	23,323	5,697,179	45.3%
1950	29,144	5,773,908	46.2
1955	32,012	6,166,348	37.8
1960	41,561	7,516,316	33.8
1963	49,796	9,269,776	36.1
1966	53,985	10,308,120	35.4
1967	55,321	10,475,869	35.2
1968	56,535	10,862,864	36.1

Sources: *Showa 42 nen, Rōdōkumiai Kihonchōsa Hōkoku* ('Basic Survey of Labor Unions,
1967'), Tokyo: The Ministry of Labor, 1968, p. 14, and previous years.
For 1968: *Japan Labor Bulletin*, Tokyo: Vol. 8—No. 3 (March 1969), p. 5.

TABLE 33

TRADE UNION MEMBERSHIP CLASSIFIED BY LABOR LAW

Labor law	1960	1963	1966	1967
Total	7,661,568	9,357,179	10,403,742	10,566,436
	(100.0)	(100.0)	(100.0)	(100.0)
(Private Sector)				
Trade Union Law	5,061,601	6,518,894	7,392,683	7,586,076
	(66.1)	(69.7)	(71.1)	(71.8)
(Public Sector)				
Public Corporation	929,666	973,031	1,023,320	1,040,481
Labor Relations Law	(12.1)	(10.4)	(9.8)	(9.8)
Local Public Corporation	130,104	166,050	169,044	172,005
Labor Relations Law	(1.7)	(1.8)	(1.6)	(1.6)
National Public Service	278,872	284,594	287,449	279,646
Personnel Law	(3.6)	(3.0)	(2.8)	(2.6)
Local Public Service	1,261,325	1,414,610	1,531,246	1,483,228
Personnel Law	(16.5)	(15.1)	(14.7)	(14.1)

Source: *Rōdōkumiai Kihonchōsa Hōkoku* ('Basic Survey of Labor Unions'), Tokyo: The
Ministry of Labor, various years.

TABLE 34

UNION MEMBERSHIP BY INDUSTRY

Industry	1960	1963	1966	1968
All industries	7,516,316	9,269,776	10,308,120	10,862,864
Agriculture and forestry	87,674	95,623	90,585	86,552
Fisheries and aquaculture	47,853	46,525	50,959	49,973
Mining	342,474	236,739	186,780	150,680
Construction	477,710	557,123	615,684	659,690
Manufacturing	2,543,749	3,477,250	3,801,646	4,024,967
Wholesale, retail	203,314	316,045	444,319	436,733
Finance, insurance	384,552	510,066	660,741	719,341
Real estate	9,949	12,560	15,157	7,144
Transportation, communication	1,456,836	1,723,018	1,915,564	2,021,149
Electricity, gas, water	185,582	201,248	207,753	210,198
Services	1,003,140	1,149,093	1,262,495	1,230,256
Government	758,376	901,220	1,013,973	1,103,308
Others	15,107	43,266	42,464	160,873

Sources: *Rōdō Hakusho 1967* ('Labor White Paper'), Tokyo: The Ministry of Labor,
pp. 296–297.
For 1968: *Japan Labor Bulletin,* Tokyo: Vol. 8—No. 3 (March 1969), p. 5.

TABLE 35

NUMBER OF UNIONS AND MEMBERS, BY SIZE
OF ESTABLISHMENT

Size	1960 Unions	Members	1963 Unions	Members	1966 Unions	Members
1,000 and more employees	7,257	2,724,323	8,811	3,493,904	9,716	4,129,769
500–999 "	1,738	417,597	2,134	569,184	2,314	606,743
100–499 "	6,170	794,247	8,434	1,127,653	9,489	1,266,121
30– 99 "	5,834	238,079	8,026	340,986	8,933	380,922
29 and less	3,418	48,706	4.260	62,026	4,518	63,802
Others	1,333	421,263	1,679	558,985	1,868	601,812
Government	15,851	2,872,101	16,452	3,117,038	17,147	3,258,951

Source: *Year Book of Labour Statistics,* Tokyo: The Ministry of Labor, various years.

TABLE 36

ESTIMATED RATE OF ORGANIZATION, BY SIZE
OF ESTABLISHMENT

Size	All industries 1960	1963	1966	Manufacturing 1960	1963	1966
All sizes	26.3	27.8	27.7	32.4	35.9	37.3
500 and more employees	69.1	60.5	64.0	70.6	69.0	78.7
100–499	38.5	38.4	31.6	40.7	42.9	35.8
30– 99	8.9	10.6	9.6	9.7	12.4	11.4
29 and less	3.2	3.4	3.8	2.1	1.9	2.1

Source: *Rōdō Kumiai Kihonchōsa Hōkoku* ('Basic Survey of Labor Unions'), Tokyo: The Ministry of Labor, various years.

TABLE 37

ESTIMATED ORGANIZATION RATE, BY SEX

Sex	1960	1963	1966
Female			
Union membership (A)	1,944,602	2,530,000	2,840,000
No. of employees (B)	6,680,000	8,280,000	9,550,000
A/B	27.2%	30.6%	29.7%
Male			
Union membership (A)	5,571,714	6,740,000	7,470,000
No. of employees (B)	15,230,000	17,660,000	19,840,000
A/B	35.9%	38.2%	37.7%

Sources: *Fujin Rōdō no Jitsujō 1966* ('Facts on Female Workers'), Tokyo: The Ministry of Labor. 1967, p. 67; *Year Book of Labour Statistics 1960,* Tokyo: The Ministry of Labor, 1961, pp. 14, 384.

TABLE 38

PERCENTAGE DISTRIBUTION OF UNIONS, BY STRUCTURE

Structure	1960	1963	1964
Enterprise-wide	88.1%	90.0%	91.4%
Industry-wide	3.2	3.7	4.9
Occupation-wide	6.6	4.9	0.7
Area-wide	0.4	0.6	0.5
Others	1.7	0.8	2.6

Sources: For 1960 & 1963: *Year Book of Labour Statistics,* Tokyo: The Ministry of Labor, 1961 & 1964.
For 1964: *Shōwa 39 nen Rōdō Kumiai Kihon Chōsa Hōkoku* ('Basic Survey of Labor Unions, 1964'), Tokyo: The Ministry of Labor, 1965, p. 22.
Note: This statistic was discontinued after 1964.

TABLE 39

MONTHLY UNION MEMBERSHIP FEES BY INDUSTRY
(1966 AND 1967)

Industry	1966 (A)	1967 (B)	(B/A)
All industries	¥468	¥521	11.3%
Agriculture	354	365	3.1
Forestry	587	635	8.2
Fisheries, aquaculture	335	364	8.7
Mining	761	843	10.8
Construction	299	347	16.1
Manufacturing	445	496	9.0
Wholesale, retail	391	442	13.0
Finance, insurance	406	430	5.9
Real estate	470	482	2.6
Transportation, communication	605	677	11.9
Electricity, gas, water	600	696	16.0
Services	448	505	12.7
Government	421	465	10.5
Others	270	214	(–) 20.7

Source: *Shōwa 42 nen Rōdōkumiai Kihonchōsa Hōkoku* ('Basic Survey of Labor Unions, 1967'), Tokyo: The Ministry of Labor, 1968, p. 23.

[303]

TABLE 40

MEMBERSHIP IN NATIONAL CENTERS AND IN UNAFFILIATED UNIONS, BY PRIVATE AND PUBLIC SECTOR

Organization	1960	1963	1966	1967
Total	7,661,568	9,357,179	10,403,742	10,566,436
	(100.0)	(100.0)	(100.0)	(100.0)
Sōhyō	3,745,096	4,191,683	4,247,493	4,208,097
	(48.9)	(44.8)	(40.8)	(39.8)
Private 1			38.5%	39.0%
Public 2			61.5%	61.0%
Dōmei	924,076	1,348,268	1,715,800	1,775,210
	(12.1)	(14.4)	(16.5)	(16.8)
Private 1			92.8%	92.6%
Public 2			7.2%	7.4%
Shinsanbetsu	46.063	49.450	65,876	69,839
	(0.6)	(0.5)	(0.6)	(0.7)
Private 1			100.0%	100.0%
Public 2			0.0%	0.0%
Chūritsu Rōren	–	895,475	1,020,751	1,037,908
		(9.6)	(9.8)	(9.8)
Private 1			99.9%	99.9%
Public 2			0.1%	0.1%
Unaffiliated unions	3,080,867	2,954,539	3,471,589	3,587,963
	(40.2)	(31.6)	(34.0)	(34.0)
Private 1			91.9%	92.1%
Public 2			8.1%	7.9%

Source: *Shōwa 42 nen Rōdōkumiai Kihonchōsa Hōkoku* ('Basic Survey of Labor Unions, 1967'), Tokyo: The Ministry of Labor, 1968, p. 19.

Notes: 1 i.e. employees coming under the Trade Union Law,
2 i.e. employees coming under the Public Corporation and National Enterprise Labor Relations Law and the Local Public Enterprise Labor Relations Law.

[304]

The Japanese Employee

TABLE 41

PERCENTAGE OF UNION MEMBERSHIP UNDER TRADE
UNION LAW, BY NATIONAL CENTERS AND
BY UNAFFILIATED UNIONS (1967)

Organization	Total	Trade Union Law*
Total	100.0	100.0
Sōhyō	39.8	21.6
Dōmei	16.8	21.7
Shinsanbetsu	0.7	0.9
Chūritsu Rōren	9.8	13.7
Unaffiliated	34.0	43.6

Source: *Shōwa 42 nen Rōdōkumiai Kihonchōsa Hōkoku* ('Basic Survey of Labor Unions, 1967'), Tokyo: The Ministry of Labor, 1968, p. 19.
Note: * i.e. employees coming under the Trade Union Law (private sector).

TABLE 42

PERCENTAGE OF UNION MEMBERSHIP, BY INDUSTRY,
BY NATIONAL CENTERS, AND
BY UNAFFILIATED UNIONS (1967)

Industry	Total	Sōhyō	Dōmei	Shin-sanbetsu	Churitsu Rōren	Unaffili-ated
All industries	100.0	39.9	16.8	0.6	9.9	33.9
Agriculture	100.0	20.0	9.7	–	4.7	65.6
Forestry	100.0	80.5	10.6	–	–	8.9
Fisheries & aquaculture	100.0	0.5	21.7	–	17.6	60.2
Mining	100.0	54.1	23.2	0.1	1.6	25.2
Construction	100.0	33.1	3.3	0.8	27.5	38.7
Manufacturing	100.0	20.6	27.8	1.4	17.0	33.9
Wholesale, retail	100.0	6.6	17.7	0.0	8.5	67.2
Finance, insurance	100.0	3.4	0.9	–	14.6	90.7
Real estate	100.0	29.1	3.0	–	–	76.9
Transportation, communication	100.0	65.7	17.3	0.3	0.4	16.4
Electricity, gas, water	100.0	22.8	62.7	–	8.4	6.3
Services	100.0	59.6	2.8	0.1	1.3	36.4
Government	100.0	85.4	1.3	–	–	13.3
Others	100.0	40.4	11.1	0.4	–	47.9

Source: *Shōwa 42 nen Rōdōkumiai Kihonchōsa Hōkoku* ('Basic Survey of Labor Unions, 1967'), Tokyo: The Ministry of Labor, 1968, p. 20.

V   [305]

Index

Index

Index

Index

Index

industrial; Management

Inventories, 32. *See* Production

Investment, 10, 33, 34, 79, 104, 132, 222; foreign, 38; of pension fund, *196–197*. *See* Capital

Ippan (一般), 24, 26. *See* Organization, company

Iryō hoken (医療保健), 183. *See* Insurance, medical

Isshōkenmei (一生懸命), 57. *See* Performance

Jidai (時代), 86

Job, 47, 52, 74, 75, 112–113, 215, 257, *258–260*, 268; classification allowance, 113; description, 47, 255, 258; rotation, 26. *See* Allowances; Incentive; Organization

Joint venture, 34, 35–37, 92, 161, 251, 263, 269–271. *See* Enterprise, foreign; Investment, foreign

Jōmu (常務), 156, 157. *See* Director; Management, top

Jōmukai (常務会), 81, *83–84*, 85, 86, 98. *See* Director, Board of managing; Organization, company

Jōmu torishimariyaku (常務取締役), 83, 92. *See* Director; Management, top

Jūgyōin-danshi (従業員男子), 104 fn. *See* Employment

Jūgyōin-joshi (従業員女子), 104 fn. *See* Employment, female

Jūyaku (重役), 77. *See* Executive

Ka (課), 92, *See* Organization, company

Kabushiki gaisha (株式会社), 12. *See* Incorporation

Kachō (課長), 24, 78, 85–86, 87, 131. *See* Section chief

Kachō kaigi (課長会議), 85, 86. *See* Organization, company

Kaichō (会長), 92, 98, 156, 157. *See* Board chairman

Kaigi (会議), 85, 86. *See* Organization, company

Kakari (係), 92. *See* Organization, company

Kakari-chō (係長), 78, 87. *See* Sub-section chief

Kami (上), 47. *See* Dynamism, up-down

Kanri (管理), 23, 26. *See* Management; Organization, company

Kanrishoku teate (管理職手当), 152. *See* Allowances; Position, allowance; Supervision

Kansayaku (監査役), 81, *82–83*, 156. *See* Auditor

Katō kyōsō (過度競争), 30, 32. *See* Competition, excessive

Keiei (経営), 23, 24, 26. *See* Management, top

Keikaku kaigi (計画会議), 85. *See* Organization, company; Planning

Keiretsu (系列), 15, 34. *See* Group, industrial

Keiretsu gaisha (系列会社), 106. *See* Group, industrial

Kenkō hoken (健康保険), 147–148. *See* Insurance, health

Kigyōbetsu kumiai (企業別組合), 71, 228, 242. *See* Labor union, enterprise

Kikō i-inkai (機構委員会), 85. *See* Organization, company

Kimatsu teate (期末手当), 141. *See* Allowances; Bonus

Kinyōkai (金曜会), 17, 21. *See* Group, industrial

Kobun (子分), 207. *See* Group

Kōdō hōshin (行動方針), 236. *See* Labor dispute

Kogaisha (子会社), 14, 15. *See* Enterprise, small

Kōin (工員), 24. *See* Employment

Kokuzeichō-chōkan (国税庁長官), 187. *See* Tax

Kone (コネ), 93

Index

Index

Index

office of the, 81, 85, *86–88;* remuneration, 156–157. *See* Executive; Management, top

Production, 11, 14, 23, 32, 49, 54, 83–84, 101, 123–124, 162, 254, 264

Productivity, 39, 57, 58, 104, 165, 167, 186, 229, 230, 232, 233, 238

Professional. *See* Employee, specialist; Occupation

Profit, 28, 141, 195, 230, 252, 255, 265; -sharing, 168. *See* Market, share; Motivation

Promotion, 25–26, 52, 53, 69, 81–82, 84, 88, 91–92, 93, 130, 237, 254, 257, 266, 269, 270; and management, 92, *152;* and salary, 137, *152–154,* 268. *See* Management; Motivation; Performance; Wages

Publicity. *See* Advertising

Quitting, *113–116,* 144, 181. *See* Lay-off; Retirement

Recruitment. *See* Hiring

Re-employment, after age limit, 24, *159–160. See* Retirement

Relations, human, 4, 54, 99, 118, 151, 211, 239, 243–244; labor-management, *69–72,* 186, 211–212, 219, 239, 242–243, 246, 265, 270; public, 23. *See* Competition; Labor dispute; Labor movement; Labor union; Management

Rent, 148, 171–172; for foreigners, 172–173. *See* Housing; Tax

Research, 12, 13, 39, 75, 84, 90, 269; operations, 84, 85

Responsibility, 24, 25, 54, 71, 74, 81, 89, 254, 256, 258, 260, 264, 266, 269; line, 84; public vs. private, 8, 10, 71. *See* Staff

Retirement, 152, 256; age, 92, 100, 115, 159, 234; and executives, 154; and

pension, *179–197;* fund, 146, 163; voluntary and involuntary, 146, 168, 298. *See* Age, limit; Pension; Retirement allowance

Retirement allowance, 100–111, 115, 126, 131–132, 140, *144–146,* 150, 159–160, 163, 168–171, 179; amount, 182, 183, 185, 297–299; and performance, 152; and pension, *179–197;* for female employees, 161; legislation, 182, 184; regulations, 182. *See* Tax

Ringi (稟議), 25, 85, 88–90. *See* Decision making

Ringisho (稟議書), 89, 90

Rinjikō (臨時工), 24, 104 fn. *See* Employment, temporary

Rōdō kyōyaku (労働協約), 242. *See* Agreement, collective

Rōdōsha-nenkin-hoken-hō (労働者年金保険法), 184. *See* Insurance, legislation

Rōdōsha shōgai hoken (労働者傷害保険), 148. *See* Insurance; Security, social

Rōshi kankei (労資関係), 69, 70, 72. *See* Relations, labor-management

Royalties, 35

Salary. *See* Wages

Sambetsu (産別), 203. *See* Labor movement

Samurai, 8, 12

Sangyō-betsu rōsō (産業別労争), 218. *See* Labor dispute

Sansuikai (三水会), 17. *See* Group, industrial

Sarariman (サラリーマン), 24, 81, 83, 90, 91, 92. *See* Employment, white-collar; Structure, social

Savings, 79, 150, 192; intracompany, 65, 131, 144, 149, 172, 174–177; rate, 33, 144. *See* Insurance

School clique. *See* Sectionalism

Sectionalism, 25, 26, *28–29, 66–67,* 93. *See* Competition

[314]

Index

Index